GW00646683

INVESTING IN
EUROPE'S FUTURE

INVESTING IN EUROPE'S FUTURE

edited by Arnold Heertje

Contributors

Michel Albert
Guido Carli
Otmar Emminger
Alexandre Lamfalussy
Ulf Lantzke
Emile van Lennep
Jean Henri Paul Paelinck
Lord Roll of Ipsden

Preface by Yves Le Portz

Published by

Basil Blackwell
for the European Investment Bank

© European Investment Bank 1983

Edited by Arnold Heertje and published by
Basil Blackwell for the European Investment Bank

First published 1983
Basil Blackwell Publisher Limited
108 Cowley Road, Oxford OX4 1JF, England

British Library Cataloguing in Publication Data

Investing in Europe's Future.
  1. Investment — Europe
  I. Heertje, Arnold
  332.6'78'094   HG912

  ISBN 0-631-13405-0

Typesetting by Santype International Ltd, Salisbury, Wilts.
Printed in Great Britain by Billing & Sons Ltd, Worcester

Contents

Preface

Yves Le Portz

The task of the European Investment Bank, under the Treaty of Rome, is to contribute to the balanced development of the Community by financing productive investment.

During the past ten years, the Bank has been providing finance first and foremost for investment designed to combat three basic forms of imbalance:

    (a) Geographical imbalance: i.e., the simultaneous existence within the Community of regions that are economically developed and others that are either lagging behind in this respect or are affected by the ageing structure of their economy;

    (b) Imbalance in energy supplies, with its implicit threat to the stability of the balance of payments, the structure of production costs and even Europe's security of supply, which came sharply into focus in 1973;

    (c) Developmental imbalance between the Community and those less-developed countries that have close relations with it.

The Council of Community Heads of State or Government and the other EEC political authorities have, on a number of occasions since the current recession set in, commended to the European Institutions the wisdom of expanding their activity and in particular the furtherance of job-creating investment. Acting on this, the European Investment Bank widened its financing operations, trebling their volume in the space of five years; the Council of the European Communities boosted the resources at the disposal of the Bank by adding to them funds raised in the market through the New Community Instrument for borrowing and lending, created in 1978.

However, there is little point to the activity of the Community's financing institutions if that activity is not dovetailed into a general Community policy. As it is, Europe finds itself celebrating the twenty-fifth anniversary of the founding of the Community at a time when the disequilibria in the European economy are becoming more and more disturbing.

Growth continues to lose momentum: that of the Community as a whole dropped to the zero mark in 1982. What ten years ago was considered to be a mere academic hypothesis, not a genuine scenario, is now actually with us, accompanied by an insupportably high level of unemployment, public finances that it has become impossible to balance, and raw material prices at levels that deny progress to the Third World.

Investment is insufficient. In 1981, the volume of Gross Fixed Capital Formation dropped by 4.2 per cent, only to shrink by a further 1.3 per cent in 1982. Moreover, blanket figures in this field tend to warp the true picture, it being quite likely that on the productive side of the economy *net* fixed capital formation, in industry especially, fell by a considerably larger margin, the trend being most marked in the private sector.

Structural disequilibria in Europe are growing more pronounced, with least developed regions getting poorer: because they are more vulnerable, they are suffering the brunt of the unemployment problem, on top of which they are having to cope with the return of a proportion of their own migrant population that has been hit by redundancy in the more developed regions. In addition, investment in the energy sector has stagnated at a far lower level than would be compatible with the pursuit of a viable Community policy of self-sufficiency in this area, working towards lasting economic recovery.

More worrying still, perhaps is this: years of inadequate investment mean that the capital equipment of European industry is growing older, while that of many competitors is being modernised. European industry faces obsolescence on two fronts: (a) in production of goods involving the application of new technology, and (b) in the introduction of modern manufacturing processes into other fields of production. Should Europe fail to make up this lost ground, the Community economy would well run the risk of serious stagnation over a long period of time.

Now, in mid-1983, signs of recovery are beginning to appear in certain Community countries, but there is as yet no guarantee that those signs will lead on a steady, long-term improvement in the situation. Overall, medium-term trends look bleak, lacking the sort of impetus that would be needed to make any real dent in unemployment. A significant improvement presupposes an adequate level of investment — to stoke recovery, give European industry back its competitive edge and expand employment. To prevent such a recovery from spurring inflation once again, moreover, a complex set of conditions will have to be fulfilled, one of the most important of which is the close coordination of economic and financial policies, especially within the European Community.

The clear implication is that the next few years of this decade are going to be decisive: either Europe will manage to get investment back to an acceptable level, with sufficient concentration in priority sectors to enable it to develop once more at the right sort of pace in pursuit of the right sort of strategy, with its economy not trapped in the inflationary spiral, or there looms a very real prospect of progressive decline. The way those active in the economy, along with governments and financial institutions, handle the situation, and exercise their judgement as to the scale and placing of investment, is obviously going to be crucial.

The European Community institutions have repeatedly stressed the need for a departure from the approach that has prevailed in this area in recent years. The rôle of the institutions will be critical when the EEC governments set about coordinating the action they must take to change the pattern of economic trends. Moreover, as productive investment steadily picks up, the Community's financial institutions, and the European Investment Bank in particular, are obviously going to have a vital part to play in pumping additional long-term capital into each country's normal financing circuits: long-term capital that is all the more attractive for being disbursed in foreign currencies.

Now that the first signs of recovery are beginning to appear, it is perhaps high time for proper steps to be taken to ensure that Europe is brought to appreciate the full implications of the need to promote priority investment and create the right conditions for the realisation of that investment.

This is the thinking behind the Bank's commemoration of its twenty-fifth anniversary: that a valid third dimension can be added to the guidelines handed down by the European Council and the action programme launched by the Parliament and the Commission, in the form of efforts to alert public opinion to the importance and the urgency of taking active steps directly or indirectly to foster the non-inflationary recovery of investment.

A viable approach, it seemed to the Bank, would be to contact leading independent figures whose abilities were acknowledged and who enjoyed undisputed international authority, asking them, with the publication of a book in prospect, to offer us their lines of thought, the questions arising in their own minds and their findings and suggestions regarding the problems of investment in the Community in the 1980s. Hence, *Investing in Europe's Future*.

To those authors who kindly agreed to contribute to this volume I should like to express my appreciation for their efforts and for the closer understanding their work will give us of a fundamental problem for the Europe of today. My thanks also to Professor Arnold Heertje of the University of Amsterdam, who generously agreed to handle the coordination and preparation of the book and see it through publication, and to my colleague on the Bank's Management Committee, Dr Arie Pais, who was closely concerned with the work of the authors.

1

The Outlook for Europe's Economic Development*

Emile van Lennep

The industrial world in which Europe has to exist has seen a decade of substantial and often painful change. Change tends principally to be painful for those who don't adapt to it. Adaptation was difficult for Europe in the 1970s, particularly because the world economy lacked buoyancy; and while European countries must share responsibility for the ending of twenty years of rising prosperity, they could not alone restore economic growth quickly once the favourable conditions had been dispersed. The process was also painful because, paradoxically, the very successes of the industrial world in the previous twenty years had built up popular resistance against change. There seems to have emerged, especially in Europe, a belief that the kinds of jobs and life-styles established during those decades had been bestowed as an immutable right, and that it was therefore appropriate to resist any challenge or modification to them.

Is the decade or so ahead of us going to be characterized by further substantial forces for change? If so, how can the industrialised countries best accommodate themselves to those changes, instead of seeking to resist them? What would happen if the main thrust of action in the industrialised world was not to accept and profit from the forces of change but was primarily defensive?

* *Author's note*: I have not burdened the text of this chapter with references to the extensive literature already existing on the matters discussed. A number of recent OECD publications deal with them in more detail and identify the more important earlier sources. Readers who wish to pursue particular aspects in greater depth may find the recent OECD studies a helpful starting-point.

This opening chapter follows, necessarily, a broad-brush and highly selective approach. And for the greater part it looks at the problems of the industrialised world as a whole, instead of confining itself to Europe. The forces for change are very similar whether one looks at Europe, North America or the advanced Pacific economies. And although the ways in which change is accommodated may differ, in detail, from country to country, the broad challenge is the same throughout most of the OECD world. The question is how Europe can at least keep pace, in its adjustment, with its economic peers—and, hopefully, play a leading role in the process.

SOME DEVELOPMENTS IN THE 1970s

The major changes taking place in the economic environment over the past decade need little discussion here. The generalisation and acceleration of inflation; the sharpness of the first oil shock and the subsequent uncertainty about energy supply and prices in general; the vast swing in international payments when the industrialised world became a net borrower overnight; the apparent difficulty of keeping recovery going in the OECD economies after the 1974–75 recession; the growing suspicion that free international trade was menaced; all combined to produce a business climate in which the dominant note was uncertainty, and which served to jog memories of the 1930s and the immediate post-war chaos.

It has been said that our advanced democratic market economies respond badly to sudden shock. But looking back, very broadly, at the size and variety of the shocks experienced over the past ten years, there seems room for more than a little surprise that industrial democracy and social and material well-being survived as well as they did. An observer with foreknowledge of the major events of the 1970s would hardly have forecast that, despite everything, private consumption in 1980 would have been some 30 per cent higher *per person and in real terms* than it was at the start of the decade—a comparison that holds good whether one looks at the OECD world as a whole, at Europe or at the Community alone. The same, privileged, observer would certainly have expressed fears, not so far borne out, as to the political and social conditions likely to be prevailing at the end of such a decade.

But if the democratic, managed-market, system has portrayed a certain ebullience and flexibility in the face of challenge, it cannot claim adequately to have adapted to change in the 1970s. The frequency, until well into the present recession, of double-digit inflation is one testimony to this. Another, perhaps more eloquent, is the inexorable rise of unemployment from under 3 per cent of the total labour force to over 8 per cent at the time of writing — and to nearly 9.5 per cent in the European Community. So steep a rise indicates, clearly enough, that industrialised countries have yet to adapt themselves fully to the changing economic environment. New jobs have been created in some sectors. But they have been insufficient — and this is particularly true for Europe — to offset job losses in the declining sectors and the growth of the labour force.

As a prelude to examining the prospects for the years ahead — the forces to which our economies may be exposed, and the circumstances that industrialised countries will have to engineer if those forces are to be accommodated — it is relevant to take stock, briefly, of some of the structural changes that took place during the 1970s, the decade that began with the catastrophic burgeoning of world-wide inflation and ended with the aftermath of OPEC II. It is important to appreciate both the direction and the speed of change to date if we are to take a balanced view of the obstacles and opportunities that lie ahead.

Changing industrial patterns

The changes packed into the ten-year stretch were substantial, on any historical comparison, and particularly difficult for an increasingly inflexible public opinion to accept. At the highest level of aggregation, at a time when total activity in the OECD was only rising slowly, the combined shares of agriculture and industry fell by over 2 per cent, with an equivalent rise in the relative importance of services. For the European Community by itself, the swing away from the two traditional sectors towards services was significantly greater — nearer 5 per cent between the end of the 1960s and the start of the 1980s. Taking manufacturing industry alone, the fall in relative importance amounted to some 3 per cent, in marked distinction to the far more gradual re-shaping of the pattern of production in the 1960s. One can remark, parenthetically, that this bird's-eye view of statistics may in one sense overstate the industry-to-service switch: the growth of services was, in part, directly related to industry, and to that extent reflects a growing specialisation in which functions previously exercised by industry itself now get taken on by service experts who offer their products in the market. But problems of statistical classification aside, the redistribution of the factors of production — and of the human and financial resources that these abstractions represent — was considerable. As a source of jobs, the importance of industry has fallen in virtually all OECD countries except those still in the process of industrialisation. Indeed, in Europe the absolute level of industrial employment has typically been falling by 1.5 per cent *a year* (and by as much as 3 per cent in Belgium). Most of the new jobs created were in the public and personal service sectors.

At a more disaggregated level, the changes stand out even more starkly, because it becomes clearer that *inside* sectors there have been highly contrasting movements. One would hardly expect all types of activity to fare equally: but in this decade of very slow growth in manufacturing as a whole, the share in the total of the textiles, clothing, leather and footwear industries fell by as much as a fifth, and basic metals lost ground almost as fast. In many cases the declining industries were concentrated in areas where alternative sources of employment were poor. It was the chemicals industry, taking all its many branches as a whole, which saw its share increase most, and in Europe the agricultural and food industries also did rather better than the manufacturing sector in general. The mechanical and electrical engineering industries saw their growth rate slowing down just about in line with that of manufacturing as a whole, but with widely differing trends between types of product. The factors underlying these widespread changes in the structure of production were many and varied.

At the most fundamental level perhaps, but felt only gradually, was the impact of socio-cultural change, which has been working in at least two directions. Industry is faced with new opportunities because of increasingly insistent demands for a better quality of life, health and working conditions, and for the protection of the environment. Hence the growing demand for leisure goods, bio-degradable products, less-polluting equipment and environment-cleaning systems. At the same time, however, certain industries and firms are faced with rising costs which, in accordance with the "polluter pays" principle, tend to get passed on to the con-sumer with consequential effects on their volume of sales.

Of more immediate impact was the steep rise in the real price of energy. In addition to its general effects on inflation and demand, this has, for example, adversely affected a number of branches of the chemicals industry and — together with the effect of slowing population growth on housing activity — has depressed many branches of the construction materials industry, despite the stimulus given to higher insulation standards. Higher energy costs have led to important inter-industry shifts (e.g. plas-tics being substituted for steel) and to changing patterns in the demand for transport equipment.

The effects of technological change on the pattern of industry have been substantial. It is perhaps most clearly seen in the growing output of goods incorporating electronics applications — ranging from information and communications and other capital equipment to household white goods and sound and image reproduction — a process that is probably still in its infancy. Also included in this category are a number of products of the chemi-cals industry such as plastics, synthetic fibres, fertilizers and (buttressed by rising demand for health-care) pharmaceuticals.

Changing patterns of foreign trade have played an important role — one that has been the subject of much public comment — in both the level and structure of production in the industrialised world. Predictably, the comment has tended to be concentrated more on the immediate and very visible losses involved than on the accompanying gains, and there has been little attempt to assess the net result of gross trade flows. Although the overall pattern is still dominated by trade between industrialised countries, changes in the pattern are increasingly coming to reflect influences from outside the OECD area. Generally speaking, the industrialised countries have progressively run into a position of comparative disadvantage vis-à-vis the developing world (particularly the newly industrialised countries, but more recently the "second tier" of new exporting countries) in certain traditional industries which tend to be labour-intensive or based on less-skilled labour and where technologies are easily transferable. The industries most affected have been clothing, leather and footwear, woodworking, non-ferrous metals, rubber and plastics — many of which, in the advanced world, had simultaneously to adjust themselves to the fact that demand for their products was limited anyway by the changing pattern of consumers' expenditure. But in recent years some of the NICs have also become increasingly competitive in certain categories of electrical equipment and instruments: their share of trade in capital goods between developing countries has, indeed, been rising. At the other end of the product-range, the industrialised countries have maintained a strong comparative advantage in industries with a high input of skilled labour — mechanical engineering, electrical machinery, transport equipment and many branches of chemicals. Indeed, the developing countries have represented an increasingly important market for OECD capital goods. By the end of the 1970s over one third of industrialised countries' exports of capital goods were purchased by developing countries, compared to only about one fifth at the start of the decade, and over half their total exports of transport and agricultural equipment and generators were destined for the Third World.

This trade has provided an important support to overall activity in the industrialised countries at a time of weak home demand. The industrialised countries have also found that even in some parts of the lower labour-skill industries they have been able to meet new competition through rationalisation of production and concentration on the types of product for which demand shows a high income elasticity and low price elasticity. Overall, it has been estimated that OECD trade with the developing world has typically led to a net creation of jobs, in which Europe has fared well. The gross loss of jobs, while the direct cause of adjustment problems, has been more than offset by the gross gains.

The loss of jobs in the less competitive sectors has, however, been the occasion for increasing public intervention, both unilateral and multilateral, in the operation of the market, of which the recent extension of the 1974 Multi-Fibre Arrangement, for a third period, is an example. Whether, across the whole industrial spectrum, such intervention (which in the case of textiles and clothing is superimposed on relatively high tariff barriers) has supported the level of employment in the advanced countries, is far from obvious, given the propensity of developing countries to use their export earnings to raise their imports. There is evidence in textiles and clothing themselves that the effects of industrialised countries' trade and industrial policies have been to increase capital intensity in the sector and to press employment down.

Changing investment conditions

One of the most significant changes in the past decade, with a marked effect on economic conditions in the period itself and likely to condition achievements in the decade ahead, was the weakening of fixed investment in Europe as in virtually all other industrialised countries. Throughout the 1960s and up to the first oil shock, gross fixed capital formation had been rising by some 5 to 6 per cent a year in real terms (and more than twice as fast in Japan). Since then the rate has been under 1 per cent, and little better in Japan. The weakness of housebuilding has already been noted. Non-residential construction was similarly flat, and investment in machinery and equipment, though slightly less depressed, showed only a modest increase. The share of investment in public expenditure tended to decline.

The shrinkage of investment in the immediate post-1973 period was sharp, and a marked feature of the years that succeeded the first oil crisis was the repeated failure of investment to respond, as it had in previous cycles, to the recovery movements sparked off by government policy. It was not until late in the decade, after a number of countries had reduced inflation considerably and their economies had become more expansive, that real signs of more buoyant investment began to appear. Even this revival, where it took place, was short-lived, because the second oil price-hike pushed inflation up again and necessitated a widespread return to fiscal and monetary restraint.

Within the generally weak investment picture, available information suggests that capital expenditure in the manufacturing sector has been particularly depressed (although the statistics available may make insufficient allowance for the growing practice of manufacturers to lease machinery from service industries). There is much evidence that such investment as there has been has been concentrated on capital deepening rather than widening. The relative importance of machinery purchases has risen, and that of construction has shrunk, suggesting that industry has invested in replacement rather than expansion of capacity; the weak outlook for total demand, and the pressures on management to become more rigorously cost-conscious, have clearly argued in favour of expenditure on modernisation of plant within the very limited total. And there is evidence that a substantial share of investment in manufacturing has been of a less directly productive nature, reflecting pressures for better working conditions and the protection of the environment.

The implications for the medium-term future of a decade of weak investment may be far-reaching. With gross investment flat, there may have been some net disinvestment, taking the capital stock as a whole, as might well be expected in a period when the growth of overall demand has been slow and when changing relative prices and increased real labour costs have created strong pressure on firms to take marginal vintages of capital (as the jargon puts it) out of operation. More significant may be the changed pattern of investment within industry, and two contrasting movements seem to have occurred. The share of basic heavy industry in fixed capital expenditure has risen, as the chemicals, iron and steel and paper industries have made efforts to modernise. The share of the capital goods industries themselves, however, has fallen, which is hardly surprising given the flatness of overall investment demand. These movements could give some basis to the belief that sustained economic recovery after the present recession would not, necessarily, be cut short prematurely by emerging scarcity of basic industrial inputs, but that strong recovery could begin to run up against capacity bottlenecks in the later processes of manufacturing.

The possible investment problems of the years ahead, and the conditions required for their solution, are discussed later in the present chapter—and form, indeed, the central subject of this volume as a whole. Looking back on performance in the 1970s, however, some reference to the profit situation seems relevant here. Available statistics are somewhat piecemeal, and not always strictly comparable. But it is clear that many industrialised countries — and particularly in Europe — saw wage and non-wage labour costs in the 1970s rising considerably faster than prices received by producers: a "real-labour-cost gap" opened up, with profit shares falling in consequence. Though these "gaps" have been reduced somewhat in the most recent years, profit shares have still, generally, remained below their pre-OPEC I levels. Through most of the industrialised world, a decline in the realised rate of return on fixed capital has been evident. Profitability, as measured by the relationship of the net operating surplus to the net stock of fixed capital, has tended either to be stable or to have declined: no upward trends are apparent, and the downward trends have been particularly evident in manufacturing. This phenomenon was not confined to the 1970s: in several countries it began earlier. There is no magic number by which rates of return on capital, or profit shares, can be judged sufficient or insufficient. The acid test probably resides in the outcome — the readiness of business to engage in capital expenditure. As will be discussed later, there is a *prima facie* case for concern when, as in the 1970s, historically low profits on fixed capital coincide with a period of special uncertainty in the minds of the business community. Investment gets caught in a vicious circle. When inflation in general has gone far beyond what corporate planners in the industrialised world have ever experienced, and when there are substantial differences between national inflation rates, risk-bearing investment programmes can hardly be expected unless profits are already high and the rewards for initiative look good in prospect. Unfortunately, the very nature of the high inflation of the 1970s ruled any such prospect out of court, because the impact fell so heavily on profits.

SOME INFLUENCES ON THE DECADE AHEAD

The recessionary starting-point

Technical discussion of the possible timing and strength of recovery from the long post-OPEC II recession would go beyond — or in a sense fall short of — the aims of the present volume. But any inspection of the years ahead must take full account of the recessionary starting-point and the special characteristics which

distinguish it from previous post-war recessions. If only because of
its duration (it cannot be said with certainty to be over at the time
of writing), the recession that began in late 1979 is likely to be
exerting its effects on economic conditions well into the 1980s.
And it has to be recalled that, when the present recession began,
recovery from the 1974–75 downturn was still far from complete.

But in addition to considerations attaching to pure longevity,
the very nature of these two latest recessions must be taken
account of when reflecting on the future, because in important
aspects they have been very different from the periods of cyclical
weakness that, sporadically, marked the previous twenty years.
They were of greater amplitude, and more nearly coincident as
between countries, than their predecessors. More fundamentally,
their origins were less clearly rooted in demand fluctuations
amenable to counter-cyclical policy.

The two recessions which, chronologically, followed the oil
shocks reflected deep-seated structural forces, many of which pre-
dated the adverse effects of OPEC I. Among these forces were
changes in income shares, the more persistent character of high
inflation, growing uncertainties about raw material supply in
general, an emerging mis-match in many countries between the
skills of the labour force and the qualifications required by technological change, and the rising instability of exchange rates. The
resulting crisis of confidence affected behaviour throughout the
economy, and seems to have been particularly marked in Europe.
Labour practices became more rigid, with increasing resistance to
change. Business became far more cautious, shortening the time-
horizon of its expenditure plans, with important consequences
both for fixed capital outlays and for expenditure on R&D and
innovation projects where the pay-off period is long. It became
increasingly attractive to invest financial savings in short-term
highly liquid assets. Perhaps the outcome is most strikingly
depicted by the productivity record. During the past ten years the
annual productivity increase — as measured by real GDP per
person employed — has slowed down from well over 4 per cent
to a scant 2 per cent in Europe, from around 2 per cent to
virtually zero in the United States, and from well over 8 per cent
to under 3 per cent in Japan.

Under these circumstances it would probably be rash to assume that economic recovery, when it is established, will be as fast as in the typical upturns of the past. After the confused decade or so behind them, policy-makers in governments and, perhaps more important, the direct actors in the industrialised market economies, will be in uncharted territory, proceeding cautiously, and ill-advised at least in the first instance to do otherwise. After so long a period of very low economic growth, and despite the level of unemployment, getting the economies moving again could encounter problems at an early stage, very much as, after a railway strike, normal services take time to re-establish because the trains and the transport workers are in the wrong places. The possibility of selective labour shortages at a relatively early stage cannot be ruled out. And the extent to which plant capacity will prove sufficient to meet the types of demand most likely to rise as recovery gets under way is highly uncertain. In short, the reserves of productivity normally brought into play in periods of cyclical upturn may by now be on the low side, historically: what has been called "the low-growth trap" may, after so long a period of quasi-stagnation, prove a reality. And until the attendant circumstances have become clearly more favourable, new capacity-enlarging capital expenditure to accommodate rising demand cannot be counted upon to take place automatically. It will probably take much more than a simple rise in demand to change the investment climate, and in the meanwhile there must be an important danger that the way that the effects of rising demand in money terms is split between higher physical output and higher prices will be biased towards the latter.

Dangers of fresh inflation

Some of the conditions that will be required if investment is to play its required role both as an *enabling* factor on the supply side and a *sustaining* factor on the demand side in an epoch of new economic growth are discussed later in this chapter. But it needs to be underlined here that there is a wide range of other problems which endanger the achievement of a new era of sustained growth, or which will present extremely difficult choices for policy-makers and for the electorates to whom they are responsible. In addition to the dangers of outrunning capacity limitations and rekindling inflation by (in the old-fashioned phrase) demand-pull, the possibility of renascent cost-push at a relatively early stage has to be borne in mind. *First*, while there may be no strong reason to fear that non-oil commodity prices will rise particularly sharply across the board in response to a moderate but progressive revival of activity, the contribution that their decline has made to the reduction of inflation since 1979 can clearly not be counted upon to continue. So far as oil prices are concerned, the weakness prevailing at the time of writing may not persist in an expanding world economy. *Second*, the outlook for unit labour costs in an economic upturn must, under present circumstances, carry a major question-mark. Recent increases in these costs reflect the fact that although wage pressures have been weakening in a climate of growing unemployment and, perhaps, growing realism as to the scope for higher compensation, productivity trends have been particularly weak. A stronger productivity movement would, in itself, reduce the danger of a new acceleration of cost-push from the wage side. But the possibility that, with strengthening labour markets, pressures for wage increases would re-assert themselves in the form of more aggressive bargaining, particularly post-tax bargaining, and in demands for the restoration of perceived real income losses and a new strengthening of indexation clauses, can clearly not be discounted. Evidence that a more favourable trade-off is developing between faster growth and wage inflation is not yet convincing. And as recovery progresses, strong pressures may emerge, on the side of prices as well as wages, to correct the distortions and changed relativities that recession — or wage and price blockages — are felt to have produced.

Exchange market conditions

In the years immediately ahead, business is likely to have to take place in international currency conditions that are still unstable in comparison with those prevailing prior to the abandonment of the Bretton Woods system. The degree of exchange rate movement will partly depend on the ability of industrialised countries to get the average rate of inflation down, and keep it down, and on their ability to limit the extent to which national rates of inflation diverge from each other. It is probably true that divergences between national inflation rates affect exchange markets more when the world inflation rate is high than when it is low, and there should be grounds for hope on this score. Nevertheless, it may well be over-optimistic to expect that narrowing inflation differentials will, at all quickly, enable exchange rate patterns to become significantly more stable. It might be similarly unreal (though this will be discussed towards the end of the present chapter) to expect that the pattern of domestic policy-mixes (and, particularly, the varying extents to which individual countries rely on fiscal policy on the one hand, as against monetary policy on the other, to influence their economies) will become sufficiently homogeneous to eliminate a potent recent source of exchange rate movements.

Unless and until there is evidence that countries are reducing such fundamental sources of national divergences, the reasonable observer may perhaps be excused for assuming that economic recovery and development are going to have to take place against an exchange-market background in which movement is still large and frequent. It may be premature to discount the possibilities of more effective official intervention on exchange markets — both inside areas where cooperative exchange rate arrangements exist, and between such areas and other currencies or currency groups. But a fair guess would be that any such intervention would be successful mainly because it entailed, as a basic condition, a greater *rapprochement* between fundamental conditions and policy-mixes, rather than because it succeeded, *per se*, in ironing out exchange rate fluctuations. Tails seldom wag dogs.

One should not exaggerate the extent to which movements between exchange rates impose obstacles to recovery and progress in the industrialised market economies of the world. Hedging facilities exist for the international trader. And after a decade of managed floating, the investor, be he borrower or lender, may be learning to take a longer-term view of exchange rate movements. Yet one cannot totally discount the extent to which exchange market instability has acted as a constraint on constructive decisions by economic agents in the decade since Bretton Woods was finally abandoned.

Throughout the past decade there have been major examples of currencies not moving when, for basic economic reasons, they should have moved. And there have been repeated clear cases where appropriate movement has led to overshooting. The vast movements of individual currencies against the US dollar — the crudest and most misleading yardstick — have probably in themselves served to reduce confidence. Far more important, however, have been the movements of competitive positions — or "real exchange rates" — as measured by the relative course of national labour costs or prices after allowing for exchange rate changes. Rational business decisions of a type likely to favour an eventual return to sustainable growth across the world can hardly have been advanced by the zig-zag course of relative competitive positions as exemplified, to name but a few experiences over the past decade, by the United States (an improvement by some 20 per cent followed, eventually, by a roughly similar deterioration); by Japan, with somewhat similar but obverse movements; or by the United Kingdom, where competitiveness fell by some 30 per cent or more over three consecutive years. It would be premature to suppose that problems of exchange rate adjustment will cease to exist in the decade ahead.

Social conditions and labour-market policies

Social conditions, and the policies required to deal with them, seem likely to confront industrialised countries with major problems. The prospects for reducing unemployment very quickly in the coming decade from its present high levels are not good unless overall growth proves much faster than it now seems prudent to expect, or unless the productivity trend is particularly weak. Achievement of the latter would seem likely to be in the nature of a Pyrrhic victory, given its probable effects on the rate of inflation: a low productivity record combined with continued high aspirations in respect of income and welfare (and, as suggested later, aspirations show little immediate sign of declining) would be a sufficient recipe for continuation of the inflation generally recognized as so fundamental an enemy of longer-run growth. In the years immediately ahead, unemployment may remain a particularly difficult problem in Europe where, unlike North America and Japan, the population of working age will still be growing strongly. And two specific factors may exacerbate its size and character: The sections of the labour force particularly prone to unemployment — women and older workers — will rise as a proportion of the total. Also, the light in which unemployment is regarded is changing: joblessness may no longer present a widespread problem of income-deprivation and queues at soup-kitchens, and to a greater or lesser extent it may be possible to provide *some sort of jobs* for the out-of-work; but the spotlight today is increasingly on *careers*, and weak labour-markets threaten to interrupt or exclude the possibility of careers even if they don't totally exclude the possibility of gainful employment.

There is thus a risk that the social climate in which the industrialised economies have to operate will become increasingly morose. This can breed conditions that reduce the flexibility of the people on which the economy depends, and impair their readiness to forego, in the interest of rebuilding economic potential, part of such small immediate consumption increases as are feasible. There may, for a time, be a sort of forced acquiescence in the unwelcome needs of the immediate situation, in the face of stark facts at the low-point of recession. But this may prove very reluctant and temporary, and be withdrawn as soon as the situation seems to be beginning to improve.

At a particularly neuralgic level, one of the results could be the progressive alienation from the rest of society of the young — who, according to contemporary surveys, still *want* jobs, however difficult they may be to obtain, and still *hope* for meaningful careers. More broadly, there must be some danger that the coming decade will be a society in which not merely are "we" progressively divided from "they" (the two divisions representing, very roughly, the labour force and management), but in which the majority groups are increasingly splintered, with the young and the relatively unprotected at odds with the better protected and more experienced members of the work force.

Governments will no doubt be continuing to search for ways in which, at least temporarily, to alleviate the burden of joblessness. The scope for temporary job-creation in the public sector may well remain limited by budgetary constraints, even though the cost is not necessarily very much greater than that of supporting the unemployed. The value of this type of action depends very much on the extent to which groups with particularly bad employment prospects receive on-the-job training relevant to their future careers — which is far from easy to ensure — and on the extent to which the expenditure involved is aimed at the provision of useful public services. The danger is that these schemes may simply provide "stop-gap" jobs, with the beneficiaries subsequently re-entering the ranks of the officially unemployed.

A more promising form of action — but no panacea in itself — may lie in marginal employment subsidies, though experience to date suggests that the net employment effect is substantially less than the gross. A major disadvantage of subsidies to maintain *existing* jobs is that they are generally of a defensive nature, protecting employment in the structurally-weak firms at the expense of the more efficient. It may be the more efficient firms, on the other hand, who are most likely to take up *incremental* employment subsidies, which can be aimed at specific disadvantaged groups in the labour force. One weakness of these schemes, however, is that they may, in part, simply shift unemployment between groups and, in a period of some expansion, subsidize firms for taking on labour which they would have hired anyway.

An important characteristic of the socio-economic situation so long as unemployment remains high is likely to be continued pressure for policies aimed at work-sharing and the reduction of working time. Social attitudes in the years ahead could evolve in directions favourable to the success of such schemes, but this is by no means certain, and until then their application can sometimes seriously complicate the re-establishment of sustainable economic growth. The basic problem is that schemes to share out work between job-holders and the jobless are only likely to bring unemployment down if they are non-inflationary in their effects, and there are numerous pitfalls. Early retirement can reduce the average level of skill in the work-force. Schemes to encourage flexible part-time work can prove disadvantageous if the weight of non-wage labour costs cannot be modified. The organised introduction of a shorter working week is likely to aggravate inflation unless specifically accompanied by suitable arrangements to raise productivity or to keep earnings lower than they would otherwise have been. Schemes which are cost-neutral (or even cost-reducing) can certainly be devised, but it may be very difficult to apply them in circumstances of slow growth and continuing inflation. Some marginal alleviation of unemployment might be achieved through removing existing impediments to job-holders who in fact want to work less and earn less — though the degree of success would depend on whether there are comparable numbers among the unemployed who would be satisfied by the offer of similar part-time arrangements.

The acid test for work-sharing in the years ahead is whether there is a voluntary movement towards more leisure at the expense of income, and this is probably more likely to develop — or be capable of encouragement — when expansion is clearly under way. Two footnotes are relevant: First, work-sharing could attract more job-seekers into the labour market and thus prolong the unemployment problem. Second, the task of reducing unemployment through work-sharing is one of the few instances where international coordination is unlikely to help. If work-sharing schemes are inflationary, no amount of international coordination of their introduction (in any case difficult to achieve) will dispel their draw-backs from the point of view of re-creating growth and high employment.

Environmental conditions

One further factor influencing business conditions in the years ahead will be the continued — and perhaps growing — pressures to protect and improve the environment. At the same time as perception of the dangers of ecological imbalances and environmental damage from some types of industrial production, energy use and transport is growing, rising incomes and evolving aspirations are increasing society's desire for less polluted surroundings.

Although some firms are increasingly taking it upon themselves to adopt less-polluting techniques (internalizing the externalities, as the literature puts it) markets do not always equate private costs with social costs. Governments have to intervene — and this is likely to continue to be the case — to ensure that tolerances are not exceeded, and that the social costs of pollution are matched by the economic costs to the polluter. And they have to intervene in ways which produce the required effect at the least possible cost to economic efficiency.

Economic efficiency today is not necessarily reduced by the

process of environmental protection, any more than it was hampered when the employment of children as chimney-sweeps was banned in 19th century Britain. The process can, and does, lead to innovation and new skills of economic as well as social benefit, just as the ending of child-exploitation led to a better educated labour force. Indeed, at a global macro-economic level, government measures in recent years to protect the environment may have had a positive effect, at least in the short term, on employment and productivity, although the effects vary as between regions and industries, with economic benefits to some and costs to others.

More costly, however, at least over the longer term, may be the decisions concerning future economic activity that governments do not take — or have to delay — because society is not ready for them. Efficiency can suffer unnecessarily from government interventions which are sub-optimally planned in the sense of hindering the evolution of new processes which are no more polluting than the old ones. It can also suffer if, by delays and lack of clarity, such interventions sow uncertainty in the minds of enterprises. The climate in which business decisions are taken in the years ahead is clearly going to be influenced by continuing concern to minimize ecological damage, and by the foresight with which governments are able to shape their interventions to this end. It is normally very much cheaper to avoid damage at the planning stage of an industrial project than to correct it by subsequent re-design or modification of production methods. And given the long lead-time required for the introduction of new physical capital, industrial structures a decade hence will depend very much on the decisions taken today. The cost of uncertainty in this field — and the difficulty of ending it — is illustrated nowhere so clearly as in the industrial application of nuclear power.

Prospective changes in industrial and employment patterns

Economic prospects for the industrialised countries, whether looked at as a single OECD group or inspected within the stricter European framework, depend heavily on how political relationships develop between the individual countries in question, and between the groups that, for short-hand purposes, we call North and South. They also depend heavily on the extent to which moral or material attitudes in the industrialised world evolve — an evolution which may either cut across national frontiers or show distinctive patterns as between countries.

It is now four years since the OECD published a study entitled *Interfutures*, in which a team of independent experts explored economic prospects over the final quarter of the 20th century. Depending on the course of relationships between North and South, on relationships *within* the Northern group and the Southern group, and on the continuity or discontinuity of value judgements inside the industrialised countries (to identify just a few of the parameters), the study put forward six contrasting scenarios which, with full reserve, it proceeded to quantify in terms of possible GDP growth rates. The interest of the study, as the authors themselves underlined, lay less in the suggested magnitudes than in the relationships between them, the differing possibilities and problems which they illustrated, and the ways in which they could help policy-makers and opinion-leaders to think about the prospects and identify the options.

For the present OECD group of countries as a whole, the suggested magnitudes ranged between a growth rate of little more than 2 per cent per annum in the case of the worst scenario (a far cry from the 5 per cent prevailing prior to OPEC I, and no better than over the past decade), and a bit more than 4 per cent in the "best case". The models might serve up somewhat different (arguably lower) numbers today, for the same scenarios, because of the events of the intervening years (which included the second oil-shock and its aftermath). But the study makes three points of particular immediate interest and, probably, of continuing relevance.

First, it points to the growing economic interdependence between the more-industrialised world and the developing countries, a relationship which accounts, to an important extent, for the great difference between the worst scenario (where North/South divisions become accentuated) and the best. The one finding common to all the scenarios is the steady shift in the relative economic importance of OECD countries and the Third World, the share of the latter in total world product rising from about one-fifth to one-third, with a mirror reduction in the share of the OECD.

Second, the study does *not* say (though it has sometimes been construed as doing so) that there are no imminent material constraints to achievement of anything approaching traditional post-war growth in the quarter-century under inspection. It produces the more important finding (which is encouraging at one level but of great fundamental concern) that although, from the point of view of raw materials, there is no ineluctible reason why availability should prove insufficient to support any likely growth rate for perhaps as long as the half-century ahead, whether in fact the necessary quantities *are made* available depends closely on the world's ability to solve a whole range of potential constraints. These include the ecological, such as the threatened loss of genetic materials and croplands and soil depletion, the socio-political, and the economic and financial circumstances which condition investment — a question which is already of contemporary significance and, as such, a major concern of the present volume.

Third, the study makes somewhat similar points in respect of technical innovation. Lack of technical innovation should not, in itself, render a slowdown of growth inevitable over the rest of the present century. But socio-economic considerations could well inhibit the incorporation of technical advance into production methods — whether because there is resistance from society, or because conditions are not conducive to the long-term expenditure decisions required of private investors.

While it is important to assess whether the industrialised countries *could* return to anything like pre-oil-shock growth rates, employment levels and productivity trends, it is also relevant to consider how far, in the decade or so ahead, their populations will *wish* to do so. It may well be that some sort of change in aspirations is taking place. The *Interfutures* study found evidence for some progressive switch from materialist to post-materialist objectives in the industrialised world, with a widening gap between the attitudes of those born before and after World War II. Among the post-war generations, something like a post-materialist outlook is probably becoming increasingly common, with rather more importance attached to the allocation of time, and less to the allocation of income: command over working methods and over the split between work and leisure hours may progressively be gaining importance compared with command over income in the aspirations of those whose experience of pre-war poverty is purely anecdotal. If organised work, in the traditional sense, progressively takes up less than the time previously allotted to it, the structure of production itself will change, with the growth of an informal production sector inside households (do-it-yourself on a more significant scale) and with less reliance on conventional market activities. But most evidence suggests that, however desirable any such movement may be, it is going to be a slow one, even in the highly-advanced countries. The decade or so immediately ahead still seems likely to be characterized by a quest for strong economic growth, for jobs for all and less material distinctions between rich and poor.

Interfutures discussed a 25-year horizon. Even for the shorter time-span of the next ten years or so, it seems unwise to indulge in any sort of quantified analysis of the evolution of industrial structures. Drawing rather broadly on recent studies by OECD governments, some qualitative assessment can be made, though here too a preliminary word of warning about the perils of projection may be prudent: because changes in trend are difficult to spot, the analyst may be over-ready to project existing trends forward.

Among the factors affecting trends in demand for the output of industrialised countries in the decade ahead, the changing population structure is likely to be important. The fall in birth-rates, and the ageing of a population that is growing more slowly, will serve to push down the demand for housing and, therefore, for construction materials. And the ageing process is expected also to reduce the growth of demand for food and clothing, but to push up demand for health-care and leisure products.

Of lesser certainty, and of a more normative character, is the expectation that domestic demand for capital goods will grow in relative importance, as investment rises to provide an adequate basis for new economic growth and a return towards high employment, as capital is substituted for energy, and as increased resources are devoted to scientific and technical research. The need for a broader capital base from which to create jobs may be particularly pressing in Europe where, in contrast to North

America, labour force growth is not yet starting to slow down and where too high a cost of labour in relation to capital may already have formed an important structural impediment to high employment. Whether the postulated increase in demand for capital goods will, in the event, materialise will depend on the many factors touched upon elsewhere in this chapter. Even with lower real interest rates, the financing of very long term or risky investments (including expenditure on R&D) on terms attractive to borrower and lender alike may prove difficult.

A third factor influencing demand for the output of the industrialised world, assuming that commercial policies are basically liberal and that international financial flows are not constricted, will be a further two-way growth in trade with developing countries. A striking point to emerge from a study of industrial prospects as seen by individual OECD countries is the extent to which each of them expects export demand to constitute a major source of buoyancy for industry in the years ahead. If this is to become a reality for the industrialised group as a whole, it would pre-suppose an important development of sales to the Third World — and (given the increasingly visible financial constraints) a substantial increase in OECD purchases from those countries. In industrialised countries this would be most likely to involve a further fall in the relative importance of, for example, the textiles, clothing, leather and footwear industries, and an increasing role for the capital goods industries in response to the pattern of developing countries' demand.

It is, thus, difficult to escape from the probability that, in the coming decade even more than previously, continued adaptation will be the price of growth. European industry seems likely to move further in the directions that became evident in the 1970s, with sectors requiring substantial human capital boosted by rising demand and the process of innovation, and the less-advanced types of activity moving progressively towards the Third World. Looking at very broad categories of industry — which necessarily leads to over-simplification — it is probable that, in the metal-related group, the relative importance of electronics products, data-processing and telecommunications equipment, agricultural machinery and some forms of transport equipment will become more preponderant, with resources gradually leaving relatively slow-growth sectors in steel, metal-working and heavy engineering. In mechanical engineering, some reversal of recent contractionary trends could become apparent as a result — if the necessary basic conditions are fulfilled — of rising fixed capital investment at home and exports to the developing world. Similar trends can be projected in the agro-chemicals-related group, where progressive sectors in the chemicals industry — particularly basic chemicals and plastics — may play the leading expansionary role. Within these rather general trends, important structural shifts inside particular sectors are likely to become apparent as technology develops; for example, the rising use of electronics-based equipment in automobile production, and, probably, an eventual rise in the importance of bio-technologies.

It is premature to pronounce on the burning question whether industry's crisis of transition is coming to an end, with structural adaptation proving sufficient to enable it to reassert itself as a driving force in the economies of the advanced countries, or whether the difficulties of securing adequate adaptation are going to linger on through the coming decade, continuing to inflict serious employment problems. So far as the present lower-labour-skill industries are concerned, it is probably justified to expect that the speed of their relative decline will be tempered by further rationalisation and productivity-raising measures, though this may support output more than employment. It is interesting — but not necessarily conclusive — that recent studies in the OECD have shown a number of countries envisaging industrial activity rising *faster than* total output in the years ahead, thus in fact restoring its leading role. One factor supporting this possibility may lie in the scope for deploying such reserves of productivity as may at present exist. But in attempting to assess the extent to which industry is able to re-establish something like its former dynamism, one soon comes back to the vital problem of ensuring sufficient fixed capital investment.

It is obviously an open question, at the time of writing, whether industry will feel encouraged to plan the investment needed if it is adequately to exploit the possibilities that technology offers, and whether it will be able to finance the capital expenditure on suitable terms. And it may be prudent to suppose that even if industry's share in GDP strengthens, productivity trends will cause employment in industry to fall, in relative though not necessarily in absolute terms.

The switch of employment patterns away from industry itself towards the service sector will partly reflect the growing tendency for manufacturing, for example, to rely on the input of service specialists, with software taking over from hardware as a source of employment. Indeed, over the years it should be expected that technological progress, by restraining costs and expanding demand, will prove a net creator of jobs, with rising efficiency producing rising real incomes. Over the economy as a whole, if productivity gains lead to lower prices and if price elasticity of demand is sufficient, employment will rise rather than fall. But the process will certainly include some job-displacement, and a greater concentration on jobs demanding the higher skills, which could well cause unemployment among the lower-qualified. An important question is whether the forces of structural change will run up against limits of tolerance on the part of individuals and society as a whole.

SOME POLICY NEEDS

Blue-prints for policy can bear an unfortunate resemblance to idealised shopping lists. It is not intended, here, to do more than attempt to identify, highly selectively, some points to which policy-makers will need to pay attention if Europe is to respond constructively to the economic influences that will be making themselves felt in the decade or so ahead. For ease of exposition, discussion concentrates, in turn, on three particular points: the stimulation of productive investment; the problem of combining economic growth in a market economy with the satisfaction of social concerns; and the need (and the scope) for an inter-governmental approach in the world of late 20th century economic interdependence. In contemporary circumstances, however, the distinction between the three points is more apparent than real.

Stimulation of investment

A basic need if fixed investment, both of a capital-widening and deepening type, is to be increased, with more risk-taking and a shift towards longer time-horizons, is to attenuate the climate of uncertainty currently enveloping the business sector. One primary requirement, if business doubt is to be dispelled, is to achieve a convincing reduction of inflation, and what is at stake here is reducing not simply the going rate of inflation, but inflationary expectations. Simply to reduce the pressure on costs and prices between two years—an area of considerable recent achievement—is only half the battle: the decisive second half is to reduce *uncertainty*, in the business mind, about inflation rates in the future. To the extent that governments and their social partners can engineer this major escape from the catastrophe of the past decade, much else of importance to capital expenditure may follow. Lower real interest rates would be easier to achieve, so long as structural budget deficits can be reduced. Also of importance, particularly if the interest rate elasticity of business investment is low, better price stability might make interest rates and their structures more *stable*: a particular disincentive to prospective business borrowers may be the disinclination to get locked into high-coupon debt when future credit market trends are very uncertain, even though the markets themselves show considerable flexibility in adapting credit conditions to meet such problems. To the extent, also, that inflation rates become lower, less unpredictable, and less divergent between countries, the constraints of exchange rate fluctuations on capital investment would be relaxed. A further condition for improved business confidence is the creation of more easily predictable market conditions in general, including the reduction of uncertainty concerning government intervention in the market system (discussed in more detail below) and progress in reducing labour rigidities which threaten future profitability of investment.

Progress in these respects may only be gradual. If that is so, the risk-premium as perceived by business may remain high, with implications for profit needs if capital expenditure is to rise. So long as perceptions of risk are historically high and profits historically low, investment by non-financial private enterprises will remain depressed. To counteract this, not only will it be necessary for unit profits to be relatively high, but expectations concerning *total* profits must be buoyant.

The fact that profit shares are still generally lower than prior to the early 1970s in part reflects the fact that productivity growth (adjusted to take the deterioration of the terms of trade of industrialised countries into account) has, until recently, decelerated more than real wage growth. Furthermore, lower rates of capacity utilisation associated with weak demand have probably lowered profit shares somewhat, and *total* profits substantially. How far profitability needs to be increased in any given country depends in part on the initial profit position, but there are probably few — if any — European countries where conditions can yet be thought conducive to an important lasting recovery of investment. Squeezed profits mean that firms are less interested in bearing the risks of re-structuring, and less able to do so. Profits could be boosted, without interrupting progress towards better price stability, either by a significant strengthening of productivity trends or by a further deceleration of real wage growth. Neither of these are likely, in the period immediately ahead, to be easy to achieve very rapidly: indeed, the problem may be of the chicken-and-egg variety. Except in the very early stages of an economic upturn, productivity stimulus itself is likely to depend narrowly on higher fixed investment. But the latter depends on profits and profit-expectations, and these could be depressed, at least momentarily, by a tendency for real wage growth — and therefore the growth of demand — to be restrained. In the foreseeable future, the scope for the traditional *deus ex machina* for raising demand and profits — higher public expenditure or large general tax reductions — seems limited, at least in most of Europe.

There may, however, be scope — varying greatly from country to country — for fiscal changes to alleviate the pressure on profits. Steps may be possible to reverse the marked tendency of the last decade or so for the tax burden to shift towards taxes on enterprises — a shift which has been particularly exacerbated by the growth of social security transfers financed by taxes on employment and profits. How far such a reverse shift could be obtained through changes in the tax structure or through the modification of social security schemes will depend very directly on conditions prevailing inside individual countries. Other directions in which support for profits could be found may include action to remove tax distortions emanating from the effects of inflation on reported company profits. And some countries may well find that investment subsidies — whether temporary and selective, or more permanent and general — have a useful role to play in stimulating capital outlays.

Innovation

In the longer term, however, encouragement of innovation may prove at least as effective as direct fiscal measures in stimulating investment, and governments may be able to contribute importantly to the ability and readiness of their economies to make use of the potential advances in science and technology. It is probable that the economic uncertainties of recent years have increased the risks normally inherent in R&D — an activity in which costs have, in any case, been rising steeply. There seem to be important directions in which governments can move to shield the innovative process from the effect of macro-economic constraints, without adversely affecting the play of market forces. But it is essential to avoid action which supports innovation in specific sectors at the cost of competition — a subject discussed in the next section of this chapter.

A first imperative is for government science and technology policy to observe an appropriate balance between short-term and longer-term objectives, and between actions that encourage innovation in specific sectors such as energy (tardy development here would mean that energy soon reasserted itself as a constraint on growth) and actions which provide more general stimulus. Indeed, in present circumstances the most important avenue for official encouragement of technological advance may not lie in "throwing more money at the problem", particularly when there is not much money to throw, but rather in the conceptualisation and organisation of policy. Considerable benefits are probably still to be gained from devising more effective machinery — involving the official and the business sectors together with the universities — for setting priorities for R&D: a difficult balancing act is involved by the need to ensure, *inter alia*, that fundamental research is not sacrificed to the pressure of current government priorities. The elaboration of national science budgets (for both the public and the private sectors) on a multi-year basis can prove extremely helpful for all engaged in this field. And since the application of technological advance is as much a social as a scientific and industrial problem, better procedures for investigating the social implications of new techniques, and for improving public understanding of them, can probably yield substantial dividends.

Nonetheless, while it is important to devise appropriate frameworks for policy, and the machinery to apply it, industrialised countries have also to assure that the volume of R&D expenditure in the economy as a whole is sufficient to enable them to meet the challenges of structural change ahead. Over the past decade the trend has been disturbing. The share of GDP represented by R&D expenditure by industry declined through the 1970s without, generally, an offsetting rise in government outlays: indeed, there was a fairly general decline in the proportion of public expenditure allocated for this purpose. Particularly at a time when overall public spending is subject to important constraints, it may well be found helpful to set up targets for the share of total resources to be devoted to R&D, and for the relative shares of government, industry and the universities. Moreover, within the limits set by their desire to reduce the general importance of public sector expenditure and borrowing, governments may find it appropriate to encourage technological progress through fiscal incentives, particularly for small firms, and risk-reduction schemes.

There are probably many domestic impediments to industrial innovation that governments can remove: regulation often has unanticipated effects, but ones which can be tempered without harm to the purpose for which the regulation was introduced. At the same time, international impediments can also have a major adverse effect. If new technologies are not allowed to flow across frontiers, there will be an increased risk of barriers to world trade and, in all likelihood, a reduction in the ability to innovate. But there is another, very positive, aspect to the international dimension from the point of view of increasing the rate of industrial innovation. Trans-frontier cooperation in scientific and technological research, such as the European Communities are currently encouraging, is invaluable in an era when R&D costs can easily run beyond the means of individual countries, and when so many industrial challenges, of which energy is only a leading example, are common to all: Europe's economic progress in the decade or so ahead is likely to depend heavily on shared equipment and shared ideas.

Smaller enterprises

To assure a climate favouring innovation by small and medium-sized enterprises (SMEs) seem to merit special attention. In most industrialised countries these account for more than half the total of industrial employment, and some of them have, traditionally, demonstrated a particular propensity to put the potential benefits of technological advance to practical use, usually by drawing upon techniques originating elsewhere. For if most industrial R&D is performed by big firms, a surprisingly high proportion of industrial innovations are introduced on to the market by SMEs. On the whole it is the small firms (when the initial expense is not prohibitive) who venture into new risky projects where the narrowness of the market in the early stages discourages their bigger competitors. Restoration and maintenance of economic growth, in Europe, North America or Japan, will certainly be greatly eased if the flexibility of response which marks the successful SME becomes more widespread, with an increased capability to apply technical progress to the satisfaction of market demand. Moreover, raising the level of technology of SMEs can help to revitalize lagging regions.

A wide range of action is open to governments to this end — concentrating, probably, more on incentive than on direct aid; beyond a certain point the latter can become counter-productive, wasteful and a source of undesirable distortion of market forces. There is important scope for helping SMEs increase their knowledge about progress outside their own immediate industrial niche, making them increasingly receptive to new technology and ensuring (to take a single example) against a replay of the experience of the European watch industry. Better higher education and training systems, the development of networks for the spreading of technical information, and arrangements to encourage collective research are directions in which micro-economic policy can play a rewarding role. Equally rewarding can be the continuous review by governments of regulatory procedures to ensure conditions likely to sharpen the competitive edge of the SMEs: easing access to markets for new products and new producers, designing and enforcing adequate anti-trust laws and simplifying patent procedures, to give but a few examples.

So far as official measures affecting the financing of SMEs are concerned, a certain modesty is desirable. Experience suggests that the odds that governments will select winners are not universally high, and the selection of losers tends too often to lock scarce funds — and commercial policies — into unprofitable protection of the original stake. Nonetheless, it has to be recognised that SMEs have small resources of their own for financing new projects, and that the pay-off time can be long. In many countries there is probably scope for action to attract the major sources of finance back into the venture-capital market and, possibly, to develop the role of risk-taking public financial enterprises. And the ability of SMEs to engage themselves in the innovation process can be increased by improving their access to official aid for R&D and to government procurement. But this, again, is an area in which action to simplify the procedures with which small firms have to comply may prove more important than big increases in the volume of government support.

Competition policy and industrial support

Whether one is looking at the role in the investment process of small companies or large, a major determinant lies in the business climate that government policies create. If the private sector is to be willing to shoulder the short-term costs of structural adaptation and development in order to obtain gains in the longer term, it must be able to operate in a reasonably stable and predictable environment: whether this exists will depend very much on the competition policies, industrial policies, and manpower and social policies applied in the decade ahead. European governments, together with their North American and Pacific fellow-members, have shown themselves in OECD discussions to be fully aware of the danger of applying defensive micro-policies which, in the end, make the necessary adjustment to macro-economic reality harder to achieve. Starting sometimes from differing social and political convictions, they have recently demonstrated a convergence of opinion on a number of important principles based on their own experience. The ability of the present industrialised world to restore prosperity over the decade ahead will depend narrowly on whether these principles are observed and the temptation to diverge from them — affording very temporary advantage — resisted.

Existing market imperfections lead governments to intervene in the field of competition for many reasons, ranging from the need to control anti-competitive developments and natural monopolies to the desire to reconcile private and social costs. Concentration, which is high in many industries and on the increase, can, if not supervised, establish positions of market-power which effectively relieve firms from pressure to innovate or cut costs. Cartels can protect high-cost firms, and discourage the more efficient members from innovation for fear of upsetting the agreements. Natural monopolies can be vehicles for inefficiency, or used largely for the purposes of social policy, or very often both.

Obviously, in the late 20th century, governments are unlikely to accord total priority to economic efficiency, at the expense of non-economic goals. They have to intervene where markets fail to perform satisfactorily from a social point of view, or where structural crises are particularly severe. What is important is that intervention should be designed to impede efficient market operation, price flexibility and factor mobility as little as possible. It needs to be designed with an overall concept in mind and to be as general and non-discretionary as possible. It has to be sufficiently clear and systematic so as not to discourage firms from long-term planning or make them more nervous of risk-taking and rigid in their attitudes towards innovation. The more firms are apprehensive about the conditions in which they will be operating in the future, the longer they will concentrate on small profits and quick returns, which is unlikely to prove a recipe for sustainable growth in an era of economic change.

Industrial efficiency a decade hence will be greatly influenced by the extent to which governments are able, in designing their policies to regulate business conduct, to avoid restricting the right of entry into industry or other production activities. A major task will be to keep individual regulations under continuous review. With the passage of time, the unintended effects of regulation can become increasingly harmful: the impact of rent control on the

availability and quality of rented accommodation is frequently
quoted in this respect. Regulation may also become less justified
because of technical advance, as current discussions in so many
countries about the future of communications amply demonstrate.
But the most far-reaching impact of competition policy, for good
or ill, on future industrial structures and efficiency is likely to
come from official attitudes towards international trade flows.
The broad arguments against artificial trade barriers hardly need
rehearsing here. But it is perhaps worthwhile underlining the fact
that, to the extent that they encourage international competition,
governments will find intervention to control the use of market-
power less necessary. Retention or introduction of international
trade barriers will increase the need for governments to intervene
to limit the process of domestic concentration, an attitude that can
run contrary to the achievement of efficiency through the exploitation of economies of scale.

A major problem for policy-making lies in the well-known fact
that the burdens that particular sectors experience from strong
competition are easily identifiable, while the benefits flowing
from the division of labour and industrial innovation are more
widely spread and less visible. There is always a tendency to
concentrate on the relief perceived to result from intervention to
protect declining industries, and to ignore the net balance of
advantage. A continuing problem for governments, in coming
years, is likely to lie in the difficulty that electorates have in
realizing that intervention in favour of something is usually at the
expense of something else, tending to erode the incentives
towards innovation and to deprive the economy of the valuable
signals flowing from the market. A linked problem is that policies
to shore up one sectoral interest tend to generate political conflicts
between groups. Unless it is possible to ensure that help for
declining sectors leads to positive remedial action by the recipients
and not simply to temporarily higher profits or wages, industrialised countries in ten years' time are likely to find themselves
housing — and paying for — considerably more lame ducks than
at present. A point which has emerged strongly from recent inter-
governmental discussion is that, where defensive aid has to be
provided, it should be subject to progressive reduction, given
preferably to industries rather than ailing individual firms, and

take the form of open and reviewable subsidies rather than less transparent price-fixing.

In most countries there are likely to be continuing pressures on governments to provide tangible support for promising new industries, despite the fact that experience in recent years has in some cases proved costly. The problems of judgment involved in specific intervention of this type are complex, particularly in the case of projects where the early promise turns out to be elusive but where it isn't clear whether it would be more wasteful to reduce (or abandon) support for them or to pay out more. Private initiative, in such cases, is clearly guided by the extent of loss; but where government finance has been involved, failure often leads to bigger subsidies. Costly dilemmas of this nature (and the cost is spread over the economy as a whole) can best be avoided by action which makes the need for specific intervention by governments in the innovation process increasingly rare — by action to improve the functioning of the markets (particularly the capital markets) themselves and by reducing inflation and the general climate of uncertainty which inhibit the private sector from selecting and backing the promising industries unaided.

Welfare and consensus

For a number of years ahead, combining growth in a market economy with the satisfaction of social concerns is likely to be a major problem for industrialised societies. There will be difficult conflicts between equity and efficiency to resolve, and some danger that they will be resolved at the expense of the structural economic adaptation that the events of the past decade have rendered urgent. In the longer run, equity and efficiency tend to be self-reinforcing. Rising social welfare requires non-inflationary growth and high employment, and achievement of these is greatly facilitated by good social conditions. Nonetheless, in at least the early years of the decade ahead, the design of welfare policies compatible with the efficient functioning of markets may pose a major challenge.

As indicated earlier, there may be growing conflicts of interest between industrial social groups, and in a period when there is going to be a clear need to devote the lion's share of marginal resources to the already overdue improvement of industrial

structures — and when some countries may wish to spend pro-
portionally more on defence — this will make policy formulation
particularly complex. In periods when, from a good starting position, general affluence is rising, governments may be able to meet
(at least minimally) a wide range of conflicting claims because, at
the margin, there is something to give away. The options in the
years ahead may be much less easy. Social welfare has to be
earned: given the slow growth of the past decade and the arrears
of investment, there cannot be much more to be distributed
through social policy until economic growth has been firmly re-
established.

With social welfare schemes now covering virtually all sectors
of the population in industrialised countries (the extension of
coverage beyond those most in need was an important factor
behind past expenditure increases) and with population growth
slowing down, some of the pressure for ever-rising social outlays
will be removed. But the demand for organised welfare seems
likely to remain strong. The slow growth and inflation that limit
the resources available for welfare are also likely to increase the
call for it. There may be rising claims for the protection of
workers thought to be particularly at risk or particularly incapable
of supporting real income depletion — the older ones, the heads of
families, those in jobs particularly exposed to cyclical weakness,
and those likely to be displaced, at least temporarily, by technological changes. Health care costs will increase with an ageing
population and the complexity of modern treatment, and new
socio-economic needs are making themselves felt. There will be
rising pressure for retraining and relocation programmes, for
programmes of public employment and recurrent education, and,
as discussed earlier, for work-sharing schemes which could be
costly. To this must be added the rising demand for expenditure
to protect or improve environmental conditions.

But though demand for social expenditure may be strong,
opposition to its growth may become increasingly marked. With
welfare absorbing 25 per cent of GDP and 60 per cent of public
expenditure by the end of the 1970s (a calculation taking no
account of the public regulations which impose economic costs
but which do not get included in conventional budget statements)
there is already an uneasy realisation of the speed of growth and

of the degree to which certain social programmes are no longer financed, as originally intended, on insurance principles. There is rising apprehension concerning the incidence of social expenditure on employers' labour costs, an emerging tax-resistance in many countries, and a greater propensity for higher taxes and contributions (not all the burden of finance falls upon the rentier) to lead to higher wage claims.

Restoration of growth and stability will thus depend on the ability of governments and the societies they represent to make agonising decisions over the next few years concerning the broad allocation of marginal resources between economic and social programmes, and between different types of social programme. The problem of choice will be exacerbated by the fact that, across the broad spectrum of the provision of social goods, there is a lack of pricing structures which permit clear signals about the efficiency of individual programmes or public preferences to be conveyed. A further complicating factor lies in rising disagreement about the degree of income redistribution now desirable.

There is an obvious emerging need to re-weigh existing social programmes in the light of changing circumstances — reduced birth rates, for example, and ageing populations. It may prove desirable to concentrate programmes rather more strictly on a guarantee of essential security and rather less on promoting equality of life-chances. And it has become increasingly important to subject the programmes to continuous scrutiny in respect of their efficiency and the extent to which they achieve the purposes they are supposed to serve. The quality of welfare services, and the efficiency of their delivery, might be improved if their administration became, increasingly, the responsibility of local levels of governments and voluntary organisations, thereby reintroducing into the concept of public welfare the local and private communal forces which were so influential in its inception.

Local administration, however, cannot conceal the problems concerning the design of social policies that central governments are going to have to solve if economic efficiency is not to suffer and if highly damaging sectoral conflicts are not to emerge. It will be important to avoid an amalgam of social interventions which, because narrowly conceived, turn out to be mutually contradictory. And if, because of resource constraints, social interventions have to become more selective, increasingly careful planning of their allocation will be required. Above all, vast changes may be needed in the machinery of government — where flexibility is normally no more evident than in the private sector — if there is to be sufficient coordination between social and economic policies, and if administrations are going to give practical recognition to the fact that neither economic nor social policy can be meaningful if pursued in isolation.

Prosperity and employment levels ten years hence will thus depend on the democratic system's ability to design welfare policies that are compatible with an efficient and flexible market economy, and to devise economic policies that help welfare. From the point of view of restoring high employment, social policy has to bear in mind that measures to increase job-security and redistribute income can prove self-defeating by making for a more capital-intensive production process, and mainly benefitting those already possessing good jobs. And in times of structural change it is particularly relevant — above all in Europe — to recall that jobs can best be preserved by a flexibility of real wages that enables profits to be sufficient to stimulate adaptation and capital-widening. In the 1970s, wage differentials actually grew in the United States and Japan but shrank in many parts of Europe. It is difficult, to say the least, for a market economy to combine low wage-differentials with the preservation of jobs in threatened sectors.

It is not yet clear whether Europe is going to be able to reconcile the needs of economic policy with the autonomy of the social partners on which modern democracy is founded. It is easy to point to the role for consensus: the agreements on the economic/social trade-off, on income distribution trends and on the breaking-down of labour-market rigidities that are needed if non-inflationary growth is to be restored. Consensus may be extremely difficult to achieve, particularly when stagflation is a major characteristic of the starting position. Meaningful *participation* in decision-making may be facilitated by the fact that rising educational standards make people both more anxious to participate and more capable of doing so. What is less certain, at present, is whether such participation is automatically going to lead to greater *consensus*. As interest groups and minorities become increasingly articulate throughout Europe, their views may become more divergent and harder to reconcile.

It is always tempting to devise new institutional structures in the search for consensus. The past twenty years or so have seen considerable growth of formal institutions to permit the exchange of views between governments, organised labour and employers, and in some European countries these have been followed by growing realization of the need to reach workable joint solutions to the economic and social problems of the day. But history to date suggests that while well-designed participatory structures can improve *understanding* of the issues at stake, they don't necessarily lead to readier *agreement* on how specific issues can best be resolved. There may well be scope for further experimentation in this direction, but it isn't clear that — in the absence of an underlying consensus produced by more normal daily political contacts — institutions can do more than delineate the openings for "a bargain", to be accepted but without relish. Beyond a certain point, institutions built up in the hope of advancing broad political consensus may suffer from the criticism once launched at the narrower concept of incomes policies: if they work, you don't need them anyway, and if you need them, they won't work.

More fundamentally, however, proposals to promote meaningful consensus through institution-building have to be seen against the perspectives appropriate to the concept of the parliamentary system. It is only through parliaments that consensus embracing all strands of the population can be achieved, because it is only in parliaments that all strands are represented. Tripartite discussions between governments, labour organisations and employers can be a useful adjunct to parliaments but cannot replace them, because they risk overlooking the interests of the biggest but the least immediately articulate interest group — the consuming public.

Inter-governmental cooperation

At bottom, however, the relative prosperity of industrialised countries in the 1990s will depend on their ability, in the immediate future, to recognize — and to draw the practical policy implications from — the irreversible strengthening of the international transmission process. With the unprecedented growth of economic linkages in recent years, national markets are increasingly sensitive and vulnerable to outside events and to the policies of other governments at both macro- and micro-economic level. Virtually anything a single nation-state does affects economic interests abroad and provokes a response therefrom.

The OECD countries as a group now rely on exports for some 20 per cent of their output, and imports provide a similar proportion of their expenditure. For the European Community alone, the proportions are as high as 30 per cent. The importance of trade *between* industrialised countries as an engine of growth has been declining in favour of trade with the developing world, which could account for something like half the growth of OECD exports in the decade ahead. Similarly, the vast growth of international financial flows in the 1970s, which followed progressive liberalization and, particularly, the emergence of important new sources of savings and new capital exporters after OPEC I, has served to shrink the world. The striking innovations in banking activity and techniques, the enormous stocks of financial assets which have been built up, and the resulting growth of international indebtedness have added to the forces that make the fortunes of the world economy narrowly dependent on the stability of its component parts. And there are other ways in which economic interdependence is growing. This is clearly apparent in the commodity markets, where pro-cyclical price movements are fostered by the increasing tendency for conjunctural developments to coincide throughout the industrialised world. And it now extends clearly into the field of the environment, with the worldwide dangers of ecological damage and the future problems of administering the "Global Commons". All countries are increasingly exposed to the danger of instability on food markets, with sharply rising world demand and the emergence of a few very big exporting countries. The world population explosion—which will continue at least into the next century—is exerting other important international effects, including migration. And the problem of energy is a world-wide one to which few, if any, countries are immune.

Economic conditions in Europe a decade hence will, thus, depend heavily not only on the balance between success and failure in securing international coordination inside the Communities, but on a strengthening of Europe's ability to work with, rather than against, the rest of the industrialised world (which will by the 1990s have spread well beyond the present confines of OECD) and with the developing countries of the Third World. Accounting, as the *Interfutures* study suggests, for only about 15 per cent of global output by the later years of the century, the Community could hardly hope to prosper in a world in which the main economic actors were pursuing divergent courses and in which the principle of comparative advantage had been largely abandoned.

Recent history suggests that there is, indeed, a desire to increase cooperation between policy-makers. The network of regional and wider inter-governmental institutions, and the parallel network of less-institutionalised contacts, is itself some evidence that the importance of reconciling the broad aims of national policies is recognized, and that there exists a certain political will to solve international economic problems. Inside the present OECD grouping of industrialised countries, the pursuit of common broad strategies has increasingly been put into practice. As a result, the severe effects of OPEC II threw the industrialised world into smaller disarray than the first oil-shock did.

But it would be rash to overestimate the potential for increasing policy coordination in the years immediately ahead: in the absence of new universal upheaval, a quantum jump of the kind experienced after World War II is unlikely. With political conditions (and the electoral cycle) differing between countries, and with strong contrasts between the ways in which individual societies react to changing political and economic events, international obstacles to economic progress will remain, and a major task of governments will be to accommodate and contain them through some mutual give and take. In some fields, indeed — and particularly in trade — there have been signs of an alarming decay which will have to be made good before economic cooperation can be said to be back on trend.

Moreover, the conditions in which the industrialised economies have to operate will be affected by more than the ability of their governments to concert their very broad strategies. Stresses can be eased if, within such strategies, governments are able to coordinate rather better than has sometimes been the case the *tactics* through which they seek to achieve their broad joint aims. It is sometimes far from immaterial to an individual country how others design their more precise mix of policies towards a general goal, and much may depend on realization of the fact that an advanced country's balance of fiscal and monetary policies, for example, or its policies in respect of investment or technology, have important trans-frontier effects. There are obvious social and institutional limits to the extent to which policy-mixes can be made identical, and these are unlikely to disappear within the time-horizon with which this volume is concerned. Moreover, since governments change, so do approaches to the problem of securing economic prosperity and social advance. What will have an important influence on market conditions in the decade ahead will be the extent to which, recognizing that differences of approach at the more detailed policy level exist, governments are ready to do what they can to prevent the inevitable ripple-effects of these differences from becoming tidal.

Industrialised economies are unlikely to be able to remain in something like a one-world liberal system unless public opinion and government action consistently recognize that there are certain minimum international disciplines to be observed, and that there are types of action that, by their nature, are unlikely to bring them profit. As a recent OECD report on Positive Adjustment underlines, an individual country can (to take a single example) alleviate its problems through export subsidies, but all countries cannot. Consistent neglect of so obvious a truth would be likely to break up the one-world system. The *Interfutures* study considered the results that this might have, envisaging a scenario in which the industrialised countries divided into three major blocks — North America, Japan and the European Community — each developing its own preferential arrangements with different regions of the South. The results would bear particularly hard on Europe: they could diminish its annual growth rate by a good 1 per cent over a 15-year stretch.

2

Growth, Investment and Employment in Europe in the 1980s

Michel Albert

During the first fifteen years of the Common Market, from 1958 to 1973, the EEC brought together a group of countries which achieved particularly spectacular economic performances, without precedent in history.

Ten years later, in 1983, the state of the European economy is completely different: for the fourth consecutive year economic growth is more or less zero, which has resulted in a rise in unemployment to a level of over 10 per cent. One of the characteristics of the European economy is that as unemployment increases and continues it tends to become an obstacle to investment, and therefore to growth, and this in several ways as will be described below. Growth, investment and employment are thus interdependent and tend to accentuate each other.

Does this mean that the whole of the 1980s will continue along the same gloomy path as during the first three years? The answer to this question is of paramount importance given the stakes involved—social harmony, economic prosperity, the future of our democratic institutions as well as our security. It would be very rash to claim to shed light on all these questions but an attempt will be made to show how slow growth, by perpetuating itself, is exacerbating the new problems which have begun to turn Europe into a zone of relative under-development.

In outlining the outlook for growth, investment and employment in Europe in the 1980s it is not sufficient to present one

41

uniform picture of the future in OECD countries as a whole. On the contrary, the largely specific nature of the difficulties facing Europe needs to be stressed:

    (a) the outlook for growth cannot be assessed on the assumption "all other things being equal" because the repercussions of errors made in the past will be borne in the years to come;

    (b) furthermore, the problem of unemployment, which has yet to be resolved anywhere, is becoming the predominant problem in Europe more than elsewhere: the rise in unemployment is having increasingly negative effects on the possibility of even re-establishing the rate of growth;

    (c) finally, potential growth in the European economy will be increasingly limited in the medium term by a technological gap which is, possibly, the most serious consequence of the belated state of European integration on the important sectors and technology of the future.

THE RETURN TO SUSTAINED AND LASTING GROWTH IS UNLIKELY IN EUROPE

The cumulative nature of obstacles to growth in the European economy

At the beginning of 1983 there was much talk of the recovery in the USA which had been expected for two years and of the fact that this time there seemed to be several indications that it was finally to come: the price of oil was falling, the dollar too, which is a double advantage for Europeans. Rates of interest were falling and each day new records were being broken on Wall Street. The media were doing their utmost to make us believe that the "run of bad luck" was at last ended.

Unfortunately, there is very little echo of these clarion calls in Mr van Lennep's report, which, in contrast, underlines the serious obstacles to a return to sustained and lasting growth in the OECD.

Similarly, medium term projections at present available paint a very black picture of the future as, for example, the projections made to a horizon of 1987 accompanying the 1982–83 *Annual Economic Report* carried out by the Commission of the European

Communities. These projections are based on the supposition that present economic policy objectives followed by most Member States will be maintained — i.e., priority given to the control of inflation, a rigorous monetary policy and the rejection of any form of expansionary budgetary policy, despite the fact that, as far as the latter point is concerned, the automatic effect of the built-in stabilisers results in a rise in the budget deficit.

On this basis, and assuming an increase in world trade of about 3 per cent, a very slight growth in output is expected (1.6 per cent per annum over the period 1981–87), continued sluggishness in productive investment — except at the end of the period — and a rate of unemployment of over 10.5 per cent by the end of 1983 (12.5 million people) reaching 11 per cent (13 million) by the end of the period. From this it can be seen that, if economic policy remains unchanged, the Community will not manage to break out of the slow growth pattern which has characterised it for many years and the problem of unemployment will simply get worse. What is more, these projections were up-dated in the spring of 1983 and the results seem to confirm these conclusions but with basic data which are even more unfavourable.

This analysis is largely corroborated by projections carried out on a national basis by certain countries. In France the scenarios prepared in drawing up the IX Plan[1] anticipate — whatever the world economy profile supposed and policy mix adopted — that the French economy will follow the same slow growth path as retained, as an hypothesis, for the world economy, and see an increase in unemployment: depending upon the scenario chosen, the rate of unemployment in France will be between 9.2 per cent and 10.1 per cent of the active population; furthermore, this increase in unemployment is expected despite the policy of considerably reducing working hours (35 hours in 1985 or in 1988 according to the case).

These quantitative models should not be ignored: whereas short-term forecasts have frequently been shown to be full of errors over the last ten years or so, in contrast, medium-term forecasts have in general correctly indicated the turning point in

---

1 *Préparation du IXe Plan: Quelques Scénarios d'Evolution à Moyen Terme*, Note de synthèse, Commissariat Général du Plan, Paris, November 1982.

the main trends — slow-down in growth, increase in inflation and unemployment etc. Nevertheless, it is important to stress that the analyses outlined above were established on the basis of econometric models which under-estimate, almost as a result of the way that they have been constructed, the enormous repercussions which the changes of the 1970s and their cumulative effect will have in the future.

Thus, for example, with respect to unemployment, it is not only the increase in the number of persons unemployed which makes this problem a difficult one, but also the length of time it lasts: the longer a person is unemployed the more difficult it is for him or her to find a job. In the EEC as a whole 40 per cent of people unemployed have been so for more than a year. The cost of unemployment in the OECD countries is estimated to amount to about US $350,000 million per annum, more than half of the total volume of developing countries' debt. This figure can but increase as the older strata of unemployment become more rigid.

Thus, in this way, economic stagnation itself automatically reinforces the factors which have caused it. It makes the deficits which it, itself, has generated both impossible to finance and inevitable; it accentuates resistance to change which has been one of its causes and it reinforces the need of firms in difficulty to have recourse to State aid; each day in Europe it increasingly confirms the rule that in a deficit economy there is only one priority, both in the private and public sector, which is to finance the deficits in order to avoid catastrophe at the end of each month.

It will therefore be much more difficult for Europe to avoid declining from stagnation into an economic depression than to avoid the rate of growth falling from 5 per cent to 0 per cent as was the case over the last ten years.

Everything has in fact become much more difficult. The price of oil, even at $25 a barrel, is still double what it was after the first oil crisis; Japan and numerous other countries have grown stronger while Europe has become weaker; and, above all, the successes as well as the errors of the past have made the problems resulting from the crisis progressively worse. The most important is the following: for a generation, thanks to high growth, the economies of Europe have been able to meet both the increase in household demand and the increase in investment made by firms, thereby permitting a simultaneous increase in purchasing power and profits. In contrast, as soon as a group of general constraints reduce the rate of growth to around zero, the system seizes up: in this case either priority is given to consumption as in Europe during the 1970s, but to the detriment of profits and investment; or in contrast, priority is given to profits — but, in this case, the stimulation given by demand to get investment underway again is lacking. Without demand, profits tend to shift into unproductive investment. Today this trend is encouraged by positive real rates of interest at an astonishingly high level which appears to reflect the *de facto* priority given to stockholders as opposed to entrepreneurs ready to take risks. This is undoubtedly the way that inflationary expectations are broken but, often, expansionary expectations are broken at the same time. Thus the cumulative chain reaction takes its course which, in Europe since the end of 1979, has resulted in continually lower growth, less investment, more unemployment and, in turn, lower growth and so on . . . .

In particular those attached to the Welfare State

The Welfare State could continue to be financed as long as it remained possible to pay the cost of the crisis with credit, through an increase in debts: during this transitory period, which ended at the beginning of the 1980s, the preference given to consumption as opposed to investment and the preference given to the present as opposed to the future appeared to be a temporary solution. It has now become a problem, as shown by the level of public and private debt, and one which will have to be resolved urgently since it is automatically self-intensifying.

This is the case as far as taxes and compulsory contributions are concerned, which continue to increase as if according to some sort of genetic code in the demography of Europe, an ageing society in which, as a result, the cost of unemployment, health and retirement as well as all social consumption tend to increase at a particularly rapid rate. In contrast, the consumption of the younger generation (housing and cars for example) tends to be much more market consumption — to the extent that the young are not unemployed.

The disadvantage which the European economy has to bear

compared with its main competitors due to the over-burden of
public finance has been stressed above. However, in addition, this
burden tends to increase very rapidly. For example, the public
authorities' share of current receipts represented more than 45 per
cent of GDP in the EEC in 1982, whereas it represented only 38.3
per cent in 1973 and 32.1 per cent in 1960. In the USA it represents about 32 per cent, but it should be added that this figure
has barely increased by more than one point between 1973 and
1982. The difference between the development in Europe and the
United States is startling: the gap between the share of all types of
taxes and social security contributions in the EEC and the USA
was no more than 5 points in 1960 but had increased to 13 points
by 1982. Over the last ten years or so these taxes and contributions have increased *seven times faster* in terms of relative value in
the EEC than in the USA. Yet, it was the Americans who elected
Ronald Reagan . . . .

Under these conditions European countries can, today, no
longer continue to finance, at the same rate as in the past, a system
which follows an invisible but relentless path and results not only
in an increasing burden of taxes on those in work (with, inciden-
tally, the risk of discouraging them) but also contributes to the
mechanical and psychological strangling of its very foundations —
i.e., the productive force itself. This effect is greater the more the
burden of social security contributions falls on firms, as in France
and Italy. In general a lack of enterprise becomes the inevitable
result of industry's lack of resources when the State takes 50 per
cent of GDP or more.

This stranglehold, this vicious circle must be broken as a matter
of urgency throughout Europe but this is particularly difficult
since the problems have become accentuated by sociological or
psychological reactions which they have engendered (corporate
rigidity, fear of the future and technical progress). In the United
States the crisis of the last few years was a profound economic
shock, comparable with the defeat of Vietnam, and aroused a
vigorous reaction on the part of firms in numerous sectors. In
contrast, the crisis in Europe is somewhat vague and lifeless.
Instead of giving a jolt, it has tended to spread discouragement or
escapism which are the products of unemployment.

UNEMPLOYMENT IS BECOMING THE
PREDOMINANT PROBLEM

The increasingly marked slow-down in growth over the last nine years is affecting attitudes towards the future. After the first oil shock, those in economic activity were still able to consider the high growth of the 1960s as the norm to which the economy could return. In the 1980s it seems more likely that this norm has been revised downwards. This change in expectations is in itself a considerable obstacle to a rapid recovery and any policy which lacks convincing grounds for an upward shift in expectations in the long-term is doomed to failure.[2] This is particularly true as far as unemployment is concerned.

Outlook

As mentioned above, the net creation of employment in the EEC was more or less nil between 1970 and 1982. What is more, the country with the worst results in this respect is the one where the economy remains the strongest: West Germany. To imagine that this trend could change of its own accord would be a profound error. Nobody can believe that the employment crisis will be resolved simply by an upturn in economic growth or even invest-ment. Nor does anyone accept the only solution with certain effectiveness in the short-term — as experienced by President Carter — a reduction in productivity. While the results obtained by several countries in the fight against inflation have been better than hoped, no-one has yet been able to reduce the level of unemployment over the last ten years.

The average rate of growth in Europe during the 1980s will probably be below 2 per cent and the active population will continue to increase by 1 per cent per annum for several years, in particular as a result of the number of women going to work, which, despite a rapid increase, still remains relatively low in Europe.[3]

2 Alfred Steinherr 1982 *The Great Depression: A Repeat in the 1980s?*, Economic Papers, No. 10, Commission of the European Communities, Brussels, November.

3 50 per cent in the EEC compared with 60 per cent in the United States; the difference represents 8 million people.

There is therefore a significant trend towards a still further increase in unemployment, at least during the coming years when the demographic pressures will remain strong. If unemployment continues to increase it will be at the expense of other social benefits. There has already been an initial attempt to control the increase in expenditure on health throughout Europe in the beginning of the 1980s. The share of the cost of medical treatment borne by the patient has been increased and the reimbursement of costs has been reduced throughout. In several countries a flat-rate payment for hospitalisation has been introduced and even in the Netherlands, the champion of social security, it has been advocated that, in 1983, a freeze should be put on all social benefits and that there should be restrictions and a return towards individual financing, for example through voluntary insurance above a certain income threshold. This is but a beginning: with the present worsening trends, in particular the increase in unemployment, most Europeans will have to pay for hospital treatment themselves within the next ten years.

Unemployment, the antithesis to investment

Faced with America, where unemployment has scarcely affected the vitality of firms nor individuals' taste for technical progress, and faced with Japan, which has been able to establish its most brilliant technological breakthroughs on employment guaranteed for life in large firms and the maintenance of full employment, Europe will be increasingly handicapped in international competition by its eleven million unemployed who are likely to become fifteen million well before 1990, particularly since in Europe unemployment is becoming a sort of drug.

In the United States, which is a society of cold and hard but dynamic individual achievement, unemployment has always existed and is more easily supported since it is concentrated among minorities and does not prevent the others from hoping that they will fulfill themselves through their own personal initiative or from continuing to believe in progress.

It is very different in Europe. Here, for the nations who, for the past generation, have staked everything· on the possibility of building, as stated by Beveridge, "full employment in a free society" by developing as nowhere else social benefits of all types, unemployment has become a mental illness. Not the physical pain of an empty stomach but the obsession of a hollow heart, a cancer of the soul. A cancer which spreads its malignant cells throughout all organs of society, which saps energy, affects the resilience of investment, provokes the rejection of new technology and leads to general demoralisation. Here are some of the examples of the *misdirection of civic values* which result from unemployment.

The first shows itself at national level and is too well known to be described in detail — *protectionism*. Unemployment has the effect, whether desired or not, of giving the most aberrant forms of protectionism the appearance of being in the national and common interest. Everyone knows that a country in a state of full employment which closes its frontiers is likely to harm itself as much as its partners. But when certain imports increase the number of factory closures and the queues of unemployed, what is in the national interest? What is the duty of politicians? Alas, it becomes dangerously less evident!

A further example of the misdirection of civic values is that which tends to inhibit technical progress in firms. What answer is given by directors of firms when asked the following question. Suppose that tomorrow you have the possibility of financing and exploiting a very profitable investment but one which would mean that 10 or 20 per cent of your workers would be made redundant: Would you hesitate before making the investment? When numerous directors in several European countries were asked this question they all had much hesitation before replying. Indeed, in Europe, when a certain level of unemployment is reached, a sort of latent civic responsibility emerges which tends to make directors of firms slow down their investment rather than reduce their personnel. This results in a *cumulative process which widens the technological gap still further*. The fact that the two countries which are by far the most advanced in the field of robots are the two developed countries which have best been able to maintain full employment — Japan and Sweden[4] — is revealing in this respect.

4 The number of robots is assessed per 10,000 workers in 1980: Sweden 8, Japan 6, USA 1.6, Germany 1.1, Italy 0.9, France 0.7, Great Britain 0.3. Michel Richonnier 1982 *Crises et Nouvelles Technologies*, Commissariat Général du Plan, Paris.

However, it is not only at national level and within the firm that unemployment causes a misdirection of civic values and the spirit of solidarity. The same happens at the deepest level of the *individual consciousness of workers:* at this level unemployment is not only a cause of social resistance to technical progress, particularly by questioning education as a means of achieving social mobility, but it spreads the idea that by working slightly less through a reduction in effort, the person with the privilege of employment helps his friends, who have to line up outside the factory or office, to find a job. This is why, almost everywhere, the system of production and distribution can be seen to be working less effectively with, in particular, a multiplication of delays and mistakes in the tertiary sector in certain countries.

THE ELECTRONICS INDUSTRY

When the Polish philosopher Krzysztof Pomian considered the "crisis of the future" in Europe recently, he wondered if we were not in the process of losing the "psychology of productive investment" which emerged here in the seventeenth century and made Europe the foremost industrial power in the world.[5] A perspective of at least a hundred years is necessary to understand both the revolutionary character of electronics and new information techniques and the sudden sterility and dramatic eclipse which characterises Europe now in this respect.

A complete revolution

It is still possible, even today, to hear economists pronouncing about the reduction in the return on capital. Are they really aware of the true economic impact of the technological revolution? Have they seen an ordinary cement factory where computerisation has resulted in a 1000 per cent increase in productivity within a few years? Do they ignore the fact that an electronic typewriter only costs $1000 and a multi-functional robot only $100,000?[6] Do they not know that the services sector which, up to now, has tended to decrease the average level of productivity in

5 *Débats*, 1980.

6 That is, much less than the current labour cost for a young worker, whereas a robot can often replace five or ten.

the economy, has now made a revolutionary step along the path of industrialisation through the use of data processing? In practically all cases, whether the factory, the bank, the hospital or administration, it is certainly not the low return on capital which is making it more difficult to lower production costs but, in contrast, mental attitudes, social resistance. In a word, the capacity of workers to accept these technological advances.

This is the crux of the problem of how to achieve growth, investment and employment in Europe in the coming ten years: reliable studies based on the hypothesis that the saving in the number of jobs will only be 5 per cent by the end of this period show that the number of jobs lost will reach 7 million.[7]

This figure alone illustrates the urgent need for the European economy to create the maximum number of jobs in the electronics industry itself. However, just the reverse is happening. The elimination of jobs due to electronics is now well underway here in Europe while the creation of corresponding employment is to be found to an increasing extent in Japan and America.

The European economy is being hit by the technological shock

All studies show the relative weakness, and above all the deterioration, in the trading position of Europe in the sphere of high technology goods. Table 2.1 illustrates this, as well as the spectacular improvement of the relative position of the Japanese and the slight deterioration in the Americans' relative position.[8]

The relative position of the countries in the European Community is undoubtedly worsened by the fact that the figures shown above include intra-Community trade which has a higher level of less sophisticated goods than extra-Community trade, which is not surprising. The trend is, however, so significant as to be indisputable: high technology goods represent a higher proportion of American and Japanese exports than in Europe, a fact which helps to shelter these countries from fluctuations in

7 Michel Richonnier 1982 *Crises et Nouvelles Technologies*, Commissariat Général du Plan, Paris.
8 The index shown is similar to an index of specialisation. It relates the importance of exports of high technology goods as a proportion of total world exports of these goods to the importance of total exports of these countries in total world trade.

TABLE 2.1
EXPORT OF HIGH TECH-
NOLOGY GOODS: COMPA-
RATIVE ADVANTAGE

	1963	1970	1980
EEC	1.02	0.94	0.88
USA	1.29	1.27	1.20
Japan	0.56	0.87	1.41

(*Source*: Services of the European Commission, *The Competitivity of Industries of the Community*, 1982.)

exchange rates and changes in the economic situation. It is true to say that in the USA and Japan there is a better industrial special-isation of exports. This is also corroborated by a recent study carried out by the Paribas Bank. This shows that the EEC is by far the most important world exporter of highly sophisticated tech-nological goods, a sphere in which it has progressed considerably over the last ten years compared with the USA, which has fallen back.[9] Nevertheless, the EEC continues to be in substantial deficit vis-à-vis the USA in trade for these goods and now is also in deficit vis-à-vis Japan; the EEC's surplus is only achieved thanks to its trade with developing countries[10] and countries in the Eastern bloc. This situation reveals an undoubted increasing state of technological inferiority compared with the most advanced countries and a greater degree of vulnerability to competition from the Third World in time. It is perhaps not an exaggeration to say that Europe has undergone a true "technological shock" similar to the "oil shock". In contrast, Japan is in surplus with all these trading zones and the USA is only in deficit with Japan.

These figures are particularly alarming since high technology goods are, in part, linked to sectors such as new sources of energy, aeronautics, space or biotechnology, in which Europe's position

9 This result, which concerns trade flows in volume terms, is not in contradiction with the former which relates to a specialisation index.

10 This is particularly clear in the case of the two great colonial powers of the last century, Great Britain and France, which continue to benefit from windfall returns in certain Third World countries. However, these advantages will be eroded in time.

TABLE 2.2
TRADE BALANCE FOR HIGHLY SOPHISTICATED
TECHNOLOGICAL GOODS IN 1980 ($1000 million)

	USA	Japan	EEC	Total
OECD	+7.1	+9	−8	8.1
of which:				
EEC	+8.1	+3.5	—	
United States	—	+2.3	−9.4	
Japan	−3.1	—	−5	
Non-OECD	+9.5	+10.5	+16	36
Total	16.6	19.5	8	44.1

Tables 2.1 and 2.2 are not comparable. The nomenclature of high technology goods used in the Commission's report is different from that used
by the Paribas Bank.
(*Source*: *Monthly Economic Bulletin of the Paribas Bank*, October 1982.)

remains strong. They do not therefore underline sufficiently the
tragic nature of Europe's weaknesses in the sphere of information
technology. It is well known that the Japanese dominate 80 per
cent of the European market in videos, but, what is worse, in
sectors such as integrated circuits as well as data-processing, the
biggest European firm (Philips in the first case and CII–HB in the
second) is only tenth at world level; and not one EEC firm is to
be found among the ten biggest world producers of robots. All
these sectors related to electronics, which are growing at a rate of
10–30 per cent per annum, are mainly benefitting Japan and the
United States.

The cost of a non-existent Europe

Europe's dependence is even greater in the case of electronics than
in the case of energy. For the first time since the eighteenth
century the main drive behind an industrial revolution is not
coming from Europe. Europe is in the process of letting the third
industrial revolution slip by just at the time when the enormous
increase in Soviet military potential is creating an Achilles heel in
western defence with serious consequences for the future of our
economy.

Yet, in the economic sphere Europe has the means necessary
but persists in rendering them unproductive.

The demand is there since, united, Europe represents a market

which is equivalent to that of the United States. The supply is
there too since Europe has as much scientific, technical and industrial capacity as its competitors. In fact, together, the countries of
the EEC spend twice as much money on research as Japan:
between 1977 and 1981 the credit provided for microprocessors
amounted to $500 million in the EEC compared with $250
million in Japan, and yet the Japanese have managed to catch up
with the United States and now supply 40 per cent of the world
market in microprocessors while Europe only supplies 10 per cent.
Why? There are undoubtedly several reasons but the most important is certainly that the word "Europe" can only be used here as
an antiphrasis. There is no Europe in this respect. There is only a
non-existent Europe in which each member still believes that it
will be able to get stronger by weakening the others. As a result,
the same expenditure which, in Japan, represents productive
investment and creates employment, in the EEC represents a
waste and serves as a welcome alibi for the loss of employment.

This is not a new development. Even as far back as 1964 a
young director of the EIB, responsible for loans in member countries, suggested to the Management Committee that a project of
common European interest be financed concerning the most
important data-processing firm in the Six at the time. This project
would have easily obtained the necessary guarantees. The majority
on the Committee at the time refused to consider it even before
examining it.

At a general level, European integration is only useful in sectors
with a future, where the economies of scale are the most important, yet a sort of sado-masochistic dissipation of energy has led to
the common institutions being specialised in sectors of the past
where there is little to be gained from uniting.

In his report, van Lennep emphasised that the overall reduction
in industrial employment in Europe of 1.5 per cent per annum can
be explained to a large extent by the fact that, given the loss in
jobs in the traditional sectors, the development in new sectors is
not rapid enough. He adds that industrial policy is mainly concerned with sectors of the past. This is true at national level, but
even more so at Community level where the emphasis has been
placed on defending the past and discouraging conquests of the
future.

It is no accident that the net flow of American investment in Europe has gone abruptly into reverse over the last few years and has been replaced by substantial European investment in the United States. Apart from the security aspect, Europe is still far from forming a real common market. The barriers and divisions which still exist present obstacles which compel the most successful European firms to prove themselves on the North American market and therefore to export their energies there.

Arriving in London for the summit in November 1981, Chancellor Schmidt declared "I have not come here to discuss eggs, butter or milk". Nevertheless, he did so since these, together with fisheries and steel, are the preferred subjects of these inheritors of our old nations' past when they meet, like a bourgeoise family whose heritage is in danger. With the exception of the establishment of the EMS, which today is under threat, there has been no important concrete initiative or creative impulse in the EEC for over ten years.

It is not Europe which is sliding down the slippery slope of relative under-development and zero growth. It is the non-existent Europe.

We are only just beginning to pay the price. Not only in the form of increasing taxes, accumulating debts, technology which evades us and jobs which are disappearing, but also, more seriously, in terms of a slackening off, deviancy, demoralisation and insecurity.

For how long will we continue to pay in this way? It is up to Europeans to decide: as has been shown throughout these pages there is no fatality in what is happening but many errors and, above all, the lack of awareness of what is going on.

An important Head of State in Europe declared recently: "If Europe is sick, it is from unconsciousness". It is of this which we must be aware if we wish the 1980s to end better than they started.

3

Investment and the International Monetary and Financial Environment

Alexandre Lamfalussy

Three elements in the international monetary and financial environment are at present (in the spring of 1983) directly or indirectly exerting a strong influence on investment in Europe. All three are so entrenched in western economic life that there is every likelihood that they will persist. They are: the inflationary legacy affecting the level, volatility and structure of interest rates; the tensions in the international financial system and the rôle of the banks in financing external deficits; and the erratic fluctuations in exchange rates.

All these elements are interrelated; they are examined separately below purely for reasons of orderly presentation.

INTEREST RATES

The most direct influence on the level and structure of investment in Europe is interest rates. Since the beginning of the 1980s the money and capital markets in the major countries of the western world, and in particular in the United States, have been dominated by the extreme volatility of interest rates, by their exceptionally high level both in nominal and in real terms and, recurrently, by the inversion of the yield curve.

Firstly, money-market rates began to fluctuate sharply. The movements were sudden and steep and involved all maturities — day-to-day, one-month and three-month. To begin with, it was mainly short-term rates that were affected, but the volatility gradually spread to capital-market rates as well.

Then, beginning in 1979, came the considerable rise in the general level of interest rates, to the extent that, in contrast with the experience of the previous few years, real rates in the major financial centres of the world became substantially positive. More significantly still, the decline in nominal interest rates since the summer of 1982 has not been much faster than that in the rate of inflation, which is the same thing as saying that real rates have still not eased from their abnormal level. In some cases they have even risen further. To put real interest rates in perspective, they must be compared with the pace of economic growth. Theory teaches us (and historical experience has borne this out) that in the long run there must be a certain correspondence between these two rates: a real economic growth rate of 3 per cent per annum can comfortably accommodate a real interest rate of the same order. Any appreciable discrepancy between the two is a source of disequilibrium, with either inflationary or deflationary consequences. Now, what do we find today? For a number of years the western economy has been stagnating, while real interest rates, depending on the country, have been in the range of 3 to 6 per cent. This is a disequilibrium that cannot last. Unless there is a rapid fall in real rates, the restoration of equilibrium will in all likelihood come about through a reduction in capital formation and, hence, in the rate of growth.

Finally, on repeated occasions over the last few years we have seen the yield curve inverted: that is, short-term rates have for lengthy periods been higher than capital-market rates.

The first of these factors has had two consequences. On the one hand, it has added to the climate of uncertainty, perpetuated by the numerous oil and other shocks that have incessantly bombarded the world economy. An additional uncertainty premium is patently having an adverse impact on investment. Secondly, the great volatility of interest rates has led to increasing use of floating-rate loans, and this has conspicuously weakened the effectiveness of monetary policy. A restrictive monetary policy dampens economic activity in two ways: rising interest rates discourage investment, but they also restrain the supply of credit from the banks by "locking in" their bond portfolios through the erosion in their capital value. Floating interest rates cancel out any erosion effect of this kind. The second factor, namely the abnormally high level of real interest rates, does not call for any particular comment: its incidence on investment is obvious. Finally, an inverted yield curve discourages the financial intermediaries from maturity transformation, or, in more positive terms, encourages them to jump on the floating interest rate bandwagon. Taken together, these three factors exert a deeply disturbing effect on the functioning of the capital markets, which is bound to act as a further brake on investment.

All three of these factors have their roots in the mounting inflationary pressures of the 1970s and the very tardy response of the authorities. For a long time monetary policies had taken an accommodating stance vis-à-vis the inflation process. This, together with the persistence of money illusion, had kept real interest rates negative. The turning-point came during 1978–79, when the US monetary authorities gradually became aware of the seriousness of the inflationary problem.

As a result of this growing awareness, the US Federal Reserve set its monetary policy on a much more restrictive course, with the adoption of more moderate growth targets for the money aggregates. From being accommodating, its policy became downright restrictive. At the same time, the monetary authorities introduced a new monetary control technique, attaching greater weight than in the past to direct control of the volume of reserves made available to the banks.

The first of these measures had the immediate effect of raising the general level of interest rates in the United States and, by contagion, in Europe. The subsequent implementation by the Reagan Administration of an unambiguously expansionary fiscal policy increased the upward pressure. The whole burden of the anti-inflationary struggle was thus shifted onto monetary policy. The new control technique, for its part, introduced an element of instability into the formation of short-term interest rates, since the Federal Reserve explicitly left it to the market to fix the Federal funds' rate from day to day. The instability of the short-term market then gradually infected the bond market. Finally, the combination of rising and more volatile rates repeatedly led to the inversion of the yield curve.

These developments can readily account for the evolution of the markets up to the beginning of 1982. But what is the explanation for the persistence of very high *real* interest rates since mid-1982 — i.e. well into a period of disinflation?

Two interrelated hypotheses can be advanced. The first would point not only to the final dispelling of money illusion but also to the stubborn persistence of inflationary expectations. For a true assessment of the real interest rate level, one must deduct from the nominal rate not the *past* inflation rate but the *expected* inflation rate. Persistent inflationary expectations mean in fact that the latter rate is still higher than the former. Given the length of the inflationary experience — the phenomenon of rising prices has not been confined to the 1970s — and the enduring doubts among the general public regarding the authorities' determination to adhere to their anti-inflationary stance, this hypothesis is, alas, quite plausible. But it is somewhat tautological, in that inflationary expectations are not amenable to any kind of independent measurement.

However this may be, it can usefully be supplemented by another hypothesis: this is based on observation of the policy mix — i.e. the combination of monetary and budgetary policy — to which reference has already been made above. Anticipation of growing budget deficits of a "structural" nature (i.e. independent of the level of economic activity) in itself exerts, via expectations, upward pressure on interest rates. This influence is further reinforced by the inflationary implications which the general public, rightly or wrongly, attributes to this policy.

Two questions can fairly be asked with regard to this tentative analysis: Does it explain the behaviour of interest rates elsewhere than in the United States? And, is it a lasting phenomenon, or is it rather a temporary feature of the current, inevitably transitory, phase of the fight against inflation? To the first question I have no hesitation in replying in the affirmative. The influence of US interest rates on the markets of all developed countries, and hence on those of Europe, is undeniable — contrary to the hopes of those who saw the floating of currencies as a means of insulating their economies from external influences. As will be noted later, these hopes have been dashed. When real exchange rates fluctuate widely in an inflationary world environment, the country whose currency depreciates in real terms is subjected to inflationary pressure from outside that it can only counter by holding its interest rates at a real level incompatible with the needs of its domestic economy. We should bear in mind the German experience of 1981–82. A transmission of interest rates from the dominant economy occurs, in fact, under any exchange rate system.

The reply to the second question has to be more qualified. In a number of major countries we have just won an important battle against inflation. But are we going to win the war? Nothing is less certain. Under-utilisation of equipment and the under-employment of manpower are moderating inflationary expectations. But these expectations are such an integral part of our life that they could well flare up again, not at the first signs of economic recovery, but perhaps during the later stages of sustained expansion. Another dose of anti-inflationary policy might then prove necessary. However, given the difficulties attaching to the manipulation of the budgetary and fiscal levers, it is a safe bet that in such an event monetary policy would again be called upon to play the leading rôle. Thus, the phenomena described at the beginning of this section have every prospect of enduring.

INTERNATIONAL FINANCIAL SYSTEM

It is obviously premature to start considering systematically and in depth the long-term effects that the present tensions in the international financial system could have on investment worldwide and, *a fortiori*, in Europe. The international financial scene is in such flux that it makes any forward-looking analysis impossible. I shall therefore confine myself to presenting one or two trains of thought.

These observations are based on two underlying assumptions: The first is that there will be continued effective co-operation between the four main actors on the international financial scene — the IMF, the Central Banks, the commercial banks, and the debtor countries. The second is that a gradual economic recovery will spread out from those major western countries that have succeeded in containing inflation, whose domestic financial management is not seriously compromised, and which are not subject to severe balance-of-payments constraints. A recovery of this nature, provided that it does not go hand-in-hand with a renewed surge in interest rates, would contribute mightily towards improving the external accounts of the debtor countries. It would thus supplement the emergency financial operations undertaken by the IMF and the Central Banks, give encouragement to the banks that have maintained or even raised the level of their international lending, and, finally, vindicate the adjustment efforts made by the countries heavily in debt. In short, the observations that follow presuppose that even if they persist, the present financial tensions will continue to be contained.

Let me begin with a brief historical review. The most important feature of the international financial scene over the last ten years has been the large-scale involvement of the western commercial banks in financing current-account imbalances (see Table 3.1). In part it has taken the form of direct recycling of the OPEC countries' financial surpluses, in particular during 1974–75 and 1979–80; but during the rest of the decade 1973–82 it went far beyond this type of international financial intermediation. Over most of this period the banks continued to finance a significant proportion of the external deficits of the non-oil developing countries, the socialist countries and the industrial countries outside the Group of Ten, even though OPEC ceased to make any substantial contribution to their resources — such as in 1976–78 or 1981. During these years their resources were provided by the countries inside the BIS "reporting area" — essentially the countries of the Group of Ten and Switzerland. In this substitution process, the lion's share was accounted for by banking capital exports from the United States. It should be added — something which is not revealed in the Table — that bank financing played a no less significant rôle within the reporting area itself, such as in the cases of Italy, France, Belgium, Sweden and Denmark, and even, in 1975–76, the United Kingdom.

By the end of the ten-year period, during which the growth of international lending by the main western banks regularly outpaced that of foreign lending, the western banking system found itself with a radically different balance-sheet structure from that in the early 1970s. The change involved both sides of the balance sheet. On the assets side as on the liabilities side the proportion of the total external component increased. Moreover, for many

TABLE 3.1

ESTIMATED FLOWS (IN US $ BILLIONS AT CONSTANT END-OF-PERIOD EXCHANGE RATES) BETWEEN THE BIS-REPORTING BANKS[1] AND GROUPS OF COUNTRIES OUTSIDE THE REPORTING AREA, 1974–82

Items	Stocks at end-1973	Flows[2]									Stocks at end-June 1982
		1974	1975	1976	1977	1978	1979	1980	1981	1st half of 1982	
OPEC countries[3]											
deposits	16.0	26.5	7.5	12.5	12.5	3.0	37.0	41.5	3.0	−7.5	145.0
borrowings	6.5	2.5	5.0	9.5	11.0	16.5	7.0	7.0	4.0	4.5	74.9
net[4]	9.5	24.0	2.5	3.0	1.5	−13.5	30.0	34.5	−1.0	−12.0	70.1
Memorandum item: Current-account balance	.	66.0	31.0	37.0	27.0	−2.0	66.0	110.0	65.0	—	.
(of which: share of bank deposits in the counterpart[5])	.	(36%)	(8%)	(8%)	(6%)	(675%)	(45%)	(31%)	(..)	(..)	.
Other LDCs[6]											
deposits	27.5	4.0	4.0	11.5	12.0	14.0	12.5	4.0	9.5	3.0	99.7
borrowings	32.0	15.0	15.0	16.5	10.5	22.0	35.5	39.0	40.0	15.0	241.7
net[4]	−4.5	−11.0	−11.0	−5.0	1.5	−8.0	−23.0	−35.0	−30.5	−12.0	−142.0
Memorandum item: Current-account balance	.	−24.0	−31.0	−20.0	−13.0	−24.0	−40.0	−63.0	−73.0	−35.0	.
(of which: share of bank borrowing in the counterpart[5])	.	(46%)	(35%)	(25%)	(..)	(33%)	(57%)	(56%)	(42%)	(34%)	.

Developed countries[7]											
deposits	27.0	0.5	5.5	1.5	4.5	8.5	7.5	6.0	3.5	—	48.7
borrowings	23.0	7.5	10.0	12.5	12.5	6.0	7.5	15.5	17.0	9.0	104.3
net[4]	4.0	−7.0	−4.5	−11.0	−8.0	2.5	—	−9.5	−13.5	−9.0	−55.6
Memorandum item: Current-account balance[8]	.	−17.0	−19.0	−21.0	−22.0	−7.0	−6.0	−14.0	−30.0	−16.0	.
(of which: share of bank borrowing in the counterpart[5])		*(41%)*	*(24%)*	*(52%)*	*(36%)*	*(..)*	*(—)*	*(68%)*	*(45%)*	*(56%)*	
Eastern Europe											
deposits	4.5	1.5	0.5	1.0	—	1.5	4.5	1.0	—	−2.5	11.8
borrowings	9.5	3.5	8.5	6.5	2.0	5.5	7.0	7.0	4.5	−3.0	54.1
net[4]	−5.0	−2.0	−8.0	−5.5	−2.0	−4.0	−2.5	−6.0	−4.5	0.5	−42.3
Memorandum item: Current-account balance[8]	.	−5.0	−12.0	−11.5	−9.0	−10.0	−6.5	−5.0	−9.0	−6.0	.
(of which: share of bank borrowing in the counterpart[5])		*(40%)*	*(67%)*	*(48%)*	*(22%)*	*(40%)*	*(38%)*	*(120%)*	*(50%)*	*(..)*	
Unallocated[9]											
deposits	7.5	2.5	4.5	3.0	5.0	7.5	5.0	9.0	5.0	(..)	48.0
borrowings	4.5	1.5	4.0	1.5	7.0	6.0	5.0	5.0	2.5		27.0
net[4]	3.0	1.0	0.5	1.5	−2.0	1.5	—	4.0	2.5		21.0
Total											
deposits	82.5	35.0	22.0	29.5	34.5	32.0	69.0	57.5	25.0	−2.0	353.2
borrowings	75.5	30.0	42.5	46.5	39.0	57.0	63.0	73.5	70.5	28.0	502.0
net[4]	7.0	5.0	−20.5	−17.0	−4.5	−25.0	6.0	−16.0	−45.5	−30.0	−148.8

Notes to Table are on page 64

Table 3.1 Notes

1 Up to 1977 the BIS reporting banks covered Belgium–Luxembourg, Canada, France, West Germany, Italy, Japan, the Netherlands, Sweden, Switzerland, the United Kingdom, the United States, and the branches of US banks in the Bahamas, Cayman Islands, Panama, Hong Kong and Singapore. Thereafter they also covered Austria, Denmark and Ireland, as well as certain trade-related items in domestic currency for banks in France and the United Kingdom not included before.

2 The total of the flow figures shown for each of the years under consideration may not necessarily be equal to the difference between the amounts outstanding at the beginning and the end of the whole period, as a result both of breaks in the series and of the method used for the calculation of flow figures.

3 Includes, in addition, Bahrain, Brunei, Oman and Trinidad and Tobago.

4 A minus sign equals net borrowing.

5 Percentage share of *net* bank deposits or borrowings by these groups of countries in financing the current-account balance; a (.) sign here means that these deposit or borrowing operations accentuated the current-account surplus or deficit.

6 Excludes offshore centres.

7 Including up to 1977 Austria, Denmark and Ireland, which are thereafter considered as part of the reporting area.

8 Current balance (excluding gold sales) in convertible currencies vis-à-vis developed countries.

9 Includes non-reporting offshore centres (Barbados, Bermuda, other British West Indies, Lebanon, Liberia, Netherlands Antilles and Vanuatu) and international institutions other than the BIS.

banks, particularly non-US banks, the process of internationalisation also took the form of an accelerated growth of balance-sheet
components denominated in foreign currencies. In the case of a
number of the major banks heavily engaged in international
business, the "degree of internationalisation" on the basis of one
or other of these criteria rose to 30, 40 or even 50 per cent.

It was with this new balance-sheet structure that the banks in
1982 were confronted with involving the external debt-servicing
problems of a growing number of countries, firstly in eastern
Europe, then in Latin America. These problems were born of the
combined effects of several developments. On the one hand, there
was the gradual drift by a number of countries into certain over-
indebtedness, made possible both by mismanagement by the
debtor countries themselves and by the banks' over-generosity in
granting loans not tied to adjustment conditions. On the other
hand, the evolution of the world economy — weak import
demand on the part of the industrial countries, a fall in commodity prices and a sharp increase in interest rates — caused problems
even for those debtor countries whose domestic management,
though not entirely above reproach, was at least free of obvious
error. In 1979–80 the financial burden of foreign debt began to
reach manifestly excessive levels for whole groups of countries.
The political "shocks" — Poland, the Falklands war — finally set
spark to tinder and spread the "risk regionalisation" syndrome.
The abrupt halt in bank lending made it impossible to refinance
the outstanding debts and ultimately created difficulties even for
those countries whose financial management had previously been
praised. These difficulties in turn led the banks to undertake a
general revision of their international lending policies.

If the change in the banks' lending policy were to prove lasting,
investment in Europe could be adversely affected via several channels.

Firstly, and indirectly, through the depressive impact of the
banks' refusal to participate in financing the future external deficits of countries outside western Europe. Even on the optimistic
assumption that a third oil shock could be avoided, a scenario
without balance-of-payments deficits, even lasting ones, in the
developing countries is hardly conceivable: how could the transfer
of real resources take place without such deficits? It is difficult to

see who would take over from financing by the banks, which, as Table 3.1 shows, represented, in terms of *net* lending, some US $30 to 35 billion a year in 1980 and 1981. The political climate would seem to rule out any revival of direct investment; increased official financing faces political obstacles; the chances are that the contribution from international organisations — the IMF and the World Bank — will increase, but the extra from this source will hardly compensate for a large cutback by the banks. The result could be a lasting check on world economic growth, either because the deficits could not be financed or because they would be financed in ways which would push world trade towards an unproductive, inefficient and retrograde bilateralism.

The change in the banks' lending policy could also have a more direct influence on European investment to the extent that it may involve a reduced supply of credit not only to the developing and Eastern bloc countries but also to the countries of western Europe and, in particular, of the EEC. It is very difficult to make any forecasts in this respect. In the spring of 1983 the contagion has not yet spread to the OECD and it is possible that it will not do so. It is even conceivable that the banks will make up for the reduction in their volume of business with the rest of the world with a sharper expansion of foreign lending within Europe.

Finally, mention should be made of the most indirect and diffuse, though not necessarily the least disturbing, influence that international financial tensions could exert on investment activity in Europe. Even if these tensions continue to be contained, an assumption that I believe to be plausible, the chances are that they will not disappear overnight and will therefore have a lasting effect on the banks' operations by instilling a sense of caution into their management which, if carried to the extreme, could discourage industrial initiatives.

EXCHANGE RATES

Apart from a few interruptions, most of the major currencies have been floating against each other for precisely ten years; that is, since the spring of 1973. Floating has been accompanied by large and very frequent exchange-rate fluctuations, whether the rates considered are bilateral or effective, nominal or real. For some years now these fluctuations have been worsening. The longer-term movements in real rates have become larger; short-term volatility has become more marked.

Let me give a few examples of fluctuations in real effective exchange rates — that is, adjusted for inflation differentials. Take the US dollar: after depreciating by some 17 per cent between December 1975 and October 1978, it then appreciated by almost 40 per cent by December 1982. As for the Deutsche mark, it depreciated by 15 per cent between December 1979 and December 1982. The yen — still in terms of real effective exchange rates — went through several cycles: a 40 per cent rise between January 1975 and April 1978; then a 35 per cent fall by February 1980; a renewed rise up to February 1981; finally, a 20 per cent decline by October 1982. Sterling first soared by almost 70 per cent between October 1976 and January 1981, only to fall back by around 20 per cent by February 1983.

Sufficient illustration of short-term exchange rate volatility is afforded by the Deutsche mark/US dollar rate. Whereas the number of days during which this rate moved by more than 1 per cent could be counted on one's fingers in 1975–77, it rose to 27 in 1980 and 62 in 1981, then fell back to 37 in 1982. During the first two months of 1983 fluctuations of more than 1 per cent occurred on one day out of every three.

It is hard to conceive how the variability of a price as important as the exchange rate could fail to have adverse effects on economic decision-making. For most of the western countries, and for the countries of western Europe in particular, no "relative" price counts for as much in the allocation of resources as the exchange rate. Even the price of energy is of less importance. The exchange rate is important not only in trade in goods and services, but also in valuing assets and liabilities, claims and debts. Extreme variability in this key price inevitably adds to the climate of uncertainty, perpetuated by so many other factors, and inhibits the whole range of decisions taken by businessmen, whether on production, trade or investment.

The large fluctuations in effective exchange rates seem to me to be even more damaging than the day-to-day variability. The fact that they have gradually eroded confidence in the basic principles of the theory of purchasing-power parity and have, as a result, caused major intellectual discomfort to both theorists and practitioners of economic policy, is the lesser evil. But they have also created new problems for the management of economies — or, more precisely, against all expectations, they have exacerbated the very difficulties that the floating of currencies had been supposed to eliminate.

For we should not forget that two arguments in particular had been put forward in favour of free-floating in the early 1970s, before the collapse of the Bretton Woods system.

The first held that responsibility for conducting domestic policies should be restored to governments. Let the authorities choose their priorites (the argument ran) and let the exchange rate suffer the consequences. If country A opts for full employment and ignores the rate of inflation — i.e. chooses a particular point on the Phillips curve, which at the time was still thought to be relatively stable — let it take the consequences of its choice in the shape of a depreciation of the external value of its currency. It will not then "contaminate" the rest of the world, since its inflationary forces will not be transmitted abroad. In this way, country B's freedom of choice in taking the opposite course and setting price stability as its priority objective is also respected. It will pursue its policy undisturbed, sheltered by the appreciation of its currency. Each country will thus preserve its independence vis-à-vis the international environment.

According to the second argument, floating was preferable to maintaining fixed parities because it would pre-empt protectionist pressures. There was, it was said, a great danger that the defence of "unrealistic" parities would push some governments towards exchange controls or, worse, towards administrative import barriers or export subsidies — in short, towards measures which would distort trade in goods and services.

Both of these arguments have been cruelly disproved by events: the large fluctuations in effective exchange rates (i.e. in countries' competitive positions) have shattered the theory of freedom of policy choice in the case of those countries whose currencies have depreciated in real terms, while they have given rise to strong protectionist pressures in those countries whose currencies have appreciated too far.

The first case was illustrated by Germany's experience in 1981 and early 1982. As we have noted, the real effective exchange rate of the Deutsche mark depreciated by some 15 per cent during 1981–82, which meant that by the end of the period Germany's competitive position was back more or less at the level at which it had stood on the eve of the collapse of the Bretton Woods system in the spring of 1973. It was generally agreed that the Deutsche mark was at that point clearly undervalued.

It is not difficult to appreciate the international implications of this development; but its consequences for Germany's domestic economic policy were equally grave. The depreciation of the Deutsche mark—even more pronounced vis-à-vis the US dollar in effective terms—gave a strong boost to domestic inflation. The import prices of oil and other commodities, together with the prices of all internationally traded goods, were pushed up sharply; in the space of two years the inflation rate, measured in terms of retail prices, almost doubled. The authorities had no other option but to tighten monetary policy—that is, to raise their interest rates at a time when the stagnation of the economy was already causing a rise in unemployment. Real interest rates became intolerably high in relation to the requirements of the country's domestic economic equilibrium. It had therefore become impossible to pursue the objective of domestic equilibrium despite—or rather *because of*—floating. Relief came only with the many realignments of central rates within the EMS, as a result of which the Deutsche mark was revalued vis-à-vis other European currencies sufficiently to offset the effects of an overvalued US dollar on its effective exchange rate.

For an example going in the opposite direction we can take the US dollar, which, in the spring of 1983, is manifestly overvalued. At no time in recent history has the surge of protectionist pressures been as strong as it is at present. This is hardly surprising: the growing keenness of foreign competition, notably Japanese, as a result of the sudden, radical change in exchange rates hits domestic producers far harder than the emergence on the domestic market of a foreign competitor working with "artificially" low costs.

The perverse effects of exchange rates which diverge signifi-

cantly and persistently from purchasing-power parity are causing
a certain awakening to the dangers inherent in the unbridled,
erratic floating of currencies. But between perception and concerted action on the part of the authorities to moderate the
excesses of floating there is a gap which will not be easy to cross.
Effective action to combat short-term exchange rate volatility —
as to combat the more fundamental distortion of real exchange
rates — would require, over and above substantial market intervention, genuine co-ordination of policies, in particular in the
matter of interest rates. Will the perception of certain dangers be
forceful enough to persuade the respective authorities to engage in
international co-operation, when experience suggests that such cooperation only operates effectively under the threat of events
whose gravity is glaringly obvious? It seems doubtful.

Even more improbable is the prospect of re-establishing a
system of fixed but adjustable parities on Bretton Woods lines.
The Bretton Woods system worked well because of, and for the
duration of, US hegemony. In the present political context, where
power is divided among several centres and where even the
biggest country cannot exert a decisive influence except by
vetoing initiatives taken by others, I cannot see how any grand
design could be conceived and negotiated, let alone how a
"rational" monetary system could be effectively managed. In
short, it is to be feared that the floating — often disorderly
floating — of the major currencies will continue to dominate the
international monetary scene in the years to come.

The negative effects of such a scenario on European investment
could be alleviated through greater stability in intra-European
exchange rates. The survival and smooth functioning of the EMS
are therefore of immense importance for capital formation within
the Community. The increasing frequency of realignments since
1981 gives no great cause for optimism. In a technical sense the
EMS has survived; and its survival has made it possible to limit
the day-to-day exchange rate volatility. This is no mean achievement. However, the more fundamental exchange rate changes
have not been prevented: unless there is a convergence of member
countries' economic performances there is a danger that the EMS
will degenerate into a sliding parity system. Is this all that can be

expected? Perhaps. The changes in intra-European exchange rate relationships have been largely nominal: on the whole, they have offset inflation differentials. There has been none of the major distortions of real rates referred to earlier. It is a limited success, but a success all the same.

4

Investment and Government Policy

Otmar Emminger

CHANGING ENVIRONMENT FOR INVESTMENT POLICY

In the last few years there have been far-reaching changes in the conditions and aims which determine the investment policy of the public authorities.

(a) On the one hand the public authorities were saddled by the ominous rise in unemployment and thereby with increased responsibility for the promotion of investment, on the principle of "more employment through more investment".

(b) On the other hand most industrialized countries have since the 1970s experienced developments which reduced the room for manoeuvre available to the public authorities. Most important amongst these are the structural rise of the State's share in the national product, the heavy budget deficits involved, with the consequent squeeze on the capital market, and the need to quell the wave of inflation that occurred in the 1970s by applying a restrictive or at least cautious monetary and financial policy.

(c) There is moreover a growing conviction that what is needed today is not just a mere fillip, nor just transitory boosts imparted by public investment programmes, but rather the creation of permanent jobs through expansion of the productive capital in the economy. When it is seen, for instance, that in the Federal Republic of Germany it would not be possible, even with maximum use of existing capac-

72

ities, to find employment for even half of those who are at present unemployed, and that today real growth potential is only around 2 per cent per year, it is evident that expansion of the productive capital stock in the economy has become a matter of urgency.

In other words, short-term considerations must in many cases take second place behind longer-term structural requirements. In cases of conflict, a policy that seeks to expand supply is usually better than a policy intended to increase demand. In most industrialized countries unemployment is largely a structural problem, the consequence of misdirected medium-term structural developments. These misdirected developments include the sharp growth of the State's share in the national product, and of the structural budget deficits, an excessively high wages ratio, the inflationary wave of the 1970s and the inevitable repercussions of the measures taken to deal with it (e.g., high real rates of interest), and the re-distributive effect of the two oil price shocks. All this led to a structural weakness in the earnings of enterprises, with corresponding consequences for investment and the capital stock available to the economy. The State's unduly high absorption of savings capital means a potential reduction in the amount of capital available to manufacturing industry, a situation which could rapidly become acute when the economy recovers. In short, the structurally high budget deficits, the structural character of a part of the unemployment figures, the prolonged weakness in the earnings of the business sector and the insufficient capital stock available in several economies has established a new set of conditions within which government investment policies must work. In what follows a picture will be given of the repercussions these changed conditions will have on the relationship between State and investment.

INVESTMENT—KEY FIGURE IN THE ECONOMY

Investment is a key figure in the economy. Economic growth and employment depend in large measure, if not entirely, on the level of investment. The intensity and quality of investments exert a great influence on the advance of productivity, on ability to adapt to structural change in the world economy and in the com-

TABLE 4.1
INVESTMENT RATIOS, GROWTH RATES, PRODUCTIVITY

	Investment ratios[1]				Growth rates[2]				Increase in productivity[3] of the economy			
	EC	FRG	USA	Japan	EC	FRG	USA	Japan	EC	FRG	USA	Japan
1967–73	22.5	24.5	18.3	34.3	5.0	5.3	3.6	9.6	4.3	4.5	2.5	8.0
1973–80	21.1	21.6	18.3	32.0	2.3	2.3	2.3	3.7	2.0	2.4	1.3	2.7
1980	21.2	22.8	18.5	32.0	1.4	1.8	−0.4	4.8	1.0	0.9	0.9	3.6
1981	19.8	22.0	17.9	31.0	−0.6	−0.2	1.9	3.8	0.9	0.5	0.8	2.1
1982	(19.4)	21.1	(14.9)	30.9	0.1	−1.1	−1.7	3.0	(1.2)	0.9	−0.9	1.6

1 Gross fixed investment in per cent of gross domestic product (GDP).
2 Annual percentage change in real GDP.
3 GDP per person in employment.
(*Sources*: OECD, EC Commission, national statistics.)

petitivity of a given economy. It is therefore not surprising that in almost all Government programmes a high priority attaches to the promotion of investment, especially in the present period of high unemployment and marked weakness of investment. A passage from the programme adopted by the new coalition which has been governing the Federal Republic of Germany since October 1982 may serve as an example: "The elimination of unemployment is today a priority task. Private and government investment must therefore be stimulated. Only in this way will it be possible to achieve the necessary structural change and to maintain the international competitivity of the German economy". After the investment ratio in the Community countries had reached its lowest ebb and unemployment had at the same time attained its highest level since the establishment of the Common Market, the European Commission put before the Member States a programme for the coordinated promotion of investment, at national and at Community level.

By way of contrast to the weakness of investment in Europe, one may cite the strength of investment in Japan. In respect of growth and of advances in productivity, Japan has for years been ahead of Europe's industrialized countries. There are many reasons for this. One of the most important is undoubtedly the far higher investment ratio of the Japanese economy. In the last few years its share in Japan's national product has been some 31 per cent, in the Community countries it averaged barely 20 per cent (and see Table 4.1). This enormous difference reflects a fundamental difference in the social and economic structure of Japan. There, the rate of saving is for various reasons far higher than in Europe, both in personal budgets and in the earnings ratios and capital formation of enterprises, so that even a relatively high budget deficit is more easily absorbed than elsewhere.

This structurally higher intensity of investment is one of the main reasons why the Japanese have for some time past beaten the Europeans to the post in the race for practical application of technological innovations. The rapid adaptation and further development of Japanese and foreign innovations is undoubtedly one of the strong points of the Japanese economy. In contrast to this, the considerably lower investment ratio in Europe points to a slower reaction to technical progress and increasing obsolescence of production plant; it also involves a reduction in the ability to adapt to new market conditions. The high level of investment in Japan is also in large measure the reason why the Japanese have so far been much better than the Europeans in coping with the problem of employment, although in the branches of industry which aim at exports they have automated more extensively than any other country. Today they employ an estimated 13,000 robots, compared with 3500 in the Federal Republic of Germany. Yet in Japan there is no question of a reduction in working hours. The length of a working life is if anything being made longer still, and the number of hours worked per year in industry is still over 2000, compared with 1700 in West Germany. Most important of all, however, is that the Japanese have in the last eight years increased their numbers in employment by over three million, while during that period the numbers in employment in the European Community marked time.[1]

Here it must however be pointed out that the investment ratio usually adopted for purposes of comparison — i.e., the share of gross fixed asset formation in gross domestic product — is a rough-and-ready and often misleading measure, for it includes not only productive investment but housing, municipal investment in swimming baths, theatres, roads and the like, and these of course vary very widely in the contribution they make to modernizing production potential and improving competitivity. But even if one compares investment ratios in the business sector (without housing), the special position of Japan is still striking: in 1979, for instance, the share of investment by enterprises in gross domestic product in the USA was barely 12 per cent, in West Germany 12.7 per cent, but in Japan 18.3 per cent.

WHERE DOES RESPONSIBILITY REST ON THE PUBLIC AUTHORITIES?

Today it is almost universally accepted that the State bears some responsibility for the development of investment activity. It must

---

1 The numbers in employment would seem to be the best measure for comparison, while the unemployment ratio given in Japanese statistics (less than 3 per cent) is, because of differences in their method of counting, not comparable with ratios given in Europe.

nonetheless be asked why the expansion of investment cannot be left to the forces inherent in the free market economy. In what spheres is intervention by the State justified, and what aims should it pursue? Where do the limits to State intervention lie?

Obviously, the State is directly responsible for investments to be made in its own public sphere — for the public infrastructure, for public transport and the like. But this raises the question whether public investments should be decided exclusively on the basis of public infrastructure needs; or are they to be, can they be, an instrument of general economic policy as well, helping for instance to iron out cyclical swings or to be part of a general programme for the creation of employment?

In most countries the State also exerts a direct influence on investment decisions in the sphere of State-owned or State-controlled enterprises. The extent of this sphere varies greatly from one country to another, as do the objectives pursued. Consequently this State-controlled or State-influenced sector gives rise to various problems.

However, the investment policy followed by the public authorities exerts an influence far beyond the strictly public sphere. The State also *influences private business investments*, and in several ways. On the one hand the public authorities promote specific investments or assist specific branches of industry, and they may help economic areas by fiscal or other incentives and reliefs. This, then, is *selective or structurally inspired promotion* of investment. On the other hand the State endeavours to influence the whole background against which businesses in general will take their investment decisions; in doing so, the State makes use of almost all the means available to economic and financial policy, including monetary and credit policy. One needs only to look at any recent budget — the budget put before the United Kingdom Parliament in March 1983 or the budgets of the West German Government that has been in power since October 1982 — to realize the extent to which public financial policy is imbued with the need for the selective and general promotion of investment. I mention the policy of these two countries because their governments favour the principle of the fullest possible freedom of the market. One might equally well cite the Reagan Administration in the USA, which is basically pro-market, but one of whose objectives is to "revitalize" the American economy; to this end it has adopted a series of measures, most of them fiscal, to promote investment. (The fact that in the first half of 1983 investment by business is still the weak point of economic development in the USA is not without a certain irony.)

Action by the State to influence investment ranges, then, over broad and disparate fields, from the slant given to its own investments, to incentives of selective character or inspired by structural policy, and to the general conditions in which industry operates. The objectives, too, are various:

(a) to meet the requirements of the public infrastructure;
(b) to control cyclical swings;
(c) general and specific structural policy;
(d) global promotion of capital formation and of productive investment by industry.

STATE INVESTMENT UNDER FISCAL CONSTRAINTS

As mentioned at the outset, the criteria for judging the investments made by the public authorities have changed decidedly in the last few years. For a long time it was considered — in no small measure owing to the influence of Keynesian doctrines — that it was up to the community, when gaps in demand appeared because of cyclical fluctuations in the private sector, to offset them by increasing its own demand (anti-cyclical deficit spending). To achieve this end the handiest instrument was of course an increase in the public investments directly controlled by the State. Today it can be said that investment by the State has largely failed as an instrument for controlling business cycles, or that for other reasons it has slipped into the background.

In certain countries, investments by the State have even proved to be a pro-cyclical element: that is, they declined during a period of slack economic activity — in West Germany, for instance, and in a number of other countries, particularly during the recession of 1980–82. One major reason was the structural deterioration of the budgets in most countries. When during the period of slack economic activity cuts had to be made because of the difficult budget situation, they tended to fall first on public investments, which are often the only flexible bloc in the budgets of the public authorities. In West Germany, for example, the share of public investment in the total expenditure of the State fell from 10.9 per cent in 1979 to 6.7 per cent in 1982 (a year of depression).

Special job-creating investment programmes too, although time and again vociferously called for by many sections of the community such as trade unions, were in the last recession undertaken on a relatively small scale. There are several reasons for this. For one thing, large-scale programmes for the creation of jobs can in most cases be financed only if the public authorities increase their borrowing; this, in view of the already high budget deficits and the high rates of interest prevailing on the capital market, they hesitated to do. The belief in an early and far-reaching auto-financing of measures to stimulate expansion has largely faded. Secondly, more and more doubts are being expressed in connection with such long-term public programmes for the creation of jobs.[2] Moreover experience had shown that because of the heaviness of bureaucratic procedures, major State investment programmes became fully effective only when a boom was already in the offing, with the result that they had a pro-cyclical effect (as happened with the 1979 German programme for "investment in the future"). Furthermore, such State measures for stimulation of the economy are inevitably concentrated on just a few areas which are by no means always suitable for raising and sustaining the rate of growth of the economy, the level of employment and productivity. These areas include motorways, barrages, bridges, canals and housing, all of which help employment in the building and construction industry for a time, but do not necessarily create permanent jobs.

In the middle term, too, direct intervention by the State has in many countries developed in unexpected fashion. In the last 15 to 20 years there has almost everywhere been a tendency for the State's share in investment to fall. For the Community countries as a whole the share of public investment in total expenditure by

2 For instance, a model calculation made by the Deutsche Bundesbank led to the conclusion that — in the conditions prevailing in the period 1974–81 — a supplementary State investment programme produced, apart from a short-lived flash in the pan, no lasting rise in the real national income (*Monthly Report of the Deutsche Bundesbank*, August 1982).

the State fell between 1960 and 1982 from 10 per cent to 6 per cent; in West Germany the fall was from some 12 per cent to 6.7 per cent. In the European Commission's programme of October 1982, to which reference has been made above, one of the demands put forward is that the share of public expenditure allotted to investment should therefore be further increased, and that this investment activity should concentrate particularly on expenditure that will improve the general conditions in which the productive sector of the economy works.

The first requirement at least, namely that there must unquestionably be an increase in the share of public investment, cannot be accepted in this general form. The medium-term decline in this ratio is in part the natural consequence of the fact that once the reconstruction boom of the 1950s and early 1960s was over, the need to catch up in public infrastructures tended to decline. Moreover the judgement reached in connection with this demand will be decisively influenced by the question of finance. If the increase in public investment is to be financed in the main through additional borrowing, this borrowing requirement will be competing with private investment for manufacturing, which is far more important, and it could keep interest rates unnecessarily high. If additional public investment is to be financed by switches within the State budget, replacing outlays for consumption by expenditure on investment, it must nonetheless be asked whether the money saved on outlays for consumption might not be used to reduce the budget deficit. Where there is a genuine and urgent demand for investment in infrastructure, its financing can indeed be made in most cases by an internal switching within the budget. And there is one further requirement in connection with public investment: if it is not possible to arrange that it shall have an anti-cyclical effect, it should at least be spread evenly over time. Eighty to ninety per cent of public investment concerns building and contracting. Here sharp ups and downs in public orders lead to considerable losses to the economy.

Approval must be given to the second of the demands put forward by the Commission, namely that public investment should as far as possible be concentrated on undertakings which improve the background conditions for manufacturing industry.

That means that this investment should not, as is often the case, be directed towards public consumer goods, but to areas such as energy, the improvement of important means of communication, etc., which really contribute to the productivity of the economy as a whole.

It could be said that in a wider sense public investment includes the investments made by State-controlled enterprises. But in the several countries this concept covers a very wide range of enterprises, from purely business undertakings to public transport and public utilities. In countries such as Austria, Italy and France, the public authorities have a very considerable stake in business activities. In such countries there are even cases where State-owned undertakings (or undertakings under State influence) have been fully inserted into the free market economy and are run in accordance with normal business principles. True, State-controlled undertakings or credit institutions in several of these countries are also used for the purpose of implementing the short-term economic policy or structural policy laid down by the State. Such cases should be looked into to see how far a specially favoured investment activity pursued by these undertakings does or does not constitute a misapplication of scarce capital.

Investigations have shown that in many countries — including the Federal Republic of Germany — the investment behaviour of State enterprises has proved to be not anti-cyclical but pro-cyclical (this was so, for instance, during the 1975 recession). In a number of other countries, however, their action, possibly influenced by directives from the State, has had an anti-cyclical effect.

The many and varied circumstances to be found from one country to another make it impossible to draw general conclusions. It would seem, however, that those countries have fared best where the undertakings subject to State influence have been made to work as fully as possible in competition with others in the market and in accordance with the principle of profitability. In several European countries the State has been prepared to cover out of State funds the continuing losses of State-owned undertakings — witness the action taken by a number of countries in the steel sector. In most cases this is nothing other than the subsidization of outmoded structures (a sort of "survival subsidy"), but at the same time a misapplication of capital at the expense of productive private investment and in many cases, too, a protectionist distortion of the common market — as can be seen in the horrific case of steel (subsidy race).

To sum up, it may be said in connection with State investment that:

(a) As an instrument for influencing the business cycle, State investment is receding further and further into the background. In various countries, including West Germany, its effect has come to be pro-cyclical rather than anti-cyclical.

(b) Far more than ever before, State investment programmes for the creation of jobs, particularly those which involve additional borrowing, will have to face up to the problem of finance. This problem stems from the structural deterioration of the public finances which is occurring in most countries, with the result that a large part of the savings capital formed in the economy is absorbed to cover budget deficits and that the room for manoeuvre available to the State is much reduced. In such a situation State investment programmes financed by borrowing prove more than ever to constitute an undesirable burden placed on the capital market at the expense of the private sector. Financing them by means of switches in the budget is, it is true, less open to this objection, but once again it must be asked whether the saving made on consumer expenditure could not be better applied to a reduction in the budget deficit and to relieving pressure on the capital market.

(c) Today there is far greater recognition than previously of the prime importance of private investment as a means of creating permanent jobs, while in most cases State job-creation programmes are credited with little or no lasting effect.

(d) This means that State investment in infrastructure — especially if it is to be financed by borrowing — should be judged primarily on the reality of the need and not in the light of arguments drawn from employment policy. The same criterion does not of course apply to the investment needs of public business undertakings, especially public utilities and transport undertakings. Their investments may in certain circumstances contribute considerably to the productive capacity of the economy and may in consequence justify the use of scarce capital resources.

SELECTIVE INVESTMENT AID FROM THE STATE

Under the pressure exerted by the economic recession, fiscal and financial incentives to invest and other forms of aid to individual enterprises, to individual branches of the economy or to regions are being increasingly used in many European countries, mainly in the form of direct aid, fiscal reliefs or interest subsidies. In France, for instance, a good 40 per cent of all medium and longer term credits are subsidized. In the current circumstances all forms of aid are particularly problematic, for in many cases they undoubtedly constitute misdirection of capital, particularly in those cases where the subsidies serve to maintain outdated structures in existence. What is more, the readiness of the State to rush in again and again with all sorts of aids when individual areas are in difficulties means that the economy concerned will not only cling to outdated plant but will also suffer losses of flexibility and readiness to adapt.

Undoubtedly there are important areas in which it is right or even unavoidable for the State to take supporting action, whether this be done through direct State investment or through State subsidies for investments made by private enterprises. They include long-term developments in the fields of energy and transport, where either the financial risk or the requisite volume of capital is too great for private enterprise. Many measures taken as part of regional development policy or for the protection of the environment, which by their very nature are not going to be profitable, may be part of the obligations resting on the State. A few years ago the Minister of Research in the then West German Government announced a "programme of selective structural change" which was to concentrate on six so-called bottlenecks: the supply of energy, housing and town planning, protection of the environment, the applications of micro-electronics, the services sector and improvement of the ability of small and medium-sized enterprises to innovate. True, even in these areas the private sector was "as far as possible" to make the necessary investments and to finance them; but — according to the programme — the

State must always invest or assist in cases where infrastructures had to be created or private investment activity proved to be insufficient. Such a thoroughly vague and ill-knit programme, in which the limits to the State's activity were extremely imprecise, is a clear example of how not to do it. And the programme has never been seriously considered. It is a mistake to cite in this connection the support given to industry in Japan; that support is aimed in far more realistic fashion at the development of certain innovations with a future; what is more, the differences in mentality and organizational form are such that the method can hardly be transposed directly for use in Europe.

Be that as it may, neither the State subsidies nor the other selective measures to promote investment can escape the restraints imposed by the changes which, as we pointed out above, are occurring in the environment. The overloading of budgets and the structural decline in the capital left available to industry mean that in this particular area a critical review and, in case of doubt, a reduction in subsidies and in investment incentives are urgently needed. Amongst the proposals on the promotion of investment which the European Commission has put to the Member States there are some which aim at concerting measures for the review and improvement of the transparency, the simplicity and the efficacy of State incentives in this field.

THE GENERAL CONDITIONS FOR INVESTORS HAVE BECOME MUCH WORSE

All the observations made so far lead to the conclusion that the major task before the State if it is to promote investment cannot be to extend State investment or selective incentives and aids, but *in improvement of the general conditions for the formation and employment of productive capital in the private sector*. The State cannot evade this task, if only because its general economic and financial policy will always, whether the government intends it or not, have an immense impact on these general conditions. And a further reason why the State cannot avoid this task is that the structural investment weakness of the 1970s and the early 1980s stems in large measure from developments for which the State bears directly or indirectly part of the responsibility.

Since the 1970s *investment risk* has risen considerably owing to *greater instability at home and abroad*. There is no need to show in detail how a high level of inflation with sharp ups and downs can distort market signals and complicate investment decisions. A recently published OECD report on *Positive Adjustment Policies*[3] put it as follows: "Inflation introduces 'background noise' that may drown out market signals". A still more serious result of the wave of inflation in the 1970s was that from 1980 on it had to be combatted with a restrictive monetary policy that had very unpleasant consequences for interest rates. A further result of inflation, namely distortions in the tax system to the detriment of firms' earnings (taxation of book profits, and so on), needs be mentioned only in passing. The sharply increased instability that has affected foreign trade since the 1970s has proved to be no less disturbing, with its sharp and often quite unpredictable swings in the rates of exchange and, even worse, the uncertainty bred by the dangerous spread of protectionism. A stable internal and external setting for business not only reduces the risk involved in investment, but it contributes to the adaptability and so to the flexibility of enterprises.

The increase in investment risks might themselves have been enough to justify giving compensation to enterprises in other fields such as finance and staff. Instead of this, the other general conditions for business investment have in the last few years deteriorated considerably. The main causes were the two *oil price shocks* in 1973/74 and 1979/80, the *sharp rise of the State's share in the national product and the budget deficits*, to which must be added the *high real rates of interest* and an evidently structural increase in the share of wages in the value added by industry—at the expense of the earnings of enterprises.

As a result, the proportion of gross domestic product devoted to investment has in many European countries been declining since the 1960s, and not merely because of a passing phase of the economic cycle, as in 1980–82, but evidently on longer-term structural grounds. At the same time the rate of growth and the rise in productivity have declined (see Table 4.1).

In this connection it should be noted that shifts, sometimes

3 OECD, Paris, 1983.

considerable shifts, have evidently occurred within the total of
gross fixed capital formation. Investment by business enterprises in
the narrow sense of the term (i.e., in the industrial sector) has
evidently been hit harder than the rest. At the same time the need
to replace obsolete or worn-out plant has risen, in part because of
the enormous rise in the cost of energy. This meant that far less
was left for *net investment* in this sector (again in the narrow sense
of the term — i.e., excluding housing and the financial sector). A
calculation covering West Germany[4] showed that in the 1970s
some 5.5 per cent of the gross national product was still devoted
to net investment in the sector concerned, but that in the first half
of 1982 only 1.5 per cent of gross national product was devoted to
the extension and improvement of plant. This is at the same time
one reason for the medium-term decline in the growth potential
of the economy; in West Germany it is today estimated at no
more than 2 per cent per annum.[5]

Consequences of the rise in the price of oil

The oil price shocks and the consequent surge in energy prices
wrought havoc in the cost calculations made by industry. Many
production plants were completely unable to work at a profit in
their existing locations. The ratio of wear and tear rose. On the
other hand, the situation offered new investment opportunities for
energy-saving investments and for alternative energy sources.

In most countries the cost of adaptation to the two bounds
made in the price of oil at first fell entirely on corporate earnings.
Both in 1974/75 and in 1980/81 the increases in wage and other
incomes continued, and at first no account was taken of the additional funds that had to be transferred abroad. Almost everywhere
the State also stepped up its claims on the national product. The
deterioration in the terms of trade therefore fell solely on enterprises, till in laborious negotiations spread over several years real
wages were brought at least partially into line with the realities of
the new situation. This meant, then, that there were two lines of
redistribution: from home to abroad, and from company earnings
to wage incomes. This one-sided burdening of company earnings

4 See *Monatsbericht der Deutschen Bundesbank*, October 1982.
5 Estimate made by the Deutsche Bundesbank.

undoubtedly had a negative effect on investment, real growth and employment. Consequently those whose incomes depended on the enterprises had in the end to accept greater sacrifices and the economy had to face a greater increase in unemployment than would have been necessary if wages and other incomes had been adapted more rapidly.

Rise in general government shares in expenditure and in structural budget deficits

Investment by industry is having to carry a particularly dangerous structural burden for which the State bears direct responsibility: namely, the share of general government (including social) expenditure in the national income. This ratio has everywhere risen steeply, and in the Community countries as a whole passed from 32 per cent in 1960 to over 47 per cent in 1980, and, partly because of the prevailing economic situation, to over 50 per cent in 1980 (see Table 4.2). In the Federal Republic of Germany the rise tallied almost exactly with the Community average. In most Community countries, and particularly in West Germany, the main cause lay in the disproportionate rise in social expenditure by the public authorities. In this connection the former Federal Chancellor wrote a letter in August 1982 to the heads of the German trades unions describing the fundamental dilemma of Germany's economic and financial policy in the following terms: "From 1970 till today the share of investment in the gross national product has fallen from 25.6 per cent to 21.5 per cent . . . . In the same period, however, the share of social transfers in the national product has risen considerably — from 26 per cent to 31 per cent". The explosion of the welfare state becomes even more obvious if 1960 is taken as the reference year, for at that time social transfer payments in West Germany accounted for only 20.7 per cent of the national income.

The rise in the State's share in the national income has inhibited investment by industry in two ways: first, by saddling enterprises with ever heavier taxes and social contributions, and secondly, because the steep rise in public expenditure has led to structurally higher budget deficits, as is apparent from the sharp divergence between the rates of increase for the State's expenditure and

TABLE 4.2

SHARES OF GENERAL GOVERNMENT EXPENDITURE AND
OF TAXES, SOCIAL SECURITY CONTRIBUTIONS, ETC. AS
PERCENTAGE OF DOMESTIC PRODUCT

	General government[1]				Taxes and social security[2]			
	EC	FRG	USA	Japan	EC	FRG	USA	Japan
1960	32.1	32.0	27.8	20.7	32.1	34.8	27.4	20.7
1970	37.9	37.6	32.2	19.3	37.5	37.5	30.3	20.7
1980	47.2	48.2	33.2	32.7	43.1	42.3	32.7	28.2
1981	49.8	51.5			45.0	(45.3)		
1982[3]	(50.8)	(50.5)			(45.8)	(45.6)		

1 Expenditure of general government (including expenditure on social services) in
per cent of gross domestic product.
2 Taxes and social security contributions in per cent of gross domestic product.
3 Partially estimated.
(*Sources*: OECD, EC Commission, national statistics.)

revenue ratios. In the 1960s the share of budget deficits in gross
national income was 0.4 per cent for the Community countries, in
the 1970s 2.8 per cent, and in the years 1981 and 1982 some 5 per
cent (partly because of the prevailing economic situation). Here
too the trend in West Germany was much the same as in the
Community as a whole, despite the fact that the share of the
German budget deficit in the national income remained a little
under 5 per cent.

Government deficits of such magnitude inevitably place a
burden on the credit markets and keep interest rates high. For
West Germany the Bundesbank has pointed out that,[6] of the total
amount of domestic monetary wealth formed at home (including
the supply of capital from abroad) the public authorities at
Federal, Land and communal level laid claim in the first half of
the 1970s to about one seventh, but in 1981 the proportion was
about one third. In some other industrialized countries this proportion is much higher still. Particularly important for the world
economic situation is the fact that in the United States the public
authorities seem to be absorbing three quarters of domestic net
capital formation in order to finance their deficit. In the *Economic*

6 *Geschäftsbericht der Deutschen Bundesbank für 1981*, p. 37.

Report of the President[7] the economic advisers of the American President wrote in this connection that "A succession of large budget deficits is likely to reduce substantially the rate of capital formation . . . . The magnitude of the crowding out of private investment is immense".

High real interest rates

The repercussions of the US budget deficit constitute not just an American but a world-wide problem, for if in the years ahead there is not a considerable reduction in these huge and menacing budget deficits — be it through fiscal measures or thanks to an unexpectedly vigorous upturn in the economy — then it is probable that American interest rates, in relation to the rate of inflation, will remain comparatively high. This could encourage flows of capital from all parts of the world to America, capital which would then contribute directly or indirectly to the financing of the American budget deficit. In all probability that would maintain the dollar at a higher level than the Americans themselves would wish in the interests of their foreign trade and lead to a lengthy period of high deficits in the American balance of current transactions. From the angle of the world economy it cannot be regarded as normal when year after year the richest country in the world covers part of its excessively high budget deficit by calls on foreign capital. It could well be, however, that in the long run the deficit on current transactions to which this must lead could place a heavier burden on the American economy than on the rest of the world.

In 1980, 1981 and 1982 the high level of America's interest rates was mainly due to the monetary anti-inflation policy. The policy of high interest rates pursued in the past was the price — and a heavy price! — which had to be paid not only by the United States, but, in consequence, by the world economy as a whole in order to recover from the sins of inflation committed in the 1970s (American rate of inflation in 1980, 13.5 per cent!). The price to be paid was especially high because America's monetary policy had to battle against inflation with no support from America's budget policy. In brief, a bad policy mix. Now that the backbone

7 *Economic Report of the President*, Washington, February 1983.

of inflation seems to have been broken, the future trend of American interest rates will depend largely on how the budget develops. Although American interest rates have fallen considerably since the middle of 1982, the real rates of interest, that is, interest rates measured in relation to the pace of inflation, are still unusually high, in particular for a period of recession.

In the United States itself, the impact on a decision to buy or to invest was very considerably softened by far-reaching tax privileges (wide deductibility from profit for tax purposes, special arrangements for business). The question is whether the high rates of interest to which these measures have contributed will in future exert an influence on the trend of interest rates in Europe, as they have done in the recent past. Fortunately this is not very probable. In the course of 1982 a number of European countries succeeded in breaking the link that tied them to the American level of interest, in particular those whose balance on current transactions improved and which managed to make progress towards stability at home. By February 1983 the real rate of interest in the Federal Republic of Germany had in point of fact fallen to around 3.5 per cent — a figure which must however be compared with 2.5 per cent in the recession year 1975. How far the countries of Europe will be able to sever the link with the trend of interest rates in America will depend mainly on their internal stability and the strength of their foreign balance. In this they are being helped by two events: first the fall in oil prices, and secondly the weakening of the dollar caused by America's rapidly growing deficit on the balance of current transactions.

The conclusion to be drawn, then, is that *the trend in interest rates in the industrialized countries of Europe will depend mainly on their own progress in stability and budgetary policy.* A further reduction in interest rates will not fall into their laps, but will have to be won by their own efforts. How important the trend in interest rates is for the re-launching of private investment activity may be seen from the juxtaposition made in Table 4.3 of the average returns on own capital in West German industry and the returns that could have been made by investing money in other ways.

Structurally higher wage ratios?

A further factor which has considerably impaired the earnings of

TABLE 4.3

	1965	1970	1975	1978	1980	1981
Returns on own capital in West German industry (per cent)	9.2	9.5	5.1	6.3	5.6	5.0
Returns on investments of capital in the financial markets (per cent)	6.8	8.2	8.7	6.1	8.6	10.6

undertakings and consequently both their financial strength and the outlook for profits that would be available for future investments is the longer-term trend in the cost of salaries and wages. It has already been shown that this was in part an unsound way of adapting to the two oil price shocks. It is, however, interesting to look closely at the consequent medium-term shifts in the relationship between the cost of staff and the returns achieved by enterprises. From 1973 to 1981 average gross hourly earnings of employees in West Germany rose by some 8 per cent per annum, the unit returns of entrepreneurs by only 5 per cent per annum. For the Community countries as a whole a glance at Table 4.4 shows that the share of persons in employment (including a calculated share of the income of the self-employed) in the total national income has risen on average from 82.8 per cent to 88.1 per cent. This change constituted a direct charge on the undistributed profits of enterprises.

TABLE 4.4

ADJUSTED SHARE OF INCOME FROM EMPLOYMENT (INCOME FROM EMPLOYMENT, ADJUSTED FOR THE SHARE OF THE SELF-EMPLOYED AS PER CENT OF NATIONAL INCOME)[1]

	1960	1970	1980	1981	1982
FRG	77.8	81.1	83.6	83.8	82.2
UK	109.0	94.5	93.7	98.4	103.7
France	82.2	79.5	87.1	88.2	86.8
Italy	89.9	86.5	90.8	94.2	94.4
EC average	82.6	82.8	87.2	88.1	87.3

1 In per cent of net national income at factor cost.
(*Source*: Commission of the EC.)

TABLE 4.5

GROSS DOMESTIC PRODUCT OF THE EC COUNTRIES — COMPONENTS
AND DETERMINANTS (VARIATION OF SHARES IN GDP, IN PERCENTAGE
POINTS AND CUMULATED OVER THE PERIODS)

	1960–1973	*1973–1980*	*1980–1982*	*1983*[1]
Public expenditure	+7.7	+7.3	+3.7	+0.7
Taxes	+6.4	+4.5	+2.2	+0.8
Real wage gap (excess over warranted level)[2]	−0.2	+3.3	−0.2	−0.9
Consumption	−1.8	+3.5	+2.6	−0.2
Investment	+2.2	−1.6	−2.3	−0.2
Real GDP (volume growth, annual average)	+4.6	+2.2	−0.1	+1.1

1 EC Commission estimate made in November 1982.
2 "Warranted level" = a development in real wages that would leave the profit share of the
enterprise sector unchanged.
(*Source*: Commission of the European Communities.)

Such a rise had on investment and employment the repercussions that could have been expected (see Table 4.5). This fact is
confirmed by an examination of the way in which wages and
profits have been developing in the Federal Republic of Germany.
It shows in particular that when real wages lagged behind the rise
in productivity, investment ratio and employment both rose, as
was the case in the 1950s and again from 1976 to 1979. When there
was a serious real wage gap, the trend was reversed. This only
confirms a classic rule, which also plays an important role in
Keynesian doctrine, even if it was usually neglected by his fol-
lowers. Under this rule *the most important means of bringing in the
unemployed is a drop in the real cost of labour; in other words, the rise
in real wages must lag behind the rise in productivity*. Not, therefore,
as we are told today by many prominent economists in the
Federal Republic of Germany and a number of other countries,[8]
an absolute reduction in real wages, but rather a merely relative
lag behind the increase in productivity till the relationship
between real costs and real earnings in industry has returned to
normal. Of course this objective can be more easily achieved

8 In the Federal Republic of Germany, for instance, by Professor Herbert Giersch,
   President of the Kiel Institut für Weltwirtschaft, and by others.

when the rise in productivity is high, as for example in the 1950s. But in the long run it will not be possible to get round observation of this rule even today, when the rises in productivity are more modest.

On the basis of several individual investigations the European Commission has come to the conclusion that "Trends in output, productivity and real wage movements strongly point to a decisive role for real wages in output determination and unemployment . . . . In the longer run real wages affect employment because of their influence on profitability and investment".[9] The future movement of wages is also of considerable importance for the nature of future investments. The relative costs of labour and of capital undoubtedly influence the decision whether the planned investments are more labour intensive or more capital intensive. Many observers have already warned against letting the level of interest sink further at the present time, as this would favour capital intensive and labour saving investment and so run counter to the target of employment. True, it would be more correct to suggest that the relation between the two elements should be put right by a suitable moderation in the development of wages. An investigation into the relationship between the cost of manpower and the cost of capital carried out in the USA, France, Great Britain and West Germany has shown that in the three European countries the ratio of labour costs to the cost of capital had approximately doubled between the 1960s and the end of the 1970s. In the USA, on the contrary, the ratio of the first of these factors to the second had risen little, and since 1970 the real wage gap has been such, apart from minor swings, that it has not contributed to a change in factor shares. This appears to explain in part why in the 1970s employment in the USA developed far more favourably than in the Community countries. It is interesting to see that in the economic report published in February 1983 by the American President (or his economic advisers) a section dealing specifically with the macro-economic problems of Europe reaches a similar conclusion: "The causes of structural unemployment are always controversial, but a key element in the

9 Cf. European economy, *Annual Economic Review 1982/83*, No. 14, p. 118, November 1982.

European employment problem was probably rapid increases in real labour costs in the first half of the 1970s in the face of declining productivity and rising oil prices". But the report also points out that it was not only excessive wage increases that were to blame for the unemployment problem in Europe, but also the European deflationary policy pursued in unfavourable circumstances — the second oil shock, the high exchange rate of the US dollar, and so on.

It is not only in relation to the United States, but even more in relation to Japan that the countries of Europe are, owing to their excessive wage gap, at a disadvantage. Here I will not discuss the advantages which the Japanese economy has for years past been enjoying thanks to its lower nominal wages and which has been maintained, particularly since 1981, by undervaluation of the Japanese yen — an undervaluation due in the main to the enormous deficit in Japan's balance on capital account, itself caused by the wide gap between Japanese and American rates of interest (and also by Japan's over-hasty liberalization of capital exports). Here we have the problem of cost structures in the several economies and the distribution of the creation of wealth between employees' incomes and the incomes of employers.

According to an investigation made by the European Commission, the share of wages and salaries in the creation of wealth by Japanese industry too has risen more strongly than in the 1960s. But while in the period 1973–78 this ratio averaged 70 per cent in the four main countries of the Community, in Japan, despite a relatively strong rise, it was only 60 per cent. In Japan, then, 10 per cent less of the wealth created had to be devoted to labour costs than in the major European countries. This is very easily explained just by the difference in the supplementary costs of labour — that is, the social expenditure to be covered by enterprises in addition to the direct cost of wages and salaries. In 1980 these supplementary outlays constituted in Japan only 26 per cent of direct wages, but in West Germany the figure was some 75 per cent. In its *Economic Review for 1982–1983* (p. 116), the European Commission comes to the conclusion that the still considerably lower share of wages and salaries in manufacturing value added "may be part of the explanation of Japan's high rate of investment and low level of unemployment compared with both the USA and the Community".

There is however no escaping the fact that *in Japan*, which is today the most successful industrialized country in the Western World, *the shares both of general government plus compulsory contributions and of wages plus salaries, are significantly lower than in all other major industrial countries*, a situation which has obviously helped Japan to attain a higher investment ratio, increased productivity and growth, and better employment.

In several ways, then, the trend in wages and salaries makes a key contribution to investment:

(a) A moderate trend in wages and salaries contributes decisively to a lower rate of inflation, and this in turn means that interest rates can be correspondingly low, which is without doubt a help to investment.

(b) Restraint in the advance of wages and salaries also contributes to a country's ability to compete with other countries; this, combined with the low rate of inflation, enables the central bank to shake off more rapidly any disturbing developments that may occur in interest rates abroad, particularly in America.

(c) As a moderate trend in the development of wages and salaries has a quite decisive influence on the way in which the creation of wealth is distributed between labour costs and the earnings of an enterprise, it can be a decisive element in the investment decisions taken in the country concerned.

(d) Finally, it also influences the type of investment made, as it reinforces the tendency to more labour-intensive as against capital-intensive investments and in this way, too, it can improve the prospects of employment.

WAYS TOWARDS BETTER GENERAL CONDITIONS

Let us not forget that in present circumstances the State undoubtedly bears a responsibility for the promotion of investment. This must not however be misconstrued as an invitation to unlimited intervention with subsidies and aids of all sorts, or to a State programme for the creation of jobs, and still less to a dirigistic channeling of investment. At a time when the State budget is for other reasons overloaded and budget deficits are already absorbing too large a share of net capital formation, the State and the economy are even less than before in a position to indulge in additional financial burdens and misdirection of capital. In the field of subsidies and aids the signals must in general be set for reductions. Governmental promotion of investment must take as its main target the extension of the productive capital stock in the economy: that is, improved general conditions for productive investment. Such improvement in the general conditions calls in particular for:

(a) Greater stability at home and in relations with other countries, but above all an economic policy consistent with itself and on which firms can rely when taking their investment decisions. The reliability of economic policy is important, for what matters is not the short-term prospect but longer-term forecasts of costs and of the outlook for earnings.

(b) A clear political decision in favour of improving the chances of profitability, in order to correct step by step the structurally low profits earned in the business sector of many European countries. It seems that this is fairly generally recognized today by politicians of all parties, as is apparent from a statement made in October 1982 by the French Minister of Economics and Finance, Mr. Delors: "Il faut un redressement du revenu brut d'exploitation des entreprises pour redonner du dynamisme à notre économie".

(c) One thing that will be necessary if this is to be achieved is a reduction in the fiscal and social burdens resting on enterprises, and in particular a measure of tax relief for profits ploughed back. It would take us too far if in this framework we were to make a detailed study of the tax problems involved; within Europe they vary very widely from one country to another. But there can be no doubt that in several countries the structure of the tax system has come to be a definite brake on investment (this is so in West

Germany too) or that the tax burden on industry is in most of the countries of Europe heavier than in either the USA or Japan. In West Germany, for example, the taxation of the earnings on an investment is, when corporation tax and depreciation have been taken into consideration, about twice as high as in the USA.

(d) In view of the overburdened state of the national budgets, such a fiscal easing of the pressures on industry seems in most cases to be possible only by means of switches within the budget or of a recasting of the tax system. It also means that the threatening dynamic of expanding social transfers must be halted; at the very least, an endeavour should be made to avoid further increasing the contributions paid under the social welfare system.

(e) Furthermore, improvement of the general conditions in which investments are made calls for a reduction both of the over-large share of the State in the national income and of the budget deficits. This would ease the strain on the capital market and bring a larger part of the wealth created in the economy back to industry. A reduction in the State ratio and in the structural budget deficit is part of the official programme of the West German Government.

(f) It is important, too, not only that capital formation should be generally promoted, but also that efforts be stepped up to ensure that the additional capital is made available to enterprises for the financing of investment. This of course calls first and foremost for a more attractive outlook for earnings in industry and an improvement in the ratio between returns on fresh investments and the interest paid on borrowed capital. But many European countries also lack a suitably structured and organized financial and banking system capable of promoting the formation and utilization of risk capital on a sufficient scale. In this field Europe still has a long way to go to catch up with the USA or even Japan.

(g) Improvement of general conditions calls in addition for the removal of administrative obstacles, in particular of those which can often lead to years of delay in reaching decisions on new investments, thereby adding extraordinarily to costs.

(h) And last but not least, an enduring structural improvement in the employment situation requires that the excessive widening of the wage gap which has occurred in the last ten years shall be gradually corrected.

This last task is perhaps the most difficult of all, for — in a number of European countries at least — wages policy is not amongst the tasks resting directly on the State. In these countries the way wages develop is primarily the responsibility of the parties to the various wage negotiations. It is not however possible for the State to evade all responsibility in this field, for again and again it has been found that when the Government and the Central Bank pursue a general policy of stability and the public has faith in that policy, this faith is not without its influence on the outcome of the wage negotiations. In West Germany, for instance, it was in the second half of the 1970s possible to combine a reduction in the rate of inflation and a partial normalization of the relationship between the wage ratio and the earnings of enterprises. At any rate the State can and must help to make the public clearly conscious of the responsibility which the several social groups and institutions bear for the trend of wages and for employment. One thing can be said with certainty: in the years ahead growth, competitivity and employment in Europe will depend largely on success or failure in combining a cautious expansion of the economy with a trend in wage costs that is consonant with stability.

JOINT EUROPEAN EFFORTS

The points set out above include measures which cannot be put through or promise to be successful from one day to the next; they mean a long haul and they call for longer-term prospects. These longer-term prospects are however essential if Western Europe is not to fall irredeemably behind other industrialized countries. In relation to Japan and other Far-Eastern industrialized countries and also in relation to the United States, most European countries are today at a considerable disadvantage because of the almost explosive expansion occurring in the social sphere and in the share of general government. The figures in Table 4.2 speak for themselves.

This is, however, not simply a matter of quantitative repercussions — that is, of too heavy a burden being placed on the earnings situation of industry by unduly high taxes and social burdens, or of the high proportion of savings capital absorbed by the State. On this last score the USA also has great problems. No less important for Western Europe are the qualitative repercussions. It can hardly be doubted that the structural developments described above have reduced the flexibility of European industry and its ability to adapt itself to the enormous structural changes that have taken place in the world economy. The exaggerations found in the European fiscal and social system therefore constitute a major problem for public policy; if the problem is not solved, Europe's economy will sink still more deeply into mediocrity.

In a publication dedicated to the jubilee of a European Community Institution, it would be right and proper to consider how far European co-operation can solve or at least mitigate the problem; but the point will no doubt be sufficiently discussed elsewhere in this work, so I would like in concluding to mention only two possible contributions that Europe can make to the solution of the problems dealt with above:

(a) Firstly, the European Investment Bank (and other European Community Institutions) can help to ensure that the scarce capital resources available are steered into the right channels — that is, where they can do most to promote the productive capital of the economies concerned.

(b) Second, the politically difficult programme sketched out above for improvement of the general conditions can certainly be made more readily acceptable and more efficacious if the various European bodies give it their unanimous approval, as has on occasion already been done in connection with the call to promote a higher level of profitability in private business. Still more important, however, is the fact that once these principles have been successfully applied in some major European States, the constant discussion of views on economic policy which goes on in the Community may make it easier for other States to follow. Example is better than precept.

5

Investment and Technological Competitiveness

Guido Carli

The preceding chapters have shown the general economic prospects for the 1980s, and have dwelt in particular on the economic, financial and monetary policies that should be developed to encourage investment. The considerations that follow are concerned more specifically with the conditions that need to be achieved to step up the pace of technological innovation in Europe, which has a key role to play in generating new business, new investment and the new jobs of the future.

As the problem of innovation has a great many facets and ramifications, the subject chosen for analysis in greater depth is the operation of the scientific and technological system in Europe, which obviously constitutes one of the mainsprings of innovation in the Community. The analysis is developed on the basis of an initial observation, namely the increasing difficulty Europe is having keeping pace with technological progress and adapting to the growing intensity of competition by means of innovation. In order to try to identify basic remedies for this phenomenon, the chapter examines both the effectiveness of the main components in the system of science and technology (university research, the public funding of research projects, R&D carried out by industrial companies) and the quality of the links or "drive belts" between the different components.

THE OBSERVED DECLINE IN EUROPE'S TECHNOLOGICAL COMPETITIVENESS

In order to delineate the question in hand and clearly determine what is at stake, it is worthwhile beginning with an examination

100

of the past trend of two particularly informative statistical indicators for the United States, Japan and Europe: that is to say performance in international trade in high-technology products and patent applications lodged by residents with their national patent offices.

Mr. B. Cardiff of the European Commission has made an interesting study of international trade in high-technology products which examines the growth of Japanese, European and American exports between 1963 and 1980 in some thirty sectors of the standard international classification of manufactured products. Although some of the categories in this selection may be debatable, the results of the study are nonetheless of fundamental significance.

The study looks at the extent to which the three economic areas under consideration have managed to substitute exports of high-technology manufactures for low-technology products. The simplest way to measure this type of performance is to consider the index of "technological specialization", which is defined as follows for a country x:

$$i_x = \frac{\text{(share of country } x \text{ in world trade in high-technology products)}}{\text{(share of country } x \text{ in total world trade in manufactures)}}$$

The following observations can be made on the basis of the development of the index, which is summarized in Table 5.1:

(a) throughout the period under consideration American industry has consistently occupied a stronger position in world trade in advanced technology products than in total world trade in manufactures;

(b) the profile of Japanese exports has been completely transformed over the last twenty years, with the emphasis moving steadily away from low-technology goods to high-technology products. Japan has therefore become the country that makes the greatest effort in relation to its size in the export of sophisticated goods;

(c) by contrast, Europe's share of the world market in advanced products was practically the same as its share in total world trade in 1963, but since then it has been unable to maintain this balanced position, so that today it trades increasingly in low-technology goods and less and less in sophisticated products.

TABLE 5.1
INDEX OF TECHNOLOGI-
CAL SPECIALIZATION IN
JAPAN, THE USA AND
EUROPE BETWEEN 1963
AND 1980

	1963	1970	1980
EEC	1.02	0.94	0.88
USA	1.29	1.27	1.20
Japan	0.56	0.87	1.41

(*Source*: B. Cardiff, *Technological Inno-vation in European Industry*, Commission of the European Communities, January 1982.)

A second general indicator that provides an interesting insight into Europe's position in scientific and technological competition consists in the number of patent applications lodged by residents with their national patent offices. This is obviously a good index of the inventiveness and technological dynamism of a nation.

In fact, national procedures for granting patents vary widely in strictness and do not yield data that are immediately comparable. A country comparison can be made only if the administrative particularities of each country are taken into account; an examination of this kind will not be undertaken here. Nevertheless, it is permissible to examine the changes that have occurred in the data country by country and to draw a number of conclusions.

Between 1965 and 1977 there was a noticeable decline in patent applications in all European countries except Ireland. There was also a slightly smaller decrease in the case of the United States. In Japan, on the other hand, patent applications by residents more than doubled. The trends are therefore very similar to those in world trade in high-technology products.

The findings are therefore clear: in the development of advanced technology as well as in the industrial and commercial exploitation of it Europe is not managing to reduce the lead of the United States and its position in relation to Japan is deteriorating rapidly and continuously. There is nothing new in this diagnosis, but in the light of the few data examined it must be concluded that the gap between Europe and its rivals has reached extremely worrying dimensions.

It is important to realise that the difficulties experienced by the Community are not fundamentally due to a lack of human or financial resources. Europe's research potential is in fact considerable. The overall R&D expenditure of the European Community of 260 million inhabitants was around ECU 40 billion in 1980, or 2 per cent of the Community's gross domestic product; within the Community as a whole almost 1,100,000 persons were engaged in research. The corresponding figures for the United States and Japan are as follows:

(a) USA: 230 million inhabitants, ECU 43 billion, 2.3 per cent of GDP, 1,520,000 research staff;

(b) Japan: 113 million inhabitants, ECU 15 billion, 2 per cent of GDP, 619,000 research staff.

Within the OECD, the R&D expenditure of the Community, the United States and Japan has developed as follows, expressed as a percentage of the R&D expenditure of all OECD countries: 1964 — Europe, 22 per cent; USA, 69 per cent; Japan, 4 per cent; 1979 — Europe, 33 per cent; USA, 43 per cent; Japan, 16 per cent. At the world level, Europe accounts for 20 per cent of the total R&D effort but has only 6 per cent of the working population of the planet.

It would therefore seem that the problem is a lack of effectiveness in applying the resources at the Community's disposal. Hence, any thoughts on ways of improving Europe's technological competitiveness must be preceded by an examination of the effectiveness of the constituent parts of the European R&D system (university laboratories, public research programmes and institutes, company laboratories) and the quality of the links between the different elements.

UNIVERSITY RESEARCH IN EUROPE AND ITS RELATIONS WITH THE WORLD OF INDUSTRY

University research is still the foundation upon which the scientific and technological system is built. High-calibre university research is vital if the long-term economic future is to be safeguarded, if only because of the essential educational role of the universities.

The European university system has continued to be held in high esteem throughout the world in spite of the rapid rise of American university research from the end of World War II onwards. If we look at the distribution of Nobel Prizes since 1946, we find that between that year and 1960 the United States received 38 citations out of a total of 78 in the fields of chemistry, physics and biomedicine, while the EEC countries won about twenty. In the period from 1961 to 1976 a total of 97 prizes were awarded, of which 47 went to American scholars and about 35 to EEC scientists.

The advantage the USA enjoys over Europe therefore seems to be diminishing, since the disparity between the two is now in the ratio of 4 : 3, compared with 4 : 2 just after the war.

Another very rough indicator of the quality of basic research can be obtained by tallying the articles quoted in scientific journals according to the nationality of their authors. Of course, much depends on the sample chosen; as this genre was developed in the United States, this criterion overstates American and Anglo-Saxon contributions and discriminates against the scientific output of other countries, particularly those in eastern Europe and to a lesser extent Japan and the Latin countries, where English is less commonly used. The results show a high degree of stability; in 1975, 1976 and 1977 38 per cent of quotations in the scientific literature of the world concerned American authors. In other words, a slightly higher percentage than that of American R&D in the total world effort.

Although it appears from this that up to now basic research in Europe has shown itself to be a strong force in the world, the future looks less reassuring. It is generally agreed that European researchers are beginning to lack mobility both in operational terms and in terms of scientific disciplines. This calls for a range of institutional, legal, financial and social measures to encourage researchers to move from one laboratory to another and from the laboratory to the lecture room or industry and vice versa. The present economic and social conditions are hardly propitious, however; rising unemployment encourages immobility and it is significant that in the large French research bodies the turnover rate was between 6 and 8 per cent in 1967, a period of boom, but had fallen to 1.5–2 per cent by 1977 — that is to say after the first oil shock.

This lack of mobility is accompanied by a marked ageing of the research staff; at present the rate of replacement of scientific staff in research establishments is scarcely above 1 per cent on average. Fresh blood can be introduced in two ways: either by increasing mobility, which entails new incentives, or by creating new jobs — some experts suggest an annual rate of growth of 3 per cent. Either course would be difficult in the present time of budget constraints, but the problem cannot be side-stepped for too long without having serious long-term repercussions on Europe's scientific potential.

The Community could usefully help stimulate the university scientific system by organising the twinning of laboratories, assisting in the establishment of transnational teams, paying some of the travelling expenses of specialists, and so forth.

The improvements in the internal working of university research outlined above should be backed up by advances in the links between university research and industrial research. Co-operation between universities and industry continues to be inadequate in Europe, even though the universities' financial problems and industry's increased need for basic research have led to some increase in joint projects in recent years.

The problem is largely a question of attitudes. The academic often distrusts the industrialist, because the latter sets too tight a schedule or does not hesitate to end an experiment early if he considers it to be inconclusive or too costly or because the academic fears he will be branded as "commercial", thus sinning against the academic ethic. The industrialist, for his part, distrusts the generalities of the academic, has the feeling that the latter regards him as a patron without really meeting his needs or fears that the publication of scientific papers is the academic's main concern. Moreover, cooperation between industrialists and academics tends to be rather informal, so that misunderstandings can arise with regard to patent rights or just rewards for the researchers, as the latter are not familiar with industrial practices and feel that they are given little protection by the university itself.

The pitfalls that result from these attitudes are very damaging: mutual incomprehension, the confinement of university research to fields that yield few marketable innovations or are linked solely to education, lack of cross fertilization. A situation such as this contrasts strongly with the dynamic exchanges that take place in the United States.

One of the best remedies would be to create liaison bodies in the universities. Their role would be to publicize the services that the university can provide for the corporate sector (training, guidance, research), to make the university more responsive to the needs of industry and to speed up the handling of industrialists' requests for assistance.

POLICIES FOLLOWED BY NATIONAL AUTHORITIES TO ASSIST R&D: ASSESSMENT AND PROSPECTS

The importance of the role of the State in stimulating R&D needs no further demonstration. The State has a considerable impact on the development of R&D through public-sector contracts, government grants for university and industrial research and also through the introduction of "contextual" measures (technical standards, legislation, etc.).

In view of the importance of this role, there has often been a tendency to believe that the disparity between government research grants in the USA and those provided in Europe (see Table 5.2) could be one of the main causes of the scientific and technological decline of Europe on the world stage.

However, at the beginning of the 1970s this diagnosis was challenged by many experts who held that public-sector initiatives in Europe suffered much more from a lack of effectiveness than from a lack of financial resources. They believed that the relatively modest grants provided by European governments could have produced much more striking results:

  (a) if a better system of coordination had been introduced both
      to avoid the duplication or triplication of effort in some
      fields and to permit parallel experimentation on a larger
      number of technological options;

TABLE 5.2

PUBLIC FINANCING OF R&D PER HEAD OF POPULATION IN 1979 (IN DOLLARS)

	Defence and aerospace	Agri- culture and industry	Energy and infra- structure	Health and social services	General promotion of knowledge	Total
United States[4]	81	3	23	20	4[1]	132
Japan	3	7	6	2	21[2]	40[2]
Germany	15	11	19	10	41	97
France	36	13	13	6	21	89
United Kingdom	50	10	8	3	18	89
Italy	4	4	7	2	9[1]	25
Canada[4]	3	15	10	7	9[1]	43
Netherlands	6	12	9	8	43	78
Sweden	22	9	19	11	45	117
Switzerland 1978[4]	6	3	6	3	11[1]	28
Australia 1978/79[3]	8	25	7	12	14	64
Belgium	3	10	9	11	14	49
Norway	4	20	10	14	37	87
Denmark	2	9	6	8	16	41
Finland	1	13	6	4	19	42
New Zealand	1	20	11	5	9	44
Ireland	1	8	2	5	9	24
Spain	1	4	1	1	2[1]	9
Portugal 1976	—	2	1	1	1	5
Greece	—	3	1	1	3	8
Turkey	—	2	1	1	1	5
Iceland	—	18	4	4	6	32

1 All or part of public GUFs are excluded.
2 R&D understated in public research establishments only, plus GUFs in the case of general promotion of knowledge.
3 Partial estimate by the OECD.
4 Federal financing only.
Note: These data permit only approximate comparisons. Only large differences between countries or between groups of objectives are significant.
(*Source*: OECD.)

(b) if the methods for stimulating and administering research had been more efficient;

(c) if greater attention had been paid to the technical and commercial stages that follow R&D, which have been seriously neglected;

(d) if economies had been more competitive and free from the damaging restraints imposed by the compartmentalization of national public-sector markets.

Developments in recent years have only confirmed this diagnosis. The rise of Japan was very rapid in spite of the fact that public financing of R&D was less in volume than in Europe, as Table 5.2 shows. Similarly, in the United States public funding was greatly reduced between 1969 and 1976 without having serious effects on the US economy.

It is generally acknowledged today that until the European governments improve their methods of encouraging R&D nationally and their arrangements for cooperation at Community level with regard to the planning, execution and maximization of certain types of R&D effort, the Community will continue to be unable to improve its position.

The measures required to resolve these problems will be approached from two angles. First, we shall examine the progress that must be made in national policies in order to provide greater incentives for projects that do not need to be directly incorporated into a European strategy. Then we shall review the types of additional cooperation that should be established at the Community level in order to allow European industry to play a significant part in developing the technologies that by their nature and implications require a concerted approach.

Policies for encouraging R&D at national level

University research financed largely by the government has already been described above and will therefore not be examined further here.

As far as State action to stimulate industrial development is concerned, it is striking to see the extent to which State support is concentrated on a small number of sectors. In some Community countries four branches of industry—electrical engineering, aerospace, computers and telecommunications—absorb 90 per cent of total state aid for R&D. It is now being realised that this over-concentration has not only hampered innovation in sectors not favoured in this way, but has also made a large proportion of these sectors incapable of rapidly assimilating the technological advances developed in the top-flight sectors receiving State support.

This financing strategy contrasts quite strongly with that pursued in Japan, where the authorities have taken care to offer incentives that are accessible to a very broad range of sectors. For example, Japanese industrialists can launch R&D activities on the basis of loans on very favourable terms, such as the provision of 90 per cent of the total finance required at an interest rate of 8 per cent for 15 years.

One of the few European countries to avoid the worst excesses of the imbalance described above is the Federal Republic of Germany, which has a system of non-discriminatory or "automatic" support for small and medium-sized firms in the shape of an annual credit for each person employed in R&D. The system has proved its worth and could very usefully be introduced in the other member countries of the Community.

A second aspect of government policies in the industrial field that needs to be corrected is the overconcentration of public expenditure on well-established firms. Enterprises with a broad financial, commercial and technical base obviously have an absolutely vital part to play in technological and economic advance; however, in certain cases the very logic of these enterprises may, for perfectly valid reasons, cause them to delay or restrict the exploitation of certain new technologies, no matter whether they have been developed within the firms themselves or outside. The reasons that may induce such behaviour on the part of some large companies are the following:

(a) they may not fully appreciate the potential importance of a radical innovation;

(b) the initial sales of a new product may seem too small in relation to the total turnover of the company;

(c) the applications of certain new technologies may extend far beyond the company's current product range;

(d) in its allocation of financial resources the enterprise may be obliged to give high priority to existing products and forms of business;

(e) some of the largest companies are interested in developing a new product only if they can win a substantial share of the national market (30–40 per cent); this may prove impossible if foreign competitors have already gained a firm foothold in the market;

(f) some large enterprises may have made considerable investments in equipment, existing technologies and production methods that they cannot afford to scrap;

(g) the principles on which companies are run and the channels for the promotion of managers may encourage them to avoid risks;

(h) the trade unions may be opposed to the introduction of certain new technologies.

In a substantial number of cases the creation of a new company (generally termed an NTBF, or New Technology Based Firm, in the specialist jargon) may be the only truly effective means of rapidly exploiting a radical invention. This has been demonstrated in numerous instances in the USA.

There is universal agreement that governments have not yet fully woken up to these problems. Incentives to create new enterprises should be greatly expanded. This could be done by emulating the American SBIC programme, for example. In addition, support must be given to the efforts developed by the European Commission to foster cooperation among bodies providing venture capital within the EEC, given the fact that in a growing number of cases such cooperation is indispensable if a radically innovative product is to be launched quickly and effectively throughout the European market.

What Community strategies should be adopted?

The size of the effort required of all interested parties if they are to adapt to the increasingly stringent demands of world scientific and technological competition can be seen from the above. The sheer number of problems involved is such that, unless one's focus is narrowed somewhat, there is no difficulty in drawing up a vast catalogue of hypothetical remedies relating to R&D itself and to its environment for implementation at Community level.

It is at this stage that it is important to make an evaluation and identify those remedies that promise to be both effective in practice and acceptable at the political level. The ideas set out below are guided by this constraint. And, although they make no pretention to constitute a panacea, the proposed activities are thought to be capable of making a substantial contribution towards improving the technological competitiveness of the Community.

If one considers first and foremost the potential role of the Community in the sphere of the direct financing of industrial R&D, it should be borne in mind — in the light of experience over the last few years — that the Community is not at present equipped to finance any class of R&D activity whatsoever. The idea of a global Community R&D policy — highly centralized and endowed with considerable financial resources — is not feasible for the time being.

Community activities would appear to have to be conducted on an even more selective basis than those of the national public authorities, in that new constraints emerge at the Community level. The acute conflicts of interest which arose in 1977–78 when the Nine were discussing draft programmes (relating, for example, to aircraft technology) which impinged too closely on the commercial realities of the market place, afford an example which militates in favour of research that is "pre-competitive" or "horizontal" in character.

A remarkable feature of the development of technology in recent years is the way in which, in a very considerable number of sectors, most enterprises are obliged to take certain routes as regards technology. If we take the motor industry, there is the matter of the mastery of new materials (composites, ceramics for the manufacture of advanced engines, etc.) and of incorporating advanced electronics into its products. In the chemical industry, there is the example of the new membrane-based separation techniques. In the field of engineering, we have the new design, surface treatment, forming and machining techniques which make use of new tools (e.g., utilizing lasers) or computer assistance (the use of robots in manufacturing, CAD). In an advanced-technology field such as the manufacture of electronic components, sub-micronic techniques have to be mastered in order to manufacture ever more miniaturized chips.

These technologies are "horizontal" in that they concern many enterprises (and in some cases even many sectors); they are termed "pre-competitive"—i.e., neutral from the point of view of competition—because if appropriate measures are taken to ensure that they are disseminated on a widespread scale they will be of benefit to the whole range of enterprises concerned while maintaining full competition as between them; the measures in fact rely on the flair and the *savoir faire* with which the individual enterprise exploits the new technological knowledge available to all.

The advantages of this approach, which has already been explored in the pilot stage of the Commission's ESPRIT programme, do not lie solely in the pre-competitive character of the activities, nor in their very extensive industrial spin-off. The sort of basic technological research involved very often necessitates industry/university cooperation; as a result, it affords an opportunity to bring these two worlds—which have drifted too far apart—closely together. In particular, Community projects would greatly facilitate cross-border cooperation between enterprises and university centres, something which is subject to barriers (chiefly of an administrative nature) over and above those which exist at the national level. In addition, the launching of effective Community projects would enable the corresponding national public programmes to be rationalized, thus obviating duplication, if not triplication, of expenditure. Finally, such activities would stimulate the public research centres, of which, at present, insufficient use is made for the purpose of the transfer of technology.

The Community should supplement this type of "catalytic" activity by a strategy designed to make the environment for private R&D initiatives as propitious as possible. In this connection, two factors spring immediately to mind: the need to strengthen the home market and the need for a more constructive EEC competition policy.

One of the lessons of the last few years is that purely national strategies calculated to enable countries to hold on to an adequate share of the world markets for advanced technology do not constitute a sufficiently effective approach. In several sectors of European industry it has come to be recognized that more intensive cross-border cooperation between enterprises must be initiated as a matter of urgency in order to back up stimulatory action taken by the public authorities.

Moreover, this tendency is not restricted merely to the European Community. Experts who have been the closest observers of the Japanese scene nowadays agree that a good deal of Japan's successes are attributable to the industrial collaboration which has taken place there — whether spontaneously or instigated by MITI — between various leading companies in the field of advanced technology. Furthermore, the Japanese Government has enacted a law, the Technology Research Association Law, with a view to modifying Japanese anti-trust law to suit the requirements of technological progress. In the United States technological co-operation groupings (covering, for example, electronic components and mini-computers) are being set up in response to the Japanese challenge. The membership of these groupings extends right up to the most prestigious companies, which no longer feel invulnerable. Moreover, the US Government's approach to competition has been substantially revised under the Reagan Administration.

In this context, European industry has begun to show signs of acute concern in the face of what it considers to be the excessively restrictive character of certain approaches taken by the Commission to the rules governing competition, particularly in the field of patent and know-how licensing agreements. Albeit based at the outset on a laudable objective — *viz.*, the alleviation of administrative constraints — the drafts currently under consideration at the Commission relating to the exemption of certain classes of patent licensing agreements are liable to have a profoundly discouraging effect not only on patent licensing agreements and technology transfer in general, but also on agreements concerning cooperation in the field of R&D, having regard to the fact that the industrial property issues raised are similar in both cases. Increasingly, R&D agreements will have to cover not only R&D proper but also its industrial and commercial exploitation. The Commission is currently considering numerous recommendations relating to the need to tackle this type of agreement in the most constructive manner possible.

The importance of a vast Community market as regards industrial and technological development (notably from the point of view of economies of scale) is too well-known to warrant a lengthy discussion here. Firstly, it is imperative that national public contracts for advanced-technology equipment be opened up more in order to give genuine opportunities for development to those European firms that have put considerable efforts into preserving a significant potential for innovation *vis-à-vis* the USA and Japan. The Commission has been making major proposals in this field for some time, and the Council's failure to act thereon must be viewed as extremely serious. To take the example of telecommunications, which has vital need of a harmonization of technical and administrative standards, in 1979 the Commission submitted very specific proposals to the Council with a view to the establishment of a harmonized basic infrastructure which would enable the various Postal and Telecommunications Administrations to take a coherent approach to the development of integrated digital transmission and switching networks for the new information services. Among other things, the Commission stressed that the national telecommunications administrations should:

(a) henceforward consult with each other before introducing any new service;

(b) implement the recommendations relating to the introduction of these new services in the integrated digital transmission and switching services which are intended to ensue from the joint studies carried out in the European (CEPT) and international (CCITT) telecommunications organizations;

(c) undertake as from 1985 to procure digital transmission and switching systems only within the framework of a harmonized Community approach;

(d) undertake as from 1981 to give users the opportunity to procure the relevant terminals freely both from industry and from the PTT.

To date the Council has taken no formal decision on the above proposals. This places European industry in a situation of commercial and technical uncertainty which is extremely prejudicial to investment and innovation. This is just one example; others could be given in the sphere of, say, data processing or transport.

The Community is generally reckoned to be three or four years behind the United States and Japan with the introduction of advanced public services merely because of the state of anarchy obtaining with respect to administrative practices and standards. It is still not too late to break with this approach, although it is more than time that this was done.

The eminently strategic role played by public contracts in relation to technological development must not cause it to be overlooked that the need to eliminate technical barriers to intra-Community trade is more general, also affecting consumer goods and goods intended for private-sector enterprises. Even though undeniable successes have been achieved in this field since 1968, the process of integration is now slowing down. This is reflected in the continuing existence of overt barriers (such as customs formalities, the cost of which, according to Commission estimates, could be as much as 5–10 per cent of the value of the goods concerned) and more covert barriers (rules on technical safety and public health, etc.). It is vital that these obstacles be eradicated if one genuinely wishes to support economic development and thereby the self-financing of R&D and innovation.

RESEARCH—INDUSTRIAL DEVELOPMENT

The third major element of the scientific and technological system, the internal operation of which is to be discussed, is R&D.

Industry as well needs to rethink the way in which it operates and its strategies.

At the scientific and technological levels, European industry continues to record some very remarkable achievements. Taking an admittedly fairly schematic view, it is reasonable to hold that the weaknesses of European industry lie rather on the marketing side.

There has been a very noticeable change in this area since the 1960s, when many European firms suffered in comparison with their US competitors from a decidedly smaller ability to recognize the complex, constantly evolving needs of the market. European industry has improved signally in this respect and the directions that it has selected for its innovatory activities are the outcome of the better use of technical and economic data. However, difficulty seems to remain at the level of the commercial promotion of innovations, a field in to which the Japanese tend to put more effort than their European — and sometimes even their US — counterparts. Increasingly, European companies will have to realize that technology is something that one has to know how to sell.

In addition, European firms will have to adopt a more dynamic, bolder stance in a situation where international cooperation is the only viable way out in the long run. While EEC competition law, on the one hand, and nationalistic policies on the part of governments, on the other, are liable to have a discouraging effect on some classes of firm, it is clear that these obstacles are less important to other classes of firm for which the main impediment to cooperation in the technological field lies in a certain lack of dynamism in the face of the — admittedly numerous, but by no means insurmountable — difficulties (language barriers, increased complexity of project management, etc.) involved in this type of cooperation.

So, it appears from this brief survey that, whereas it is clear that enterprise needs Europe, it is equally clear that Europe needs enterprise.

6

Investment and Energy

Ulf Lantzke

The present easy oil market (in early 1983) has tended to divert international attention from energy to more pressing issues. Indeed, in 1981 equilibrium was finally restored to the international oil market that had been shaken by the revolution in Iran in 1978. The equilibrium, however, was achieved at a very high economic cost. While oil prices increased by 170 per cent in 1979 and 1980, the economies of the OECD countries went spiralling downward. Still trying to adjust to the first oil price shock of 1973–74, this second shock contributed even more to inflationary pressures, high interest rates and the staggering increase in OECD unemployment, from 19 million people in 1979 to almost 32 million by the end of 1982. Overall, it has been estimated that the loss of income to the OECD countries due to this second oil price shock amounted to around US\$ 1,000 billion (in 1980 dollars) or a loss of US\$ 1,300 for every person in the OECD region.

The current weakness of the oil market does not mean that the energy problem has been solved. It is only partly due to more efficient use of energy and the displacement of oil by other fuels in OECD countries. But it is also due to current low levels of economic activity which are themselves in part a result of the two oil-price shocks. The following analysis will show that there are no grounds for complacency about the world and the European energy outlook.

WORLD ENERGY OUTLOOK

In 1981, world oil demand of 47.7 million barrels per day was already significantly below possible production. In 1982 it fell to

117

45.6 Mbd, and it is expected to decline futher. As a result of low demand, the average price paid for crude oil by OECD countries declined from US$ 36 per barrel in early 1981 to about $ 29 in March 1983. Further price decreases are possible. But the effects of this price fall should not be over-estimated. It should be remembered that the average crude oil price paid in early 1983 still was 125 per cent above the level of the end of 1978 in nominal terms. Moreover, until recently the rise in the value of the US dollar, in which crude oil sales are transacted, has led to a nominal or even real increase of consumer oil prices in most local currencies, despite the sluggishness of activity. Western economies are far from having adapted to these cost increases.

Decisions in the energy sector, particularly on investment, need to take account not so much of the situation today as of the likely long-term outlook for energy supply and demand. To contribute to this process, the International Energy Agency published in October 1982 a book entitled *World Energy Outlook*,[1] the second such study published by the IEA. This study concluded — under various scenarios for economic growth and oil prices — that world energy markets, and the oil market in particular, are likely to remain easy until the second half of the 1980s. Thereafter the position will become increasingly difficult. Demand for energy in the OECD area is likely to rise as the economy grows and as opportunities for new measures to promote energy efficiency lessen. Production of oil in the OECD area is likely to decline as a result of falling output in North America and the United Kingdom, partly offset by rising Norwegian production. At the same time, oil import requirements are expected to rise in the Third World as a result of economic development, increasing urbanisation and industrialisation. Even on optimistic assumptions about the development of alternative fuels, particularly coal and nuclear power, the demand for oil from the OPEC countries seems likely around 1990 to become uncomfortably close to the levels of production which those countries are able and willing to maintain. The world will again be vulnerable to an oil price shock.

1 IEA/OECD, *World Energy Outlook*, Paris, 1982.

ENERGY PERSPECTIVES FOR EUROPE

The 19 European member-countries of the OECD have made considerable progress in improving the structure of their energy economies. Oil imports of the group fell from 735 million tonnes in 1973 to about 430 Mt in 1982. Even taking account of the economic recession, this is an extraordinary success. Over the same period, the amount of energy required to produce one unit of GDP in OECD Europe has fallen 16 per cent, and oil use relative to GDP has decreased 33 per cent.

Despite this progress, the energy scene in Europe is still dominated by a high level of oil dependence and by continued dependence on imports. In 1982, OECD Europe depended on oil for 49 per cent of total energy requirements, and 73 per cent of this was imported. Except for Norway and the United Kingdom, virtually all European countries depend on imports for 95 to 100 per cent of their oil use. To a lesser extent, OECD Europe is also dependent on imports of natural gas (15 per cent of total consumption), and even in the case of coal, the basis on which European industry developed, about 63 million tonnes of oil equivalent (Mtoe), or 22 per cent of total requirements, were imported in 1982. By far the greater part of the uranium necessary for nuclear power generation is also imported. On the basis of latest government projections, prospects for European energy demand and supply until 1990 can be summarised as in Table 6.1.

The main features for the remainder of this decade are:

(a) Total energy requirements are expected to increase, reaching almost 1500 Mtoe by 1990. In contrast, oil use will continue to fall.

(b) There will be radical shifts in the balance between fuels, with oil's share falling from 49 per cent in 1981 to less than 40 per cent in 1990. The share of solid fuels is expected to increase from 23 to 25 per cent, growing by one third in absolute terms. The share of nuclear energy should increase from the current 6 per cent to more than 12 per cent. However, oil will continue to be by far the most important single energy source.

(c) At the same time, domestic energy production is expected to rise by 2.5 per cent per annum. This is essentially due to

TABLE 6.1

OECD EUROPE'S PRIMARY ENERGY DEMAND AND SUPPLY 1973–90

	1973	1980	1981	1985	1990
Total demand[1]	1199.2	1248.5	1214.3	1349.5	1499.2
solid fuels	278.7	285.3	285.7	310.7	374.2
oil	704.6	643.8	590.6	612.6	592.0
gas	122.6	178.6	175.2	200.4	221.6
nuclear	18.7	50.3	69.7	119.2	182.9
hydro/geothermal	74.6	90.1	92.7	97.2	108.0
other	0	0.4	0.4	9.4	20.5
Total demand (per cent)	100.0	100.0	100.0	100.0	100.0
solid fuels	23.2	22.9	23.5	23.0	25.0
oil	58.8	51.6	48.7	45.4	39.5
gas	10.2	14.3	14.4	14.8	14.8
nuclear	1.6	4.0	5.7	8.8	12.2
hydro/geothermal	6.2	7.2	7.6	7.2	7.2
other	0	0	0	0.7	1.3
Domestic production (Mtoe)	473.8	654.1	684.5	764.2	853.4
Net imports (Mtoe)	771.5	649.5	558.1	614.4	677.8
Import share in TPE (per cent)	64.3	52.0	46.0	45.5	45.2

1 Total primary energy (TPE), in million tonnes of oil equivalent (Mtoe). Including stock changes and excluding marine bunkers.

the expected further development of North Sea oil and gas
and to nuclear expansion. The share of imported oil alone
in total energy requirements is forecast to fall from 39 per
cent in 1981 to around 30 per cent by 1990. However, due
to increasing imports of coal and natural gas, overall import
dependence of OECD Europe will fall only slightly to a
level of 45 per cent of total energy demand.

This outlook is based on the Low Oil Demand Scenario of the
World Energy Outlook, which assumed moderate economic growth
for the OECD (2.4 per cent per annum, 1980–85; 2.7 per cent per
annum, 1985–2000) and a relatively high real oil price path (−3.3
per cent per annum, 1980–85; +3.0 per cent per annum, 1985–
2000), as adjusted for current economic growth conditions (1.5
per cent per annum, 1980–85) and real oil prices (−7.7 per cent
per annum, 1980–85).

Current projections for the longer term suggest the following
development until the end of this century:

(a) European energy production could grow by almost 40 per
cent, with nuclear being the single most important contribution.

(b) Coal use could almost double and coal imports could grow
four-fold, although current developments make this estimate seem optimistic.

(c) Natural gas would probably not exceed a relative share of
15 per cent, but imports may grow more than four-fold.

(d) As a result, the oil share could be held to some 32 per cent,
and oil imports could drop to around 25 per cent of total
energy requirements.

Since the first oil price shock in 1973–74, IEA countries and
member countries of the European Community have indeed committed themselves at various occasions to improve their energy
economies along such lines. Members of the IEA, for instance,
adopted twelve Principles for Energy Policy in 1977, Principles
for Coal Policy in 1979 and Lines of Action for Energy Conservation and Fuel Switching in 1980.[2] Energy problems also were

2 For more details, see IEA/OECD, *World Energy Outlook,* Paris, 1982, pp. 46–55; and
European Community Council Resolution of 9th June 1980 on the Community's
energy objectives for 1990 (OJC 149, 18 June 1980).

given repeated focus at the meetings of the Economic Summit, in particular at the Venice Economic Summit in June 1980. Agreed energy policy objectives focus on increasing energy efficiency and emphasise the need for structural change to reduce dependence on imported oil through oil substitution, rapid expansion in the production and use of coal, natural gas, nuclear power and other available energies.

PROSPECTS FOR ENERGY INVESTMENT

The transition to better balanced energy economies will require substantial investment in additional energy supply sources, in developing alternatives to oil and in improving the efficiency of energy use. In 1981, the Commission of the European Communities estimated that the total of energy investment programmes of its member countries for the period 1981–90 would be some European Currency Units (ECU) 500 billion, of which 80 per cent were planned for energy production and 20 per cent for measures to increase energy efficiency.[3] These programmes would represent some 2 per cent of GDP as compared with about 1.5 per cent in the period 1968–80, or about 9 per cent of total investment compared with 6.8 per cent. However, these figures can only indicate the orders of magnitude involved. Many changes in the underlying assumptions and in energy and investment policies have occurred and require continual revision of investment prospects.

The viability of investments in both energy supply and demand has been affected adversely in 1981–82. Investors' expectations of future oil price movements are becoming lower. However, new energy plants, such as the development of new but more costly marginal resources of conventional fuels or of synfuels, usually require an increasing oil price scenario before they can commence. The decline in demand for oil products and the decline in the demand growth rates for other forms of secondary energy has created uncertainty in planning to meet future demand and the cancellation of new plants, particularly in the synfuels, electric utility and nuclear power industries. Finally, recent economic developments in member countries have resulted in low operating

3 Fifth Medium-Term Economic Policy Programme of the European Community (COM(81)344 final).

surpluses among companies who would normally be interested in investing in new energy projects, high levels of interest rates which increase the cost of capital intensive projects with long lead times, and high rates of inflation, which have tended to increase the uncertainty surrounding future cost estimates.[4]

Indeed, the past year has seen a downward revision of investment plans. Following the domino-like collapse of major synfuels projects in the United States, major energy supply projects were also cancelled or postponed in Europe. They include, for instance, the £2.7 billion British North Sea gas gathering scheme, two coal gasification projects of Shell in Wilhelmshaven (West Germany) and Moerdijk (Netherlands), and two major co-operative coal gasification and liquefaction projects of the United States, Germany and Japan (Wycoal gas and SRC II). It must be assumed that there has been a similar reduction in energy efficiency and fuel switching projects.

In principle, such retrenchment reflects a healthy ability of economies to respond to changing market signals and avoids wasteful use of resources on sub-optimal investment. On the other hand, there remains a danger that an over-reaction could set in. This could lead to economically justifiable energy investments being delayed or cancelled. Given the long lead times of energy supply projects and the relatively short time in which the energy market can change, it must be questioned whether such responses are helping to set the foundation for a more secure and stable energy future.

IEA Ministers called attention to these risks in May 1982. They expressed their concern that concentration on short-term oil market conditions is deterring producers and consumers from taking the investment decisions necessary to meet probable long-term trends. While recognising that the short-term energy situation has changed, they agreed that the longer-term situation remains uncertain and stressed the important role that energy investment must play in assuring energy security. In their meeting in May 1983, IEA Ministers reaffirmed this assessment.

Quantification of future energy investments is very difficult, given the uncertainties about major factors that influence them.

4 See also Symonds, Energy financing—reappraisal after the boom years, *Petroleum Economist*, 1982, p. 219.

Such uncertainties are changing economic conditions, changes or cancellation of exploration and development projects, prolongations of lead times for authorisation and construction, changes in legislation, taxation or administrative procedures, cost over-runs and the development of investment and financing costs. Therefore, the following analysis[5] should not be regarded as a forecast but as an attempt to seize the nature and the orders of magnitude of energy investments that will be required to bring about the necessary structural improvement of European energy economies.

INVESTMENT IN THE OIL MARKET

Outlook for European Oil Supply and Demand

The oil industry is in the midst of fundamental change.[6] A decade ago, Europe was almost totally dependent on oil imports, mostly from the Middle East. In 1973, member countries of OECD Europe used 705 Mt of oil — one quarter of the world's total — but produced only 20 Mt. In 1982, annual production, essentially from the North Sea, was running at 149 Mt, while demand had fallen to 590 Mt. Latest government projections indicate that this trend will continue. Both the United Kingdom and Norway should continue to raise the level of oil production, at least until about 1985, while European demand should remain constant (Table 6.2).

The expected shift in market shares of the major fuels will probably feature a significant decline for oil from 49 per cent in 1981 to less than 40 per cent by 1990, with Belgium, France and Sweden likely to show the largest absolute reductions — though considerable gains for oil can be expected in Portugal, Spain, Turkey and the United Kingdom. But oil will remain the most

5 For earlier analyses, including questions of investment financing, see Chase Manhattan Bank, *Capital Investments of the World Petroleum Industry, 1980*, published mid-1982; Bauer, Häfele, Rogner, Energy strategies and capital requirements, *11th World Energy Conference*, Munich 1980, Vol. 4B, p. 395; Christians (Deutsche Bank AG), International aspects of the formation of capital to cover energy-related financing requirements, *World Energy Conference 1980*, Vol. RTB, p. 433; Diel, Radtke, Stößel (Dresdner Bank AG), Investment requirements in the energy sector and their financing, *World Energy Conference 1980*, Vol. 4B, p. 431; *Revue de l'Energie*, Paris, 1980, special issue on Energy Investment Finance.

6 For more details see Schürmann, Neuorientierung und Anpassungsprozesse in der internationalen Ölversorgung, *Oel-Zeitschrift für die Mineralölwirtschaft*, 1982, pp. 312–21.

TABLE 6.2
OECD EUROPE'S OIL MARKET 1973–90

	1973	1980	1981	1985	1990
Consumption (Mtoe)	704.6	643.8	590.6	612.6	592.0
Oil share in total primary energy demand (per cent)	58.7	51.6	48.6	45.4	39.5
Domestic production (Mtoe)	19.5	123.5	131.7	153.4	147.0
of which: Norway	1.6	24.5	23.7	27.5	33.5
United Kingdom	0.4	82.2	91.4	104.0	87.0
Others	17.5	16.8	16.6	21.9	26.5
Net imports (Mtoe)	734.9	564.6	471.2	488.2	477.0
Import share in TPE (per cent)	61.3	45.2	38.8	36.2	31.8

important energy source in Europe. Thus, any unchecked momentum of overall energy demand would continue to have a direct upward impact on oil demand.

Starting in the second half of the 1980s, domestic oil production in Europe is likely to fall, with the main decline occurring in the United Kingdom. As a result, the proportion of imports to demand is expected to rise again to its 1981 level of 80 per cent by 1990, after a small decline around 1985.

Investment Perspectives

Even at depressed demand levels, enormous oil investments are required just to replace depleted reserves and to develop new supply. But the volumes and pace of oil investment will depend essentially on the prospects and investors' perceptions of future demand and prices, on future development costs as well as national depletion and taxation policies. Currently the European oil industry is making heavy downstream losses, due to the combination of weak demand, which leads to under-utilisation of capacity, high crude-oil import costs, relatively low spot-market prices for oil products and strong competition in a shrinking market. In some countries relatively inflexible government price controls are adding to these problems. These factors, together with rising investment costs, tend to jeopardize investment plans.

In this situation two main areas of oil activity still show significant investment perspectives: namely, further development of North Sea oil, and conversion of refineries which will be combined with closures of obsolete capacities.

North Sea Oil Production

The greatest efforts by far, in the technical and financial regard, will have to be made for oil and gas exploration and development in the North Sea. Over 85 per cent of OECD Europe's oil production and almost 90 per cent of its reserves are in the North Sea.[7] However, further development will be more difficult and more expensive since exploration is now moving to greater water depths and more remote and hostile environments. Moreover, the size of oil and gas deposits tends to diminish. As a consequence, production costs for new oil fields are expected to reach more than US$ 15–20 per daily barrel, while they are around one-half of this for existing fields.

Oil production of the British sector of the North Sea between 1975 and 1981 amounted to a total of 354 Mt. In 1982, the annual production went up to about 105 Mt. As to future production, the British government has indicated a possible range of 95 to 130 Mt for 1985.[8] It can be assumed that production will reach its peak around 1985 or somewhat later, and gradually decline thereafter. The United Kingdom may therefore return as a net importer of oil in the first half of the 1990s.

The gross capital investment in the oil and gas exploration and production industry of the British North Sea sector as a whole, including that of drilling and other contractors, was in the order of £26 billion (1981 prices) for the period 1965 to 1981. There has also been exploration expenditure amounting to some £5 billion.[9]

Future investments that are necessary to maintain the United Kingdom's oil output at about 75 to 80 Mt between 1982 and 1990 — roughly in line with the country's current oil demand —

7 For more details, see *World Energy Outlook*, pp. 229–32; North Sea oil and gas fields in production and planned, *Petroleum Times*, 1982 pp. 16–22; Quinlan, UK North Sea — development slowing down, *Petroleum Economics*, 1982, pp. 232–36.

8 UK Department of Energy, *Development of the Oil and Gas Resources of the United Kingdom ("Brown Book")*, London, 1982, p. 61.

9 UK Department of Energy, *op. cit.*, p. 22.

have been estimated at £14 billion (1981 prices) for existing oil and gas development projects, £3 billion for exploration and appraisal drilling, and £13 billion for new field developments. An additional £10 billion could go on operating costs. According to industry estimates, investments required to develop the next generation of oil fields and to maintain self-sufficiency into the late 1990s could even reach the very high total of £30 to £40 billion (1982 prices).[10]

Latest developments demonstrate that offshore development is continuing. Exploratory drilling hit new heights in both Britain and Norway during 1982. Other examples are the recent decision by Britoil to go ahead with the £1 billion Clyde Field project, due to start producing in 1987 and the £1.2 billion development application recently submitted for the North Alwyn oil and gas field by French companies Total and Elf Aquitaine. On the other hand, important projects such as the US$ 4 billion project of Phillips in the "T-Block", were postponed recently,[11] and the eighth licensing round in January 1983 showed a much smaller number of applications than the previous round.

Investment behaviour of the oil industry not only depends on future oil price perceptions, but also on the tax and royalty regime. Tax and royalty changes since 1979 had brought the marginal tax rate on proven oil and gas fields to a very high level of almost 90%. This was thought to delay or hamper exploration and development activities, especially in marginal and more expensive new fields. Therefore, the government has recently introduced some tax concessions to encourage exploration and stimulate new field developments. These concessions are generally expected to accelerate the development of second generation oil fields. This illustrates that government action is required to ensure that taxation, royalty and depletion policies, some of them designed when oil prices were increasing rapidly, are appropriate to the high cost/lower profitability developments now being considered.

In the Norwegian zone of the North Sea, oil production

10 Shell Briefing Service, *The Offshore Challenge*, London 1983, p. 8; Harms, Nordsee '82, *Oel-Zeitschrift für die Mineralölwirtschaft*, 1982, p. 257.

11 For more details on development projects and investments, see Harms, *op. cit.*, pp. 284–96, *North Sea Annual Report*, Noroil No. 1, 1983, pp. 25–46.

between 1971 and 1981 amounted to a total of 128 Mt. In 1982, it reached some 24 Mt. Plans and forecasts for future production have been revised frequently. In a White Paper submitted to the Storting (Parliament) in December 1982,[12] the Norwegian Petroleum and Energy Ministry presented provisional plans for the development of new oil and gas fields to offset anticipated declines in offshore investment from 1984, and a sharp fall in production in the 1990s. According to the report, oil and gas output from fields already producing or scheduled for development are estimated to rise from the current 49 Mtoe (of which 24 Mtoe are oil) to 60 Mtoe by 1990 (of which about one half could be oil). Production would fall steeply from 1990, unless new fields are brought on stream. Final decisions will probably be made in 1984 on the development of the Sleipner gas and Oseberg oil and gas fields.

Total investment for Norwegian oil and gas production including pipelines, between 1970 and 1981, amounted to 115 billion Nkr (1982 prices). Total exploration costs were 16.6 billion Nkr.[13] Future investments in oil and gas fields scheduled for commercial development are estimated to peak at 18–20 billion Nkr (1982 prices) per annum in 1983 and 1984. Thereafter, investment will decline sharply to levels of 16 billion Nkr in 1985 and 2 billion Nkr per annum by 1990. If further exploration and development projects are approved in 1983–84, investments will increase above these volumes and could attain 15 to 20 billion Nkr per annum by the end of the decade.

However, as in the case of British North Sea development, it is not certain how much of these projections will actually materialise. A commission appointed by the Norwegian government is currently reviewing the future level of oil and gas activities with a view to defining a depletion policy that will be tied more closely to overall economic policy considerations. The commission's report is expected in the spring of 1983. Ensuing policy decisions will influence future oil and gas development.

An important factor will again be the level of taxation which is currently viewed by the oil industry as being too high to permit

12 Norway, The Royal Ministry of Petroleum and Energy, *Report No. 40* (1982–83)
   Relating to the Perspectives in Petroleum Activity in the Coming Years, Oslo, 1982.
13 *Op. cit.*, pp. 8/9.

profitable exploration and production at the pace envisaged by the government.

The small Danish section of the North Sea also has some oil and gas resources. Oil production was 1.7 Mtoe in 1982, but the Danish "Energy Plan 1981" expects it to increase to 4 Mtoe in 1985 and to be maintained at that level until the end of the century. This would require total investments for offshore oil and gas development of 13 to 15 billion Dkr (1981 prices) between 1981 and 1990, most of which will occur in the first half of the decade.[14]

The Netherlands are developing some oil and gas fields in the Dutch section of the North Sea, and exploration also goes on in various areas of the Mediterranean. However, so far development and investment prospects in these areas appear much less important than British and Norwegian potentials.

Synthetic Fuels

Only two years ago, prospects for synthetic fuels were viewed much brighter than they appear today. Lower oil price expectations and large cost escalations currently close off most of the options for developing alternative fuels from tar sands, oil shale, gas and coal conversion on a strictly economic basis.

Since oil prices have ceased to rise and governments are reassessing their priorities for RD&D expenditure, a number of large synfuels projects have been cancelled or postponed in Europe, as in other parts of the world. However, a considerable number of projects are going on, for instance the DM 600 million plant of Rheinbraun in Germany, designed to convert about 2 Mt of lignite into 1 billion cubic metres of synthesis gas and some 350,000 tonnes of methanol annually as of 1988. This project is remarkable in that it does not benefit from specific government subsidies. Other large projects that will be realised, mostly with high government and EC aid, are Kloeckner and the Australian group CRA's DM 750 million coal gasification plant at Bremen, two French coal gasification projects at Le Havre (FF 500 million) and Carling (FF 1 billion), a British 600 tonnes per day slagging

---

14 Onshore investments for gas transport and distribution are estimated at 10.5 billion Dkr between 1980 and 1990.

gasifier and some smaller pilot and demonstration projects.[15] This development is encouraging, at least with respect to coal gasification. But if synthetic fuels from this and other technologies are to be a viable alternative later on, the long lead-times involved mean that more pioneer plants will have to be built now so that technically and economically viable commercial-scale plants are available in the 1990s when they may be needed. Since in the short-term, industry would find this investment very difficult, government assistance would be helpful to make synfuels a viable and economic alternative.

Oil Processing Sector

The anticipated decrease in oil demand and increasing losses of the refinery industry have brought about a rash of oil refinery closures in Europe, above all in Germany, France and the United Kingdom. In the EC area, for instance, it brought down crude oil distillation capacity from 814 Mt per annum in 1973 to some 700 Mt at the beginning of 1982. This trend accelerated in 1982.[16] Nevertheless, capacity utilisation continued to fall. Most of the remaining plants now operate at less than 60 per cent of their capacity. Therefore, considerable further refinery closures are in prospect. A specific European problem is the imbalance of the restructuring process among European countries in the area of refinery closures and upgrading which calls for improved international co-ordination.

While closing primary distillation capacity, the oil industry also adapts to changes in crude oil supply and to an increasing share of lighter products in total demand by installing secondary processing capacity (reforming and cracking).[17] This may lead to a strong increase in total conversion capacity, depending on further development of supply and demand and on product prices.

15 See also: IEA/OECD, *Coal Liquefaction — A Technology Review*, Paris, 1982; Commission of the European Communities, *Evaluation of the Community Demonstration Programmes in the Energy Sector*, Brussels, 1982, pp. 70–75, 129–32.

16 For more details, see Report of the World Petroleum Industry, *Oil and Gas Journal*, 80(52):82 (December 1982).

17 For more details see IEA/OECD, *Refinery Flexibility in the OECD Area*, Paris, 1981; Worldwide report on industry construction projects, listing new facilities under way in refineries, petrochemicals, gas processing and pipelining, including investment costs, *Oil and Gas Journal*, 80(43):105 (October 1982).

An important factor will be the impact of product imports from OPEC and other oil producing countries. Although still modest in size, Middle East sales of petroleum products to Western Europe almost tripled between 1974 and 1981, and they continued to grow between 1980 and 1982 when crude oil exports to Europe were falling. Further increases of these exports can be expected. This will be an important development for future international oil relations. For instance, it could spur more joint ventures and market sharing between oil producing countries and the European oil industry, such as the recent participation of Venezuela in refinery and petrochemical activities of VEBA or the purchase of Gulf refining and marketing assets by Kuwait. Obviously, this would strongly affect European refinery investments.

Overall investment volumes cannot be predicted with certainty, all the more since conversion plant is not constructed in isolation but is integrated into the refinery process. As an illustration of the orders of magnitude involved, investments required to build conversion capacity over the 1980s have been estimated at DM 10 billion in Germany[18] and some 8 to 10 trillion lire for Italy.

Transportation, Marketing and Petrochemicals

The other traditional downstream businesses, shipping and marketing, are equally characterised by large over-capacities. Therefore, apart from the new pipeline investments included in North Sea development projects, these sectors are likely to show disinvestment rather than investment. Scrapping of oil tankers has reached an all-time high in 1982 and is expected to continue.[19] British Petroleum, for instance, announced in 1982 that it would sell or scrap a third of its tanker fleet — 16 vessels totalling 1.25 million deadweight. Likewise, over-extended retailing networks are being reduced. In Germany, for instance, 17,000 gasoline stations were closed during the last ten years, and more will follow.

The petrochemical industry, which accounts for more than 10 per cent of Western Europe's total energy consumption equally suffers from overcapacity. This was mostly built or planned before 1973, based on the expectation that oil prices would remain

18 Deutsches Institut für Wirtschaftsforschung, *Der Investitionsbedarf der Energiewirtschaft in der Bundesrepublik Deutschland*, 1982, p. 365.
19 See Tanker markets — decade of change, *Petroleum Economist*, 1982, p. 93.

stable and economic growth would continue at previous rates. The industry is now amidst a process of shutting down excess capacities and adapting to the increase in oil and aggregate energy prices. As in the refinery sector, the development of product imports from the Middle East and other areas will affect the European petrochemical market and its investment prospects.

Finally, it should be noted that as a result of changed oil prospects, the oil industry is also engaged in a process of diversification into other energy and non-energy sectors such as coal-mining and trading, nuclear energy, minerals, trading and manufacturing. Given the scale of many of these new activities, considerable investment is involved outside the energy sector. However, it would exceed the scope of this article to analyse this development in more detail.

INVESTMENT IN THE NATURAL GAS MARKET

Outlook for European natural gas supply and demand

Natural gas will play a critical role in reducing European oil dependence over the next twenty years. Starting with the huge gas finds in the Netherlands, its use increased from almost nothing in 1960 to 175 Mtoe or 14.4 per cent of total energy use in 1981. It is expected to increase further into the 21st century. According to latest government projections, the European gas market in the 1980s may develop as given by Table 6.3.

To the year 2000, West Europe's gas demand may increase to a range between 255 and 320 Mtoe, depending on the development of economic growth, oil prices and energy policy.[20]

Increased supplies will be required to meet this demand. In 1981, Western Europe as a group produced 155 Mtoe or 88 per cent of its gas requirements, and imported 23 Mtoe or 13 per cent of total supplies from outside sources. Up to the year 2000, Western Europe's domestic production is expected to fall to between 107 and 133 Mtoe, with major declines occurring in the Netherlands, Italy and Norway. Therefore gas imports would

20 For more details, see IEA/OECD, *Natural Gas: Prospects to 2000*, Paris, 1982, pp. 38–41, 49–51; *World Energy Outlook, op. cit.*, pp. 380–81.

TABLE 6.3
OECD EUROPE'S NATURAL GAS MARKET 1973–1990

	1973	1980	1981	1985	1990
Consumption (Mtoe)	122.6	178.6	175.2	200.4	221.6
Gas share in TPE (per cent)	10.2	14.3	14.4	14.9	14.8
Domestic Production (Mtoe)	116.4	159.1	155.0	148.7	140.7
of which: Netherlands	54.8	70.2	65.2	56.0	45.8
Norway	0	23.3	23.2	26.5	30.5
United Kingdom	24.9	31.9	31.8	35.0	35.0
Others	36.7	33.7	34.8	31.2	29.4
Net Imports (Mtoe)	6.6	19.9	23.4	51.7	80.9
Import share in gas consumption (per cent)	5.4	11.1	13.4	25.8	36.5

have to increase substantially. They could grow more than four-fold by the end of the century.

The actual size of future gas use and imports will depend on the extent to which appropriate solutions can be worked out with respect to the two major issues associated with gas trade: price, and security of supply. Gas use will increase in consumer markets only if competitive prices make it attractive as an alternative to other fuels. At the same time, utilities considering long-term supply contracts and investment in capital intensive gas long-term supply contracts and investment in capital intensive gas infrastructure depend on a reasonable outlook for secure returns from their projects. Prices at the producer level will have to make allowance for these concerns if gas trade is to grow. This objective may have suffered a setback as European gas prices increased sharply since 1980. This has reduced the previously existing price advantage of gas over competing fuels, in particular fuel oil, and may seriously limit the scope for increased gas use.

Arrangements will have to be made to avoid that oil dependence, while being significantly diminished, would simply be replaced by a new vulnerability to disruptions in external gas supply. Possible risks could be contained by a number of preventive measures such as integration of existing gas grids, additional storage and surge production capacity. Also, fuel-switching possibilities at the level of individual power or industrial plants can contribute to greater supply security.

Investment Perspectives

Development of new gas fields offshore and increasing exploration of deeper strata onshore is necessary to offset the inevitable decline in production from existing fields. Government exploration and development policies have been generally positive in this area.

The Netherlands is the third largest world gas producing region after the United States and the USSR. It accounts for 37 per cent of Western Europe's gas supply. However, apart from some new development activities in the North Sea, investment seems to be on a downward trend, since the Netherlands has adopted a gas depletion policy which will result in output declining from 70 Mtoe in 1980 to 46 Mtoe in 1990 and 19 Mtoe in 2000. Most of reduced output will come from cessation of gas exports, which are projected to decline from 33 Mtoe in 1981 to 10 Mtoe in 1995 and to end by 2000.

In contrast, very large investments will be required for further natural gas exploration and development in the Norwegian and British sectors of the North Sea. Norway is the European country with the brightest natural gas prospects. Proven reserves stand at 1,318 billion cubic metres (1,084 Mtoe) — that is almost 50 times the current output — but total resources are much higher. One field alone — the gigantic Troll discovery — is thought to contain sufficient gas to transform the European supply picture. But water depths of 300 metres and complicated geology mean new technology must be developed for exploitation, and this field will be more expensive to develop than any other field before. Moreover, Norwegian development and depletion policies will have to be defined more clearly before future gas production and export levels can be assessed.

British gas production is now expected to increase somewhat beyond its current level of 32 Mtoe, but will probably remain stable around 35 Mtoe after 1985. British Gas needs new supplies in the late 1980s and appears ready to pay substantially higher prices for new gas than so far. This development has clearly spurred the interest of the gas industry to explore and invest into new gas fields in the North Sea.

The patterns of future European gas imports, which will also affect investment activity, are still developing. Apart from the large import contracts that were recently concluded between various European partners and the Soviet Union and Algeria, other contracts (e.g. between Belgium and Algeria, or Italy and the Soviet Union) are currently being negotiated. Major gas trade negotiations are also being held among European countries, for instance over the sale of Norwegian gas from the Sleipner field, for which there is competition among British and continental utilities. Another far-reaching idea is to improve the interconnecting gas network transport system of western Europe which is now being discussed as a measure to increase European supply security. It could involve connecting Norwegian gas fields to Europe's gas line network, either directly or through the British pipeline system.

Prospective investment volumes for the development and production of North Sea gas are included in the above-mentioned figures for off-shore oil development. Additional investments will be required for on-shore gas transport, storage, processing and distribution. In the past, this sector showed a strongly rising investment trend up to a level of ECU 4 billion in 1981. For the period until 1985, on-shore investments in western Europe as a group are foreseen to remain at over ECU 4 billion per annum, but will probably decrease afterwards, due to declining growth rates of gas penetration and progressive completion of gas pipelines. Also, the pipeline industry foresees a slump for gas pipeline construction before the end of this decade.[21] In any case, the projected increase in OECD Europe's gas consumption by 46 Mtoe between 1981 and 1990 will require significant investments to maintain and expand on-shore transmission, distribution and storage systems.[22]

21 *Oil and Gas Journal*, 80(43) : 88 (October 1982).
22 Average investment costs of US$ 5.10 per million Btu of additional gas-throughput for industrial use and $13.60 per million Btu for residential/commercial use have been estimated in IEA/OECD, *Natural Gas: Prospects to 2000*, pp. 54–55.

TABLE 6.4

OECD EUROPE'S SOLID[1] FUELS MARKET 1973–90

	1973	1980	1981	1985	1990
Consumption (Mtoe)	278.7	285.3	285.7	310.7	374.2
Share in TPE (per cent)	23.2	22.9	23.5	23.0	25.0
Domestic production (Mtoe)	244.6	231.1	235.3	239.0	257.2
of which: France	19.0	14.6	14.8	14.7	20.0
Germany	96.3	91.9	93.0	87.0	89.0
United Kingdom	87.8	74.8	73.2	73.0	71.0
Others	41.5	49.8	54.3	64.3	77.2
Net imports (Mtoe)	30.0	64.6	63.1	71.8	117.0
Import share in consumption (per cent)	10.8	22.6	22.1	23.1	31.3

1 "Solid fuels" include hard coal and lignite (accounting together for about 95 per cent of the total) and other solid fuels such as peat and wood wastes.

INVESTMENT IN THE COAL MARKET

Outlook for European Coal Demand and Supply

The oil price increases in 1973–74, and especially those of 1979–80, gave coal a strong competitive advantage which it still retains. Indeed, coal use in Europe started increasing in 1979, as industry and utilities sought coal to replace oil. OECD governments were equally enthusiastic and frequently reiterated commitments to increase production, trade and use of coal as a medium to diversify energy supplies. At the summit conference in Venice in 1979, the Heads of State and government even set the objective of doubling the production and use of coal by the early 1990s.

But, as in other energy markets, the economic recession — in particular the decline in European steel production — combined with falling oil prices, has diminished previous expectations of the role that coal could play over the 1980s.[23] In the EC, coal production and use are now lower than they were in 1973. Since 1980, producers' stocks have continued to grow at a tremendous rate, reaching a total of 51 Mt of coal and 14 Mt of coke at the end of 1982. Operators at all stages in the coal chain are reluctant to invest in new facilities for coal production, infrastructure and coal use. However, in the longer run there are good prospects for coal, provided it is secure and remains competitive. European governments project development of the coal market as shown in Table 6.4.

A substantial increase is anticipated in production of solid fuels in the course of the 1980s. But European consumption of solid fuels is projected to increase by a much greater amount, from 286 Mtoe in 1981 to 374 Mtoe in 1990. However, this would still be far from the Venice objective, which was defined in a period of higher economic growth. Coal's share in total energy supply will rise slightly from 23 per cent in 1981 to 25 per cent in 1990. The incremental coal would come primarily from an increase in coal imports of about 54 Mtoe per year by 1990, and from a fall in intra-European coal trade of about 10 Mtoe. By the year 2000, the

23 For a more detailed analysis see IEA/OECD, *Coal Prospects and Policies in IEA Countries*, Paris, 1982; Commission of the European Communities, *The Role for Coal in Community Energy Strategy*, OJC 105/2, 26 April 1982.

share of coal in European energy use could reach around 30 per cent.[24]

The most favourable sectors for expanded coal use are industry, electricity generation and district heating. Almost 60 per cent of total European solid fuels' use is now burned in power plants, and electricity will continue to be the main contributor over the next two decades. In fact, coal will gain access to other sectors, mainly through transformation to secondary forms of energy such as electricity and, to a lesser extent, heat in district heating systems. As electricity demand is projected to grow faster than overall energy demand, it will provide a sizeable potential for, but also an upper limit on additional coal use in power plants. Solid fuel use for electricity generation in OECD Europe is now projected to increase from 169 Mtoe in 1981 to 200 Mtoe in 1990.

The growth in industrial coal use has been disappointing. It is currently constrained by the subdued outlook for many energy-intensive industries, such as iron and steel. While a rapid conversion to coal has taken place in recent years in the steel and cement industry, existing boiler stocks in other industries will only gradually be replaced or converted. Industrial use of solid fuels in Europe is expected to grow from 65 Mtoe in 1981 to 103 Mtoe in 1990. But the major part of a new industrial coal use is expected to come on-stream during the 1990s only.

Investment Perspectives

As a result of the increasing role of oil and gas, and to a lesser extent, low priced coal imports from third countries, European hard coal production capacity has shown a steady decline since the 1960s. In the EC, for instance, it fell from more than 500 Mt annually in 1965 to 246 Mt in 1980. The investment trend, however, after a long period of disinvestment, has been clearly upwards since the first oil shock. Starting in 1974, coal-mining investment in the EC (excluding processing and transport) rose steadily from a level of less than ECU 500 million annually to about ECU 1.8 billion in 1982.[25]

---

24 *World Energy Outlook*, pp. 439, 449.
25 Commission of the European Coal and Steel Community, *Investment in the Community Coal Mining and Iron and Steel Industries*, 1981 Survey, Luxembourg, 1982, pp. 15, 43, 45; 1982 Survey.

In the future, European coal production potential is not likely to increase, as costs to maintain the industry have risen to unprecedented heights. In 1982, for instance, member states of the EC and the Community itself provided ECU 3.4 billion in subsidies to the coal industry. High subsidies will continue to be granted, but costs must be stopped from escalating by modernising the coal industry. The industry will have to restore its profitability and, to reach this target, close uneconomic pits as fast as is politically and socially possible.

The process of modernisation is going to require large investments and social expenditures. If current production capacity was merely to be maintained — which is not likely to happen — almost half the existing capacity might need to be replaced by the early 1990s.[26] Since the time horizon of new deep-mined coal production capacity is of the order of ten years, investments required to develop new capacity for the 1990s should be decided very soon.

In 1981, EC coal producers estimated that achieving the then-envisaged production objective of 270 Mt by 1990 would require an annual level of investment in new and existing mines, including ancillary industries, of more than ECU 3 billion, of which ECU 1.4 billion would fall to Germany and ECU 1.2 billion to the United Kingdom.[27] However, given the lower production levels that are now projected, decreasing public aids and the critical cash-flow situation of the coal industry, it is unlikely that actual investment activity will reach this level.

For lignite and peat investment prospects are generally better than for hard coal as the industry involved is generally healthy. In Germany, which accounts for 86 per cent of the European Community's lignite production, the industry is under way to develop new fields. These projects may require further investments of DM 10 billion for the period 1981–90. Also, Greece and Spain are extensively developing their lignite resources. Peat will play a

26 IEA Coal Research, *Constraints on International Trade in Coal*, London, 1983, p. 57; Emerson, Investing in coal, *Revue de l'Energie*, 1980, Energy Investment Finance, p. 9.

27 *Communication by Comité d Etude des Producteurs de Charbon d'Europe Occidentale*, Brussels; Woronoff, The investment needs of the coal industry of the European Community, *Revue de l'Energie*, 1980, Energy Investment Finance, p. 180.

major role in Ireland. Most lignite is used for electricity generation. At a later stage it could also play a role as a basis for
synthetic gas or fuel production.

In order to ensure future coal supply, Europe will have to
import increasing quantities of coal from third countries. Gross
solid-fuel imports of OECD Europe are projected to increase
from 87 Mtoe in 1981 to 131 Mtoe per annum by 1990. By 2000
they could reach a level of 300 to 320 Mtoe.[28] However, realisation of these projections depends not only on future growth in
electricity and industrial demand for coal, but also on the ability
of exporting and importing countries to upgrade coal handling
and inland transportation systems on time. In some European
countries, major improvements of coal handling capacity have
been made or are under way, such as in Germany, France, the
Netherlands and Denmark. Other countries, for instance, Greece,
Ireland, Italy and Portugal, are planning to build coal handling
ports with a view to importing more coal.

The Italian National energy plan of 1981 contains the most
ambitious coal import plan in Europe. It intends to expand the use
of coal nearly three-fold, from under 18 Mt in 1980 to about 50
Mt in 1990, all of which has to be imported. Overall investments
envisaged to fulfill this plan stand at 12,800 billion lire (ECU 10.8
billion in 1980 prices), including 7,800 billion lire (ECU 6.5
billion) for thermo-electric power stations.

Investment in the end-use of coal — being the ultimate link of
the coal chain — will be crucial for the future role of coal.[29] In the
main commercial outlet market of coal, electricity generation, 12
GWe of coal-fired (and substantially more multi-fired) generation
capacity is currently under construction in the EC.

The expected increase of coal use in industry will have to overcome a number of obstacles.[30] The current heat-price advantage

28 *World Energy Outlook*, p. 323; IEA Coal Research, *Constraints on International Trade
in Coal*, London, 1983, p. 12.

29 The above-mentioned IEA Coal Research study, pp. 56–58, says the end-use facility
(mostly utility) typically accounts for 80 per cent of total capital costs of a coal chain.
It estimates aggregate capital costs for coal developments from production to
end-use in OECD Europe at US$ 400 billion (1981 prices) for the period 1980–2000.

30 For a more detailed analysis see IEA/OECD, *The Use of Coal in Industry*, Paris, 1982;
World Energy Outlook, pp. 301–11; Commission of the European Communities,
Substitution of Coal for Oil in "Other Industries", COM(81)229 final.

of coal over oil is not by itself sufficient to persuade potential investors to switch to coal. Industrial energy consumers often feel insecure about future economic trends in general and relative fuel price developments. Environmental and safety requirements in a number of countries tend to constrain conversion of oil burning facilities to coal. The costs for conversion are high and industry often prefers to use scarce investment funds for productive equipment rather than boiler conversion. Moreover, investors often apply very short pay-back periods for conversion measures. To accelerate the conversion process, the EC and some countries (e.g. France, Spain, Sweden and the United Kingdom) provide various financial incentives for conversion investments.

INVESTMENT IN THE ELECTRICITY MARKET

Outlook for European electricity demand and supply

Electricity generation in OECD Europe rose from 1396 TWh in 1973 to 1769 TWh in 1981. Electricity demand has consistently grown at rates higher than overall energy demand. However, projected growth rates and capacity plans have been revised downwards steadily. For the present decade, electricity demand of OECD Europe is forecast to increase by an annual average of 3.1 per cent, while total energy requirements are expected to grow by 2.4 per cent. As a result, the share of electricity in total final energy consumption will continue to increase, from 14.6 per cent in 1981 to 16.5 per cent in 1990.

Electricity is clearly expected to be a major medium for structural improvement over the 1980s. Oil use in electricity generation in OECD Europe has declined by almost 20 Mtoe per annum between 1973 and 1981, and its share in the fuel mix fell from 26 per cent to less than 16 per cent. However, oil use still amounts to more than 60 Mtoe in OECD Europe.

Further progress in achieving a better balanced and more economic fuel mix is expected (Table 6.5).

The market share of oil is expected to decline further to 8 per cent in 1990. Nuclear power generation is expected to grow more than two-and-a-half times, leading to a rise in the nuclear share from 17 per cent in 1981 to 32 per cent in 1990. France, Germany

TABLE 6.5
OECD EUROPE'S FUEL INPUT INTO ELECTRICITY GENERATION
1973–1990

	1973	1980	1981	1985	1990
Total (Mtoe)	329.1	411.1	418.5	468.5	564.5
solid fuels	126.4	168.9	169.4	162.5	200.3
oil	85.3	77.2	65.7	62.7	45.2
gas	24.1	24.6	21.0	25.1	22.4
nuclear	18.7	50.3	69.7	119.2	182.9
hydro/geothermal	74.6	90.1	92.7	97.2	108.0
other (solar, wind, etc.)	0	0	0	1.9	5.7
Total (per cent)	100.0	100.0	100.0	100.0	100.0
solid fuels	38.4	41.1	40.5	34.7	35.5
oil	25.9	18.8	15.7	13.4	8.0
gas	7.3	6.0	5.0	5.4	4.0
nuclear	5.7	12.2	16.7	25.4	32.4
hydro/geothermal	22.7	21.9	22.1	20.7	19.1
other (solar, wind, etc.)	0	0	0	0.4	1.0

and Spain are projected to provide three-quarters of the increase in nuclear generation. Coal use should grow by 18 per cent, based on the assumption that all new power plants will be nuclear, hydro or coal-fired, and that oil and gas will be gradually reserved for peak-load and for certain environmentally sensitive areas. By the end of the century, nuclear energy might have a 35 per cent share in OECD Europe's fuel input for electricity generation. In contrast, the oil share may fall to less than 3 per cent.[31]

However, achieving such structural improvements will require resolute action by electric utilities and governments. It is true that the oil price increases in 1979–80 resulted in a clear economic advantage of nuclear power and coal in producing electricity. For instance in the Member countries of the EC, under presently prevailing fuel costs the cost of nuclear power generation is 50 to 77 per cent lower than that of electricity generation from oil-fired plants. The cost advantage of nuclear over hard coal, in particular for base-load stations, ranges between 20 per cent and 50 per

31 *World Energy Outlook*, pp. 438, 448, 466, 470.

cent.[32] However, there are risks that expansion plans will not proceed as rapidly as envisaged. The overall economic stagnation, high costs of financing, and uncertainty about future levels of electricity demand are leading governments and utilities to defer expansion plans. Tariff policies in some countries (e.g. Italy) make it difficult for utilities to raise adequate revenues to finance new capacity. Increasing concerns about safety and the environment in most countries have resulted in regulatory regimes that entail lengthy and costly delays in plant construction. These problems may jeopardise electricity development as it is now envisaged.

Investment perspectives

Investment in electricity generation. At the beginning of 1982, Member countries of the EC had installed electricity generation capacities of 337 GWe. At the same date, new capacities of 90 GWe were under construction and 75 GWe projected, partly to replace decommissioned old plant, partly to expand capacity. Out of new capacities under construction and planned, 93 GWe are nuclear, 24 GWe coal-fired and 14 GWe hydroelectric generation sets. Almost 10 GWe of monovalent oil burning capacity are still in construction (mostly in Italy and the United Kingdom), but no further monovalent oil or natural gas capacity is planned.

Latest government projections for construction of new electricity generation plant can be summed up as in Table 6.6. 65 GWe of new thermal power stations (including nuclear) are scheduled to be in service by 1985 and 52 GWe by 1990.

It is obvious that these investments are essential not only from the point of view of energy policy, but also as a contribution to overall investment activity. However, a substantial part of projected capacity additions is at risk. Of the projected 32 GWe of new conventional thermal capacity, only 8.5 GWe are decided, while 24 GWe are in a preliminary stage of preparation. Of the projected 37 GWe of nuclear capacity additions, only 6.7 GWe are decided.

According to a recent study of the IEA and the Nuclear Energy Agency,[33] Member countries of OECD Europe are projecting to

32 IEA/NEA, *Nuclear Energy Prospects to 2000*, Paris, 1982, pp. 55, 58; *World Energy Outlook*, p. 354.

33 IEA/NEA, *Nuclear Energy Prospects to 2000*, p. 23.

TABLE 6.6
PROJECTIONS FOR EC EUROPE'S ELECTRIC POWER CAPACITY
(GWe GROSS)[1]

Type of plant	In service 1 January 1982	Under construction[2]	Projected[2]
Total installed capacity	336.7	89.9	75.2
Conventional thermal:	243.8	25.6	32.2
solid fuels (monovalent)	74.5	11.7	11.9
oil (monovalent)	62.3	9.6	0
natural gas (monovalent)	10.6	0	0
multi-fired	58.5	4.3	20.3
Nuclear	43.7	55.7	37.3
Hydro-electric	49.2	8.6	5.7

1 *Source:* EC Commission, *Annual Report on Investment Projects in the Electricity Sector of the Community*, Brussels, 1982.
2 Thermal generating sets of 200 MW or more; hydro-electric sets of 50 MW or more.

increase their nuclear power capacity from 44 GWe in 1980 to 133 GWe in 1990. But almost all the countries with nuclear programmes, except Belgium, France and Sweden, may not have all of this capacity available at this point of time. Altogether, some 13 GWe are at risk.

If all capacities currently under construction and firmly decided are actually built, a construction volume of about 105 GWe of new generation plant in the EC could materialise over the 1980s, of which 62 GWe would be nuclear and 8 GWe coal-fired. In this case, total investments[34] of roughly ECU 110 billion in the EC could materialize over the 1980s.

Investment for electricity transmission and distribution and for the nuclear fuel cycle. Over the past decade, the proportions of investments in

34 Assuming average construction costs (including price variations and interests during construction) of 1,200 ECU/kWe (1981 prices) for nuclear plant, 600 ECU/kWe for coal-fired plant and 550 ECU/kWe for other plant. Actual unit costs vary considerably from these values, depending on site conditions, degree of plant standardization, safety and environmental requirements, lead times, interest rates, etc. See International Union of Producers and Distributors of Electric Energy (UNIPEDE), *Generating Costs — Assessment Made in 1981 for Plant to be Commissioned in 1990*, Brussels, 1982.

electricity generation on the one hand and in transmission, distribution and related facilities on the other have shifted substantially. This is due mainly to relatively stronger increases in con.truction costs of generating capacity, especially nuclear plant, and to progressive completion of transmission networks. While during the 1970s a ratio of 1 : 2 among generation and transmission investments prevailed, it is now about 1 : 0.8. In future, this ratio may turn around further in favour of generating capacities. In the European Community, a total of 4,125 circuit kilometers of transmission lines and cables[35] was under construction at the beginning of 1982, and almost 7000 circuit kilometers were planned.

Assuming the above-mentioned growth of nuclear electricity generation, the nuclear fuel cycle, including uranium exploration in Europe and overseas, enrichment and fuel fabrication, transport and storage of spent fuel, reprocessing and disposal of waste will equally require considerable investments. These are difficult to project since many of them are fraught with political uncertainties. To illustrate the orders of magnitude involved, for Germany the investments required to secure nuclear fuel supply for the projected expansion of nuclear capacity from 8.6 GWe in 1980 to 25 GWe in 1990 have been estimated at DM 28 billion,[36] that is about 40 per cent of projected investment for nuclear generation plant.

The only two factories in the world that currently receive, store and reprocess spent nuclear fuel from over 100 nuclear reactors in Europe and Japan, British Nuclear Fuels, and Cogema in France, also plan major investments to increase their capacities and to adapt them to higher safety standards.

INVESTMENT IN THE RATIONAL USE OF ENERGY

Outlook for improvements of energy efficiency

Industrialised countries have committed themselves to improving the overall efficiency of energy use in their economies and to slackening the link between economic growth and energy con-

---

35 Including all voltages and types (overhead, underground, underwater cables).
36 Diel, Radtke, Stößel, Der Investitionsbedarf der Energiewirtschaft und seine Finanzierung, *World Energy Conference 1980*, Vol. 4B, p. 443.

sumption.[37] They have made considerable progress along this way. But in the current market situation, investments on the energy demand side appear to be under threat, just as energy supply investments.

The real incomes of consumers have fallen and this may affect the readiness to invest, even in items which will produce overall savings. Petroleum product prices have started to fall, and the price gap between petroleum products and alternatives has narrowed in 1982. This affects the economics of energy saving investments and fuel substitution.

Despite progress achieved, substantial scope still exists for further cost-effective improvements of energy efficiency. For the remainder of this century, it can be estimated at 25 to 30 per cent of current consumption in industry, 20 to 25 per cent in transport, and up to 50 per cent in the residential and tertiary sector.[38] However, considerable time will be required to exploit this potential since the capital stock is renewed only slowly and various constraints and obstacles must be overcome. Specific constraints, apart from general economic uncertainties, are the lack of information and training on energy use and opportunities for efficiency improvements, cash-flow and financing problems, stringent pay-back requirements and low priority in industrial investment programmes.[39]

Investment perspectives

Assessing past and future investment volumes for improvements of energy efficiency is difficult because investment in this area is in very much smaller blocks than in energy supply and it is undertaken by a very large number of enterprises — many small — and private consumers. The EC Commission has estimated that the total of national investment programmes of EC member countries for measures to improve energy efficiency may be some ECU 100

37 See for instance, *IEA Lines of Action for Energy Conservation and Fuel Switching of 1980;* IEA/OECD, *Energy Demand Management in the 1980s,* Paris, 1981, pp. 16–17; EC Council resolution of 9 June 1980 concerning *Community Energy Policy Objectives for 1990 and Convergence of the Policies of the Member States,* OJC of 18 June 1980.

38 *World Energy Outlook,* pp. 126, 128, 131; Commission of the European Communities, *Investment in the Rational Use of Energy,* COM(82)24 final, annex 5, p. 4.

39 For more details see IEA/OECD, *Energy Demand Management in the 1980s; World Energy Outlook,* pp. 125–33.

billion in the period 1981–90.[40] In the Commission's view it would be a reasonably ambitious objective to see energy efficiency investment increasing from ECU 7 to 8 billion in 1980, to ECU 19 billion by 1985, and ECU 25 billion by 1990. Market opportunities are certainly important. The British House of Commons' Select Committee on Energy, for instance, has recently estimated the potential market for cost-effective conservation investments in all energy use sectors at £20 billion for the next ten years.[41]

Governments, individual consumers and industry should avoid the risk of under-investing in this area. Otherwise, they would increase the existing imbalance between energy supply and demand investment and not use the limited capital resources available to the best advantage in achieving better balanced energy economies.

ENERGY RESEARCH AND DEVELOPMENT

After seven years of ever increasing public spending on research, development and demonstration covering all areas of new energy technologies, public expenditure is now levelling off. Research is becoming more focussed as each country sees more clearly its priorities and where its funds promise the greater return on investment. In the short to mid-term, there has been a growing realization that coal, gas and nuclear, together with continued efforts towards improving energy efficiency, will continue to be the principal substitutes for oil to meet the energy supply/demand balance to the year 2000.

The sheer volume of European government expenditure — more than ECU 2.7 billion in 1981 — demonstrates that governments continue to regard investments in energy RD&D as important to their energy policy objectives. However, RD&D investment may be too slow in rising in some key areas, in particular in coal technology, given the ambitious projections for increasing coal use.[42]

40 Commission of the European Communities, *Investment in the Rational Use of Energy*, pp. 3, 4, annex 1.

41 United Kingdom House of Commons, Select Committee on Energy, *Energy Conservation in Buildings*, London, 1982, p. XIV.

42 See IEA/OECD, *Energy Research, Development and Demonstration in the IEA Countries*, Paris, 1982, p. 17; for more details on the EC demonstration programme, projects, investments and financial support involved, see Commission of the European Communities, *Evaluation of the Community Demonstration Programme in the Energy Sector*, Brussels, 1982.

Government expenditure is complemented by increasing industrial RD&D expenditure. Governments are developing a tendency to have private industry take on a larger share of development costs, not only for budgetary reasons but also based on the premise that market-oriented decisions by the private sector may be a more effective means of determining cost-effective priorities for investment.

In the future, budgetary constraints are likely to persist for a number of years. This will probably reinforce the trend of greater reliance on private sector involvement in energy technology development. However, it is important to stress that energy research and development remains inherently a long-term endeavour driven by the need for fundamental change to substitute for fossil fuels in the decades ahead. Since the cost–benefit criteria applied by the private sector may lead to postponing important RD&D projects, governments will have to remain involved if they want to achieve progress in timely development of new energy technologies.

CONCLUSIONS

Following the oil shocks of 1973–74 and 1979–80, western Europe has made considerable progress in improving the structure of its energy economies. Oil demand and oil's share in total energy supply have fallen considerably. The balance among oil and other energy sources, and the efficiency of energy use have improved. Domestic energy production, in particular oil, coal and nuclear, has replaced large amounts of energy imports. But these structural improvements and the present weak oil market situation should not give Europe a false sense of security. Oil will remain the most important energy source until well into the 1990s. Energy imports of all kinds and origins will continue to be the main feature of the European energy scene. Nearly half of European energy needs will still be met by imports, with a fall in imported oil's share offset by higher coal and gas imports.

Meanwhile, the expected growth in European energy production is largely dependent on the expansion of nuclear power. It accounts for almost 70 per cent of the forecast increase in domestic energy production. In the past, nuclear progress has consistently fallen short of ambitions. Any further short-fall will directly affect the expected structural improvement of European energy supply.

Moreover, not all of the structural improvements achieved since 1973 are guaranteed to remain. Much of the decline in oil consumption and the current pressure on oil prices is due to the continued economic recession and to changes in consumer behaviour that may well change back with more optimistic energy supply and price expectations. In particular, energy investment perspectives appear to be clouded by expectations of further declining oil prices. As a result, many of the energy developments anticipated after the last oil shock — oil substitution, domestic oil and gas development, alternative energy sources — have been scaled back, postponed or cancelled. But whatever the short or mid-term development of oil prices will be, actual market conditions show no evidence which would justify price levels approaching those the world faced five or ten years ago. What would seem the most plausible in the current situation would be a modest reduction in oil prices, with some assurance of a substantial period of price stability in nominal terms. Such a development would give a badly needed boost to the world economy. Simultaneously, it would improve the climate for economically viable energy investment.

Low economic growth has reduced the pressure on energy and oil markets. But it has also contributed to the slowdown in energy investments. When the economy picks up — a development which is essential to combat unemployment — and as incomes rise, there is likely to be a substantial increase in energy demand. The only energy source which can be readily turned on is oil. Therefore, there is a real risk that economic revival will give rise to increasing demand for oil from the OPEC countries. This will already mitigate some of the reasons for the recent fall in oil prices. Later on, around the 1990s, oil demand may again become uncomfortably close to the level of production which the OPEC countries are able and willing to maintain. This would obviously increase Europe's vulnerability to supply disruptions and sudden oil price rises, as we have experienced them before. However, the world economy cannot and must not tolerate a third oil shock in this century.

Europe has the resources and the technical and economic means to guard against these risks. It should maintain or increase domestic energy production, in particular North Sea oil and gas, coal and nuclear energy, synthetic fuels and, to the extent possible, renewable energies. It must increase and diversify its energy supply scene by additional imports, particularly of coal and gas. In doing so, European countries, working with other countries, will also have to see how the economic advantages of certain energy supply contracts can be enhanced from the viewpoint of supply security. Europe also must use its important potentials to improve the efficiency of energy use and to develop new energy technologies.

To achieve these objectives, European governments should continue to refine their energy policies, particularly in the following areas:

(a) Market forces and the price mechanism should be used to their full extent and supplemented where necessary to check underlying energy demand trends. In particular, efforts to remove constraints on economic energy pricing and improve price transparency must continue.

(b) Full weight needs to be given to long-term energy policy considerations in the development of other government policies: for example, on taxation, resource depletion, revenue requirements, environmental, safety, and other regulatory controls.

(c) Careful attention must be given to the issue of the price of natural gas. Gas prices should reflect the costs of production and be competitive in consumer markets.

(d) Because of its relative abundance, coal deserves particular attention as an effective substitute for oil. On the demand side, conversion of oil-fired power plants to coal or their early retirement should be pursued vigorously where technically feasible and economically viable. Industries should be encouraged to recognize and realize the advantages of using coal instead of oil. At the same time, efforts should be made on the supply side to modernise coal mines and transport infrastructure in line with growing demand.

(e) Further penetration of electricity should be recognized as one of the major avenues for the use of non-oil fuels, and utilities should be encouraged to invest in new non-oil based generation capacity.

(f) In order to widen the scope for public acceptance of nuclear, governments should elaborate and speedily implement satisfactory schemes for final disposal of nuclear waste. At the same time, the outlook for investment in nuclear power plants needs to be improved in the face of soaring capital costs due to lengthening and uncertain lead-times and high interest rates. Licensing systems, in particular, should be rationalized so as to shorten costly lead-times. Electricity tariffs must be adapted so as to cover the cost construction of new facilities.

(g) Continued energy efficiency gains at the end-use level must be achieved by both appropriate pricing policies and government action to remove institutional barriers to the operation of market forces.

(h) With the changing energy supply mix, Europe must also consider what new potential supply risks, particularly in coal, nuclear and natural gas supplies may develop and take corrective steps where necessary to minimize them.

These measures will need to be implemented by governments, assisted by international co-operation. Moreover, energy producing and consuming industries, utilities and private consumers have responsibility to realise opportunities for economically viable energy investments. These investments are necessary if Europe is serious about maintaining adequate energy security. The key issue is, in fact, whether continuing efficiency gains and substitution of other fuels for oil can be brought about by further development and more effective implementation of energy policies, or whether they will be forced upon European economies by recurrent sharp increases in oil prices at the cost of huge losses in national income and economic growth.

7

Investment and the Development of Backward Regions

Jean Henri Paul Paelinck*

Regional policy-makers have been much concerned about regional disparity, especially since the end of World War II. But even before 1940, some countries, the United Kingdom among them, already had reason to keep a vigilant eye on certain regressive regional developments, first and foremost in employment. The important thing to note is that, at that time, policy changes were introduced if and when the situation seemed to require it. A systematic study of the causes of disparity was not yet possible because, for one thing, there was no adequate theory, and for another, there were no adequate statistical data.

Indeed, regional phenomena have only been studied properly and systematically in the last thirty years; the collection of statistics, following the theoretical efforts, has proliferated in the way we all know. The flourishing of regional statistics can really be said to date from the 1960s.

Employment, regional product, and other indicators,[1] all show that, notwithstanding a certain convergence in the last thirty years, there are still appreciable disparities among the regions of the European Community, the data on which we will concentrate. For instance, the disparity indexes of regional product per inhabitant in 1979 are found to vary between 225 (Hamburg region) and 35 (Calabria), with respect to an average of 100 for

---

* The author is grateful to J.-P. Ancot for the precious help he has given in the preparation of this study, and to A. J. Hughes Hallett, W. T. M. Molle and A. Sallez for very useful comments on a first version.
1 Eurostat, 1979; Keeble *et al.*, 1981; Molle *et al.*, 1980; Molle and van Haselen, 1980.

the European Community of Ten. Corrections for purchasing power carries the disparity from a factor 6.43 to one of 4.02 (193 Groningen in the Netherlands; 48 for the same Italian region mentioned above).[2]

In the next section we follow the statistical approach in a first attempt at integrating long-term data and confronting regional product with sectoral specialisation. Because there are great gaps in time-series of data on investment — either directly productive or environmental — we will choose a *result* of the spatial allocation of investments as relevant object of study; to wit, the spatial dispersion of employment.

But we must not stop there. We then try to find an *explanation* for the regional specialisations, for only in that way can we identify the mechanisms commanding the effectiveness — or lack of it — of all the interventions that have been made in favour of the so-called "retarded regions", and sometimes to the detriment of regions considered "too far advanced".

Following on from this, starting from the results obtained with one particular model, we will present an entirely new method which we hope may help to solve the problem of *optimum allocation of aid* to regions. Moreover, that same model — known by the name of FLEUR (factors of location in Europe)[3] — will enable us to make not only a diagnosis but also a prognosis; the latter in the form of a tentative forecast on the assumption of constant policies. In the same terminology, the supplementary allocation of aids can be named a "therapy".

Our conclusions will round off the discussion; and the last two sections of this paper contain a technical appendix and the references.

REGIONAL DEVELOPMENTS IN EUROPE: SOME NUMERICAL RESULTS

We pointed above at the unequal distribution of GDP per inhabitant across the European Community. The observation that inequality has diminished in the course of the last twenty-five years is not sufficient; we also need to find a structural explana-

2 Banque Européenne d'Investissement, 1982; the special position of the province of Groningen is due to the production of natural gas there.
3 See on the subject the works of the Netherlands Economic Institute, and in particular NEI, 1982, the last report of the series; also Molle, 1983.

tion of the phenomenon. In fact, that would be one step towards analysing how the regional and sectoral orientation of investment is linked to its results in terms of creating regional purchasing power.

Some very simple hypotheses come to mind:

(a) The structural composition of regional activities is an explanatory factor of the overall regional productivities observed;[4] indeed, the product per inhabitant — or better, by person employed — of each region is a sum of weighted productivities depending on the region's "product mix", which in turn is an important structural factor for the explanation of the level and development of overall regional productivities.

(b) Sectoral and regional productivity levels may be influenced by macro-economic, sectoral and regional policies of the national government; hence our desire, right from the outset, is to integrate in the analysis, and to test carefully the impact of national characteristics.

(c) Productivity averages may develop at rhythms that differ from country to country and from period to period; careful testing on that score is necessary to keep the analysis realistic.

These three hypotheses have indeed been tested; the appendix presents the technicalities of relating total regional productivity (regional product per employed person) to the sectoral division of employment into four, major categories: agriculture, industry, market services, non-market services. From this analysis, which refers to the years 1950, 1960 and 1970, the following conclusions can be drawn.

With respect to our first hypothesis: the coefficients corresponding to the employment in manufacturing industry and market services (in technical terms, the "elasticities") rise slightly between 1950 and 1970; they are positive, below unity, and all of them statistically significant. Meanwhile the elasticities corresponding to agricultural and public-service employment, low in absolute value, do not differ significantly from zero. Note also that the industrial parameters, after rising between 1950 and 1960, have

4 See Hoffman *et al.*, 1977.

been practically stable since; the parameters of market services, stable at first, rose between 1960 and 1970.

With respect to our second hypothesis: the national parameters are again statistically significant and show a very steep rise in the course of the period under observation, indicating that their levels have shifted substantially through time. The differences in parameters observed among groups of countries in each separate year are less striking but still almost invariably statistically significant. The rankings of those groups of countries with respect to those level constants are very nearly stable through time, with the Federal Republic of Germany tending to come abreast of the vanguard (France, Benelux, Denmark), and the group composed of the United Kingdom and Ireland tending to fall back to a lower level in the course of the years. That implies the verification of our third hypothesis.

The numerical details are shown in Table 7.9, later (see the technical appendix).

TOWARDS THE EXPLANATION OF DIFFERENTIAL REGIONAL GROWTH

In the previous section a link has been made between the structural orientation of the economies of the European regions and their participation in income creation.

The strategic question is, however, for what *motives* is the regions' orientation in a certain direction, and with what *intensity?* To answer those questions a theory of regional development has to be first developed and then submitted to tests; in other words the theory will have to be confronted with regional reality as expressed in the statistics.

A theory of multi-regional development

The first hypothesis rests on the current observation that regions are in fact easy to arrange in two groups by an indicator of their overall growth, or the growth of certain sectors of activity, industrial or otherwise. The two categories are, broadly, the stagnant, the weakly expanding or even declining regions on the one hand, and on the other the freely expanding regions. The idea of a *growth threshold* suggests itself,[5] a critical level of certain elements responsible for regional development, a concept to which we will come back later on. This apparently simple idea will prove very rich in the analysis; indeed, as we hope to show later on, the same concept may help to diagnose in a workable manner the "pathological" state of stagnant regions, and thus to identify the elements which, if acted upon in a programme of regional policy, might raise those regions above the critical threshold and set in motion a spontaneous process of (possible sector-specific) growth. Once again, the notions of a diagnosis and a therapy are cropping up!

Figure 7.1 gives a schematic survey of the principal elements presented above. In this diagram the tentatively S-shaped curve suggests a possible empirical description of the relation observed between sectoral regional growth and an indicator — probably specific to the sector studied — which will come to be called the "regional attractiveness potential". The crosses in the Figure correspond to possible positions of stagnant and growing regions within the diagram; the figure also suggests that there is a potential saturation level for the phenomenon of regional growth, a level which may vary from one sector to another and from one country to another.

A second general idea, from which much of our reasoning about regional growth has evolved, is that of the "potential of regional attraction", mentioned above. New firms will settle in a given region, or existing firms develop their activities there, if that region is adequately endowed with factors conducive to the expansion of their type of activity; such factors are called *location factors*, and the set of all such potential factors defines the concept of a *regional location profile*. The elements of such a profile will be developed later on; let us just say briefly that they are associated with factors of supply and demand — markets of finished products, intermediary products, and raw materials; with other production factors — manpower, capital, land, access to energy sources; with advantages associated with industrial and urban agglomerations, socio-cultural factors, policy factors — sectoral, regional, or related to town and country planning; and with

5 This idea was first put forward by the author at a conference devoted to effectiveness thresholds of regional intervention; see Paelinck, 1976; it was taken up and used in Ancot and Paelinck, 1979, and in Ancot, 1979.

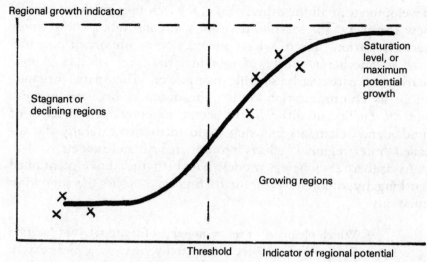

Figure 7.1. *Relation between regional sectoral growth and an indicator of the regional attraction potential.*

conditions for protecting the environment and nature. Two important points can be made: first, the intensity of these different elements varies among the individual regions; and second, the relevance of each element for the location and expansion of specific sectoral activities varies from sector to sector. So the problem is to identify the elements in a regional profile that appear relevant to the growth of each sector, and to arrange them for each sector in a quantified hierarchy. Only thus can the profile of the deprived regions be remodelled in the way, and to the extent, that they surpass one or more of their critical thresholds, and thus initiate spontaneous growth processes.

Given these two basic ideas — that of a growth threshold and that of a regional profile — a third element is of crucial importance, namely, the *interdependence in space* of regional activities. That interdependence must be clear to all who observe the movements that enliven economic space: transportation of people and goods, commuting and migration, communication at long distances. It means that in observing and explaining regional growth or decline one needs, from the very beginning, to consider a system of regions, and the impact each of them may have on the

development of all the others. Take, for example, the location of a
new company: the location decision will constitute a compromise
between various sites of which one may be an important potential
market, another a source of raw materials, yet another a local
market of particularly suitable manpower. The spatial organisation, its communication routes, the distances between regions,
and the facility or difficulty of access, together form a series of
fundamental elements inducing us to introduce carefully the so-
called "inter-regional" effects into our analysis and models.

As argued elsewhere,[6] models based on the above-mentioned
working hypotheses are meant to find answers to the following
questions:

(a) Which elements of the regional profile are relevant location
    factors for each sector of activity, is there a hierarchy of
    those factors for each sector, and which elements of the
    regional profile appear to exert no influence at all on the
    location decisions of that type of industry?

(b) Among these relevant location factors, are there any that
    apply universally to all sectors of economic activity, and are
    there any others that are specific to certain sectors?

(c) What is the spatial range of relevant factors for each sector,
    in the sense that one could, for instance, distinguish groups
    of factors with a purely local, regional, national or interna-
    tional zone of influence?

(d) What level of the regions' overall sectoral attractiveness
    indicator is the growth threshold?

(e) What is the relevant position of the different regions in
    respect of that threshold, and what means can be applied —
    and with what intensity — to modify the profile of
    deprived regions to lift them above the critical threshold
    and initiate one or more growth processes?

Before proceeding to elaborate these general ideas, let us define
somewhat more closely the concrete contents of the so-called
attraction profiles.

6 Ancot and Paelinck, 1983(b).

Location factors, regional profiles and
regional attractiveness

The idea of location profiles is not perhaps the latest novelty; in fact, for several decades American companies have been known to base their location decisions on check-lists, listing all the location factors a company might consider of particular importance to its establishment. Entrepreneurs will select the regions where they expect those factors to be adequately represented, perhaps after sending out inquirers to check locally the presence of the various elements offered.

We have taken up that idea of check-lists, rendering it systematic and introducing it into the analysis of regional growth in the shape of the "regional profiles" already referred to. Let us consider the main headings; the following classification may not be unique, but because it has been well-proven in practice we reproduce it here.

A first group of elements could be called the *market profile* of the region. Why that name? It indicates that this part of the regional profile is the set of demand levels of the regional activities and of supply levels by groups of products and services. Why those indicators? An investor looking for a site will want to know first the different market potentials for the products or services he supplies himself, as well as for the products or services he will need in his production processes. The future links of the new establishment with product and factor markets imply transportation costs, or, more generally, communication costs. To study how the tastes of consumers evolve, to have fast access to spare parts for his investment goods, or to get an order for raw materials promptly executed, suppliers and clients need to establish and maintain close connections. That is why communication costs play a role in the analysis.

Together with the market profile comes the sub-profile relating to *other factors of production*, encompassing such factors as the availability of manpower, their wage level, and their professional quality. As will be argued later on, the relative importance of the elements of these sub-profiles varies among activities; the order in which they are presented here is not necessarily hierarchical.

A third sub-profile that characterises a region refers to the elements of its *socio-cultural structure*. These elements are of a peculiar nature: on the one hand they may be desirable in themselves because they contribute to the socio-cultural satisfaction of the populations for which they are meant; on the other hand, the socio-cultural equipment may become indispensable to certain economic activities because they tend to attract the very groups of people upon whose collaboration those activities depend.

A fourth element could be associated with the regional *environment* such as it manifests itself in the region, either in a positive sense (touristic attraction of certain sites) or in a negative sense (pollution problems).

A fifth element, finally, encompasses the various instruments of *regional policy;* let us simply say that measures of regional policy modify in some sense the location profile of a region, and thus affect its future development. We have already hinted that infrastructural measures deserve a more individual treatment.

How, indeed, does the infrastructure enter into location decisions? Roads, railroads, navigable rivers, telecommunication, airports, etc. — all such infrastructural facilities influence in some way or other the calculations, in terms of costs and benefits, of a potential investor. Each new layer of infrastructure modifies in some way the industry's *access* to the markets of factors and products, or in simpler terms, the relative accessibility of the different regions. We have pointed out that an investor will choose his location partly in function of a multi-regional potential, either of markets for his own production, or of markets for the various production factors he needs. Clearly this potential will differ according to the infrastructural conditions; indeed, as access is easier or more difficult, as transportation and communication are faster or slower, markets will carry more or less weight in the investor's calculation. So, infrastructural changes on the map translate themselves into changed variables in the economic model describing location behaviour.

The remarks just made with respect to infrastructure can be fitted into a wider frame of thought;[7] namely, that of the relations between regional policy and that of physical or spatial planning. In general terms, regional economic policy aims at

7 For more details, see Klaassen and Paelinck, 1974.

stimulating the development of new activities at certain places with the help of instruments that seem to have nothing to do with the objects of spatial planning. The latter's concern is the optimum arrangement in space of a set of physical elements: not only new additions to capital stock (investments) are at stake, but the arrangement of the entire stock of capital. Moreover, physical capital stock means more in a context of spatial planning than in other economic considerations; physical planning is much more than economic planning, being intimately concerned with such elements as nature, centres of education, health care, leisure, culture, etc.

However, two links unite regional policy and physical planning. First, the distribution of human activities in space is a consideration central to physical planning, and is partly governed by acts of regional policy. Second, the elements of physical capital mentioned above figure in the regional profiles, and for that reason they help to attract economic activity; the special role of transport and communication infrastructure has been underlined.

Regional policies and spatial planning as location factors;
the variety of these measures

The conclusion from the foregoing may be that the growth opportunities of regions are ultimately influenced by a wide variety of measures of public intervention.

In the European FLEUR model — to be described in some more detail in the next section — four groups can in fact be distinguished.

The first group of variables are the "traditional" measures of *"regional economic policy"*, to be split into four categories:[8]

    (a) loans and guarantees;
    (b) subsidies;
    (c) fiscal concessions; and
    (d) measures with a negative impact.

Figures 7.2 to 7.4 reproduce the intensity of an indicator constructed from those four variables for three years (1950, 1960, 1970), the indices running from -1000 to $+4000$; the gradual

8 Netherlands Economic Institute, 1981(a), p. 55.

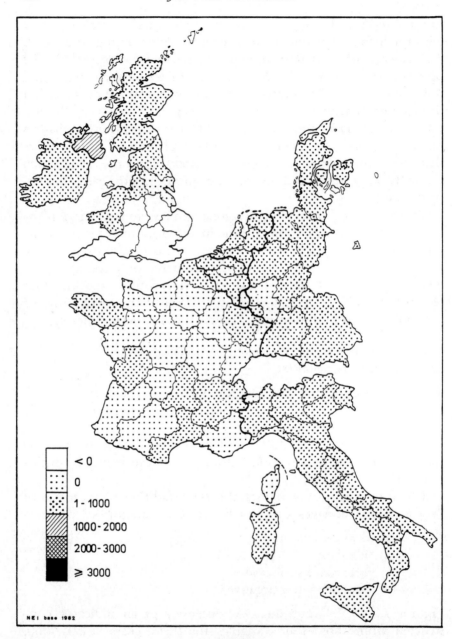

Figure 7.2

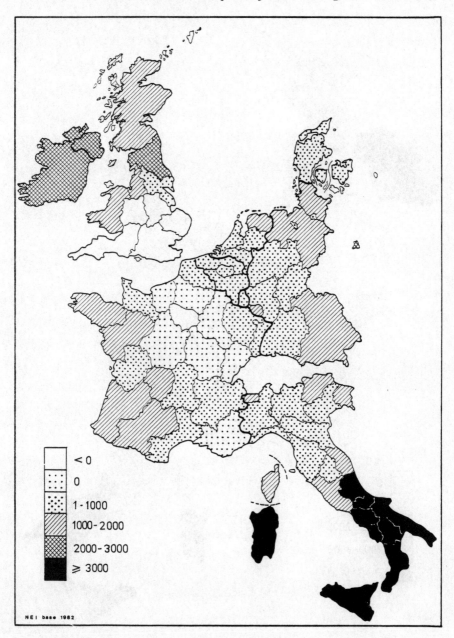

Figure 7.3

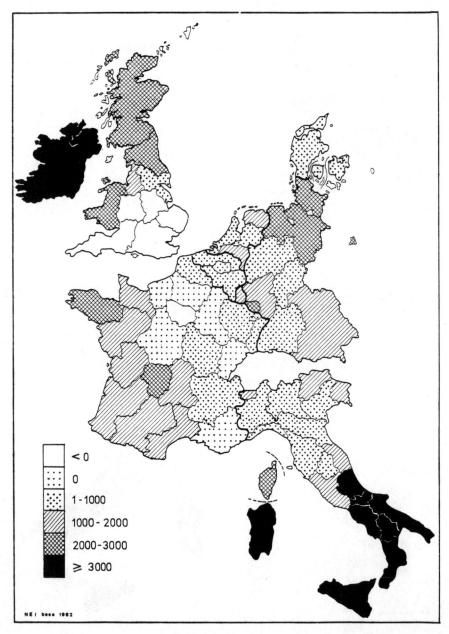

Figure 7.4

relative disparity of these measures is so clearly shown as to make comments superfluous.

However, as argued above, measures of *spatial planning* also have their impact on the relative evolution of the regions within a system; their results have also been measured and aggregated within the framework of the FLEUR model, by seven criteria:[9]

    (a) size of the population (various definitions);
    (b) population density;
    (c) urban structure;
    (d) presence of a capital city;
    (e) presence of international organisations;
    (f) presence of business centres; and
    (g) presence of facilities for air transportation.

Contrary to the maps of regional policy, the maps referring to spatial planning — in the form of a synthetic indicator — show great stability through time, which is why only one map — relating to 1970 — is presented (Figure 7.5), scaled from 0 to 1. Given the nature of the variables involved, this stability will surprise no one. Unless the marginal effectiveness of certain measures is exceptionally great, their effects will become manifest only after a very long time.

A less obvious group of variables, appearing only indirectly in the model, are the distances among regions, which determine their mutual *accessibility*. We will not reproduce the matrices, which are too technical for our purpose; suffice it to say that they contain, in terms of access time, information about the relative distances within a system of regions.

Finally, direct intervention in the *creation of activities* constitutes an instrument of stimulation particularly relevant to the activity of the European Investment Bank. Unlike the previous policies, activity-creating policies stimulate directly the birth of specific activities, which in turn become a potential future location factor to new activities, as has been remarked above.

But let us now take a few moments to consider how the relations mentioned translate themselves in modelling terms.

9 Netherlands Economic Institute, 1980, p. 21.

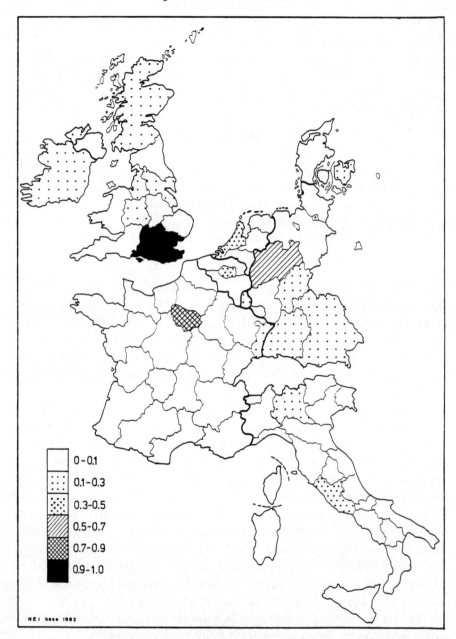

NEI base 1982

Figure 7.5

COMPUTING RATIONAL AID TO EUROPEAN REGIONS WITH THE HELP OF THE FLEUR MODEL

Without going into the technical details, we will now describe the fundamental structure of the European FLEUR model.[10]

The growth-threshold model FLEUR

The FLEUR model sets out to explain how employment in the sectors chosen (40 out of an original total of 53) developed in 76 regions of the Community of Nine through three ten-year periods. The model is dynamic as well as inter-sectoral and inter-regional: dynamic because it addresses the problem of growth (or decline) of employment; inter-sectoral because its specification refers to the demanding and supplying sectors of a given sector; and inter-regional, because the two kinds of sectors mentioned above are defined for a set of regions within the accessibility range of a given region.

The explanatory variables take up largely the systematics presented above; over and above those of supply and demand already mentioned, the following variables appear in the model:

    (a) the labour market;
    (b) physical planning; and
    (c) regional policy.

For the purpose of the present study the model has been re-estimated in terms of only two aggregated sectors: (a) employment in manufacturing industry; and (b) employment in market services; employment being the variable to be explained. Table 7.1 gives the results of the analysis for the period 1950–70, with two sub-periods (1950–60 and 1960–70). We will not go into the details of the econometric exercise on which Table 7.1 is based; suffice it to say that the adjustments were all statistically highly

10 Reference is made to Ancot and Paelinck, 1983, for the econometrics of FLEUR, and to Molle, 1982, for a synoptic description of the model.

significant. The coefficients of Table 7.1 represent the reactions to
the various location factors and are all of comparable orders of
magnitude.

TABLE 7.1
RESULTS OF THE TWO-SECTOR ESTIMATION OF THE FLEUR
MODEL

	Industry		Services	
Coefficients	1950–60	1960–70	1950–60	1960–70
Dynamic adjustment	0.241	0.211	0.231	0.208
Propensities				
demand	5.47	9.50	22.40	6.63
supply	1.62	1.81	1.64	1.79
wages	1.13	2.05	0.84	1.57
unemployment	2.13	2.39	2.28	1.66
urbanisation	3.57	3.71	3.23	3.24
regional policy	1.52	1.72	1.48	1.62

Locational diagnosis

From the results of the calculations of which only a part has been
shown in Table 7.1, and on the basis of the critical threshold
introduced previously, the European regions can be divided into
the two categories mentioned before: potential growth regions
and potential stagnant regions, and that for the two activities—
manufacturing industry and market services—distinguished
earlier. Table 7.2 gives the list of potential growth regions,
divided into two groups by the degree of their retardedness; the
arrangement will serve as a basis for the application to be presented later.

We strongly underline the provisional nature of the present
demonstration exercise, which rests on preliminary calculations;
far more profound studies ought to follow. No rash conclusions
should at all be drawn from the results now to be commented
upon!

In the course of the period 1950–70, out of the set of 76 regions
of the original division, 23 showed strong signs of potential lags,

TABLE 7.2

POTENTIAL GROWTH REGIONS WITH RESPECT TO INDUSTRIAL AND SERVICE ACTIVITIES IN THE COURSE OF THE PERIODS 1950–60 AND 1960–70[1]

Regions	Industry		Services	
	1950–60	1960–70	1950–60	1960–70
Very backward regions				
Valle d'Aosta	×	×	×	×
Trentino–Alto Adige	×	×	—	—
Umbria	—	×	×	×
Molise	×	×	×	×
Basilicata	×	×	×	×
Franche-Comté	—	—	×	×
Limousin	×	×	×	×
Corse	×	×	×	×
Fyn	×	×	×	×
Backward regions				
Bremen	×	×	—	—
Saarland	×	×	—	×
Northern Ireland	—	—	—	×
Friuli-Venezia Giulia	—	×	—	×
Marche	×	×	×	×
Abruzzi	—	—	×	×
Calabria	—	×	—	—
Sardegna	×	—	×	×
Champagne	—	—	×	×
Basse Normandie	×	×	×	×
Poitou-Charentes	×	×	×	×
Auvergne	×	—	×	×
Languedoc-Roussillon	×	×	—	—
Nederland-Noord	×	—	×	×

1 A cross indicates that the region considered is (strongly) retarded for the corresponding sector and period.

TABLE 7.3

RELATIVE REGIONAL INVESTMENTS, BY COUNTRY
(IN PER CENT OF THE NATIONAL TOTAL)

Federal Republic of Germany (total), averages 1974–78

Schleswig-Holstein	3.8
Hamburg	3.9
Niedersachsen	10.9
Bremen	1.5
Nordrhein-Westfalen	25.5
Hessen	9.6
Rheinland-Pfalz	5.9
Baden-Württemberg	16.1
Bayern	18.6
Saarland	1.5
Berlin (West)	2.8
(100.0)	

France (categories 06 + 30), averages 1974–78

Ile de France	17.9
Champagne-Ardenne	2.6
Picardie	3.2
Haute Normandie	5.5
Centre	5.5
Basse Normandie	2.1
Bourgogne	2.6
Nord et Pas-de-Calais	9.3
Lorraine	5.8
Alsace	4.1
Franche-Comté	2.3
Pays de la Loire	3.7
Bretagne	2.3
Poitou-Charentes	1.9
Aquitaine	4.1
Midi-Pyrénées	2.6
Limousin	0.9
Rhône-Alpes	11.9
Auvergne	1.9
Languedoc-Roussillon	1.9
Provence-Alpes-Côte d'Azur	7.9
Corse	0.0
(100.0)	

United Kingdom (categories 06 + 30), averages 1974–80

North	9.7
Yorkshire et Humberside	8.5
East Midlands	4.9

East Anglia	1.9
South East	17.3
South West	3.9
West Midlands	7.4
North West	9.3
Wales	5.1
Scotland	11.3
Northern Ireland	2.0
(Extra Regional)	18.7
(100.0)	

Italy (categories 06 + 30 + 68), averages 1975–78

Piemonte	10.1
Valle d'Aosta	0.3
Liguria	3.9
Lombardia	18.0
Trentino–Alto Adige	1.8
Veneto	8.9
Friuli–Venezia Giulia	2.6
Emilia–Romagna	8.6
Toscana	6.3
Umbria	1.4
Marche	2.5
Lazio	7.4
Campania	5.6
Abruzzi	1.7
Molise	0.5
Paglia	6.6
Basticata	1.0
Calabria	2.6
Sicilia	6.6
Sardegna	3.7
(100.0)	

Netherlands (categories 1 + 20 + 84), averages 1974–78

Noord–Nederland	13.4
Oost–Nederland	14.9
West–Nederland	48.2
Zuid–Nederland	23.5
(100.0)	

which were particularly serious for nine of them. Except for two regions (Trentino-Alto Adige and Franche-Comté), the problems of the latter group occurred in both sectors of activity and throughout the two decades observed. The fourteen remaining regions had to cope with more localised problems in either one or the other sector or for one of the periods studied.

To illustrate the effect of the investment analysis just presented, Table 7.3 resumes for some years the relative regional investments by country.

These figures in Table 7.3 have been taken from the *ESA Regional Accounts* published by EUROSTAT,[11] where they are expressed in national currency and are far from perfectly comparable. Thus for the FRG total investments (including public investments) had to be taken; for the United Kingdom, France and Italy items 06 + 30 (energy, water and industry); and for the Netherlands, items 1 + 20 + 84 (agricultural products, metal products and machinery, vehicles). The figures for Belgium, Denmark, Greece, Ireland and Luxembourg, not being regionalised, are not reproduced here.

In spite of the poor comparability with Table 7.2 and the need to normalise the regions in some way, the facts are clear: in the study period, problem regions tended to attract relatively less investment than others.

Growth thresholds, location factors and regional policy[12]

A *decision model*, elaborated and quantified for objectives and instruments as well as for the impact of the latter, is a useful device for constructing rational programmes of economic policy and comparing their effectiveness. In agreement with the specification of the FLEUR model, the fundamental structure of which has been roughly described above, our primary objective will be to boost employment in the backward regions. Moreover, once that objective is achieved, some others, such as better spatial resource allocation, and better distribution of income among regions, will also come within reach.

11 See Eurostat, 1980, 1981, 1982, 1983.
12 The ideas presented in this section have been borrowed from Ancot, 1983; we refer
    to that article for more technical developments.

The priority of one type of objective does not mean that only one kind of instrument is put to work; on the contrary, a whole range of different instruments may contribute to that objective. Instruments of an economic nature, such as taxes, subsidies and controls, are supplemented by a wider array of instruments attacking sub-profiles of location, such as the quantitative and qualitative development of the infrastructure. They will be the more effective as the location factors they affect are more relevant and important to regional employment; we have already observed that the impact of location factors is sector-specific.

To make measures of regional policy fit their specific purpose even better, the instruments adopted may be adjusted to specific regional situations. For instance, the height of subsidies to employment can be determined in relation to excess supply of labour in the regions;[13] the fiscal instrument could then serve to tax the factor in direct proportion to its excess demand. Evidently a large number of instruments may be refined in that way: subsidies to investment lend themselves naturally to such refinement. By the same token measures to control the creation and expansion of establishments may be replaced with a system of taxes on industrial development like the one practised in the Paris Region in France.

The explanatory variables of the FLEUR model have been enumerated previously. On the other hand, as emphasised before, some of them (e.g. the variable of regional policy in the strict sense) constitute direct and relatively short-term instruments, while for others (such as physical planning) the impact of policy is assumed to be indirect and/or more long-term.

Once more, the methodology presented previously may provide a quantitative starting point for modelling the process of political decision-making;[14] in this methodology, certain instruments of economic policy must be put to work to change the location profiles of declining regions in such a way as to help them surpass the critical threshold and to create in them condi-

---

13 See for instance Hutton and Hartley, 1968.
14 Modelling policy decision-making is at least as important as that of the economic system itself, which after all is but a constraint on the process; such questions, and others, have been dealt with in Hughes Hallett and Ancot, 1982.

tions favouring certain types of growth. The choice of the instruments and the intensity with which they will be applied should satisfy some criterion of effectiveness, which should be a function of: (a) each instrument's own nature; (b) the relationship of the instruments to location factors and to sectoral growth; and (c) the initial regional profiles. Finally, the programme should be set in a dynamic perspective.

Formally, our model to prepare a programme of regional development can be written as the optimising of an effectiveness criterion under the constraint that the regions involved attain at least a critical threshold, account being taken of the initial profiles and all other exogenous data. Such a programme can be solved for a "planning period" with a fixed horizon.

Application to the regions of the EEC

Starting from the results presented in Tables 7.1 and 7.2, we have used the above approach *ex post* to prepare an imaginary programme of sectoral aid to regions in distress in the course of the period 1950–70; let it be emphasised that our exercise has been set up for purposes of orientation, albeit one of the first of its kind. For this demonstration we will take the variables of the FLEUR-model characterising the infrastructure, supply, regional policy, and level of urbanisation as instrumental variables. Each instrumental variable may be set to work in each of the sub-periods considered or in the course of the whole period; moreover, a variable associated with the supply of products and services may be specialised with respect to the sectors — industry and services — governing the aggregation level of the present application. Having thus introduced a sectoral and temporal specialisation as well as a division into two groups of the backward regions (see Table 7.2), we can distribute the aid to be granted to these regions according to nine orientations, corresponding to the columns of Table 7.4.

From the eighteen possible cases, six have been selected for the present exercise:

(a) support to all 23 backward regions throughout the whole period (1950–70) and for all sectors (industry and services);

(b) selective aid to the most seriously backward regions, throughout the whole period for all sectors;

TABLE 7.4
POSSIBLE SPECIALISATIONS OF AID TO BACKWARD REGIONS

Regions	Two sectors			Industry			Services		
	1	2	3	1	2	3	1	2	3
Very backward regions (9)	(b)	(d)							
Backward regions (23)	(a)	(c)		(e)			(f)		

1 1950–70.
2 1950–60.
3 1960–70.
(a)–(f): see text.

(c) as (a), but only for the first decade, 1950–60;
(d) as (b), but limited to the first decade;
(e) aid to all backward regions for the entire period 1950–70, directed towards industrial activities only; and
(f) as (e), but oriented to service activities.

For each case the instrument variables have been refined in the following manner:

(a) Infrastructure: a general effort to improve the infrastructure in the retarded regions of Europe by a maximum of 10 per cent in respect of the initial situation;
(b) Supply: investment in favour of supply activities of products and services in the regions where the factor is deficient; for each region and for each sector the intervention is limited by a fixed amount;
(c) Regional policy: as for the preceding instrument variable, a special effort is made within the framework of European regional policy in those retarded regions that in the course of the periods considered have not particularly benefited from such aid; the complementary contributions are also limited to a maximum;
(d) Urbanisation: in regions where the quality of services associated with urbanisation is found to be inferior to the European average, an effort is made to remedy that situation in respect of the European average.

To indicate how direct or indirect and at what delay these instruments work, their relative costs were hypothetically set in

TABLE 7.5
AID PROGRAMME ACCORDING TO SCENARIO (a) FROM TABLE 7.4[1]

Regions	1950-60					1960-70				
	Infra-structure	Industrial supply	Supply of services	Regional policy	Urban-isation	Infra-structure	Industrial supply	Supply of services	Regional policy	Urban-isation
Valle d'Aosta	10.00	—	100.00	—	—	10.00	—	100.00	—	8.78
Trentino-Alto Adige	10.00	—	—	—	—	—	—	—	—	3.44
Umbria	10.00	—	100.00	—	—	10.00	—	—	8.10	—
Molise	10.00	—	—	—	—	10.00	—	100.00	—	7.52
Basilicata	10.00	—	—	—	—	10.00	—	—	—	5.92
Franche-Comté	10.00	—	—	—	—	10.00	—	100.00	—	—
Limousin	10.00	—	100.00	9.72	—	10.00	—	100.00	—	—
Corse	10.00	100.00	100.00	25.44	—	10.00	100.00	100.00	—	—
Fyn	10.00	—	—	—	—	10.00	—	—	10.92	—
Bremen	—	—	—	—	—	10.00	100.00	—	6.54	—
Saarland	10.00	—	—	4.86	—	10.00	100.00	—	—	—
Northern Ireland	10.00	—	—	—	—	—	—	—	—	1.74
Friuli-Venezia Giulia	10.00	—	—	—	—	10.00	—	—	—	2.10
Marche	10.00	—	—	4.86	—	10.00	—	—	—	—
Abruzzi	10.00	—	—	—	—	—	—	—	—	3.14
Calabria	10.00	—	—	—	—	10.00	—	—	—	2.44
Sardegna	10.00	—	—	—	—	10.00	—	—	—	2.44
Champagne	10.00	—	—	—	—	10.00	100.00	100.00	4.32	—
Basse Normandie	10.00	—	—	—	—	10.00	—	100.00	5.06	—
Poitou-Charentes	10.00	—	—	—	—	10.00	—	100.00	4.34	—
Auvergne	10.00	100.00	100.00	—	—	10.00	—	100.00	—	2.42
Languedoc-Rousillon	10.00	100.00	100.00	5.68	—	—	100.00	100.00	—	—
Nederland-Noord	10.00	—	100.00	—	—	10.00	100.00	100.00	—	2.78

1 Infrastructure improvements are expressed in percentages of the initial situation, urbanisation improvements in percentages of the European average; for the other instruments the percentages refer to the maximum amount allowed.

the ratio 3 : 1, on the assumption that actions on the supply market and on regional policy are three times more "effective" for development aid, or (which comes to the same thing) three times "less expensive" than efforts to improve the infrastructure or stimulate urbanisation. Finally, the constraints have been imposed that the development initiated by the aid to backward regions should take them up to the critical growth threshold. The horizon is thought to lie just beyond the end of the programme period.

Tables 7.5 and 7.6 present the results of these exercises; the following comments are in order.

From Table 7.5, summarising the results obtained with scenario (a), improvement of infrastructure is the most generally adopted instrument; in accordance with its long-term character it was applied throughout the period; improving the supply conditions for goods and services is another form of aid used at maximum intensity but selectively for regions and sectors particularly deprived in that respect. Those two fundamental instruments are joined by the complementary instruments of regional policy and urbanisation, applied across space in a selective manner and, as far as urbanisation is concerned, in the second period only. That hierarchy in the relative use of the different instruments is notice-able both for the most retarded group of regions and for the others, though for the latter group the instruments characterised as "complementary" are applied with less intensity.

The results corresponding to scenario (b) are identical — on account of the linear form of the programme and the structure of the problem — to the first part of Table 7.5, with respect to the "seriously" backward regions. Of course, the hypothetical total cost of the programme is different, but we shall come back to that later on.

The results associated with scenario (c) are given in Table 7.6. Some of the above comments to scenario (a) remain valid; the principal difference between the results of these two scenarios is that the "complementary" instruments — regional policy and urbanisation — tend to be applied with more intensity when the period of application is shorter (scenario (c)).

Again, the results of scenario (d) — apart from the hypothetical

TABLE 7.6

AID PROGRAMME ACCORDING TO
SCENARIO (c) FROM TABLE 7.4[1]

	1950–60				
Regions	*Infra-structure*	*Industrial supply*	*Supply of services*	*Regional policy*	*Urban-isation*
Valle d'Aosta	10.00	—	100.00	9.00	—
Trentino-Alto Adige	10.00	—	—	3.54	—
Umbria	10.00	—	100.00	9.02	—
Molise	10.00	—	100.00	—	7.70
Basilicata	10.00	—	—	—	6.10
Franche-Comté	10.00	100.00	100.00	8.92	—
Limousin	10.00	—	100.00	9.74	—
Corse	10.00	100.00	100.00	25.46	—
Fyn	10.00	—	—	12.18	—
Bremen	—	100.00	—	7.32	—
Saarland	10.00	—	—	4.86	—
Northern Ireland	10.00	—	—	—	1.78
Friuli-Venezia Giulia	10.00	—	—	—	2.14
Marche	10.00	—	—	4.86	—
Abruzzi	10.00	—	—	—	3.22
Calabria	10.00	—	—	—	2.50
Sardegna	10.00	—	—	—	2.45
Champagne	10.00	100.00	100.00	4.86	—
Basse Normandie	10.00	—	100.00	5.68	—
Poitou-Charentes	10.00	100.00	100.00	4.86	—
Auvergne	10.00	100.00	100.00	—	2.50
Languedoc-Roussillon	10.00	100.00	100.00	5.66	—
Nederland-Noord	10.00	—	100.00	—	2.86

1 See note at the bottom of Table 7.5.

total cost of the programme — are the same as those of scenario
(c) comprised in the first part of Table 7.6.

The results of scenarios (e) and (f), which are directed towards
industrial and service activities, respectively, are not interesting

enough to be reproduced in a separate table. Indeed, but for one result the numerical components of scenarios (e) and (f) are the same as those of scenario (a), and as will be shown below, even the "costs" of the three scenarios are equal. Keeping in mind the scope of this introductory exercise we may conclude that the selective use of an instrument aiming at improving supply conditions (the only element distinguishing scenarios (a), (e) and (f)) does not affect the optimum programme for the other instruments, neither as regards the intensity with which they have to be put to work, nor as regards the relative effectiveness of those scenarios.

Table 7.7 compares the "costs" (hypothetical, as pointed out) of the various scenarios in indices based on the cost of scenario (a).

TABLE 7.7

HYPOTHETICAL RELATIVE COSTS OF SCENARIOS (a) TO (f) (SCENARIO (a) = 100)

Scenario:	(a)	(b)	(c)	(d)	(e)	(f)
Cost:	100.00	60.88	103.38	62.80	100.00	100.00

The conclusions to be drawn from the comparison are evident: scenarios (a), (c) and (f) are absolute equivalents, which confirms the earlier comments. Scenario (b) is the cheapest; indeed, the additional aid given to relatively less retarded regions in scenario (a) implies considerable additional costs. On the other hand, concentration of the support in a shorter period as in scenarios (c) and (d) is only marginally more expensive than spreading it over a longer period (scenarios (a) and (b)).

Obviously the results presented above are purely indicative and can only serve as a starting point for more specific exercises, either with respect to individual regions or with respect to disaggregated sectors.

These results, admittedly hypothetical but representing the first data obtained by original analysis, have been compared to information relating to the loans and commitments of the European Investment Bank (Table 7.8).

TABLE 7.8

QUALITATIVE CLASSIFICATION OF INDIVIDUAL LOANS AND CREDIT COMMITMENTS ON OVERALL LOANS (1958–81) OF THE EIB FOR THE REGIONS OF TABLE 7.2.

Region	Infra-structure	Industrial supply	Supply of services	Urban-isation	Comments (project(s))
(a) LOANS					
Valle d'Aosta	X				X
Trentino–Alto Adige	X	X			X multi-regional infrastructure
Umbria					T multi-reg. industrial
Molise		X			T multi-reg. infrastr.
Basilicata		X			T multi-reg. agriculture
Franche-Comté		X			T multi-reg. water
Limousin	X	X			
Corse	X				
Fyn					
Bremen					multi-reg. fishery
Saarland		X			T multi-reg. infrastr.
Northern Ireland	X	X			T
Friuli	X	X			X
Marche		X			XT multi-reg. water
Abruzzi	X	X			T multi-reg. water/infrastr.
Calabria	X	X	X	X	T water
					multi-reg. water/infrastr.

Table 7.8 continued
on page 182

Region						Type
Sardegna		X				T multi-reg. ind.
Champagne			X	X		T* multi-reg. infrastr.
Basse Normandie		X	X	X		T
Poitou-Charentes		X				T multi-reg. infrastr.
Auvergne			X			T*
Languedoc						T multi-reg. ind. / multi-reg. agricult.
Nederland-Noord		X				T multi-nat. infrastr.?
(b) CREDITS						
Valle d'Aosta						X
Trentino-Alto Adige		X	X			X
Umbria		X		X		T
Molise		X				T
Basilicata		X				T
Franche-Comté		X		X		T multi-reg. ind.
Limousin	X	X				T
Corse	X					T
Fyn				T*		
Bremen						T
Saarland						X
Northern Ireland		X				T
Friuli-Venezia Giulia		X	X			X
Marche		X		X		T
Abruzzi		X		X	X	T construction

Table 7.8 continued

Region	Infra-structure	Industrial supply	Supply of services	Urban-isation	Comments (project(s))
Calabria		X		T	
Sardegna		X		T	
Champagne		X		T*	
Basse-Normandie	X	X		T	T*
Poitou-Charentes	X	X		T	
Auvergne	X	X		T	T*
Languedoc-Roussillon	X			T	
Nederland-Noord					

The following symbols have been used in the comments: T (regions qualifying entirely on regional considerations), T* (regions partly qualifying on regional considerations), and X (regions not qualifying on regional considerations). Some regions are only partly eligible on regional considerations: there is not always a clear distinction between administrative regions and the regions defined by various national schemes. Moreover, among the projects financed by the EIB in regional aided zones, there are also some investments financed by virtue of paragraphs b) and/or c) of Article 130 of the Treaty of Rome which may or may not be at the same time eligible by virtue of paragraph a).
We thank Mr. H. Leroux, Director of the Department of Economic Studies of the EIB, for kindly putting at our disposal the data on which this Table is based.

The infrastructure variable, appearing systematically in Tables 7.5 and 7.6, is matched by some of the multi-regional projects; the same is true of the variable "supply of services", which is less frequent in the EIB data. In addition one may wonder whether it would not be useful in future to consider what we have called the "urbanisation" investments, however general that expression may be. Certainly, such "externalities" enter the picture only in the longer term, but the econometric calculations do seem to suggest that an adequate-access infrastructure is a systematic regional attraction factor. Even if detailed location factors for "end-of-the-century" (high-technology) activities came to be appreciated differently from what can be inferred from the past, within the framework of a still valid FLEUR-specification, an adapted "environmental structure" could remain a primary element of stimulation for the regions whose growth one wants to accelerate.

FUTURE INVESTMENT TRENDS

That there will still be considerable regional disparity in the future can be illustrated by use of the earlier model of regional developments. By extrapolation of its coefficients and use of FLEUR employment projections for the year 1990,[15] the remaining gap in terms of GNP per employed person has been calculated at 2.54 (between the Grand Duchy of Luxembourg and Northern Ireland).[16]

So, as long as the reduction of that gap is still thought desirable, stimulating the proper investments remains important. We have previously suggested — albeit cautiously, because a demonstration exercise is all we have to go on so far — that efforts to improve the regional facilities for the reception of new activities might also, in the long run, prove an adequate instrument of a European policy of regional aid. Certainly, more detailed studies will be necessary, but we hope we have opened up a useful mode of

15 Netherlands Economic Institute, 1982(a).
16 The difference between these regions and the ones mentioned in our introduction is due to the fact that here we have product per employee, and elsewhere product per inhabitant.

analysis.

The reasoning presented also enables us — by way of a general conclusion — to propose a systematic and differentiated hierarchy of the regional policies pursued in Europe. On the EEC level we see an obvious task for the responsible agencies: to bridge the gap as far as possible between the value of the regional profiles of the weakest regions and the value of the critical *threshold*, which were the key notions of our study; it is in those terms that we give a new interpretation to the idea of developing the "endogenous factors" of the European regions put forward by the services of the European Commission. It will then be up to the individual countries to construct the differential *employment* policies they would wish to put in motion, and to the regions to take care of their local infrastructural *equipment* (which we will not go into a detailed analysis of).

Diagnosis, prognosis, therapy: these three notions of intervention have after all not been treated exactly in the order in which they had been mentioned at the end of our introduction. They have appeared, however, in the course of our exposition, which we hope has helped certain ideas to become clearer and will inspire action in the future.

TECHNICAL ANNEX: THE MODEL OF REGIONAL DEVELOPMENTS IN EUROPE

For a region r and a year t let:

p_{rt} be the domestic regional product per person employed;

a_{rt} be the proportion of agricultural employment;

i_{rt} be the proportion of industrial employment;

s_{rt} be the proportion of employment in market services; and

o_{rt} be the proportion of employment in non–market services.

A possible equation explaining the average regional productivity p_{rt} may then be formulated as:

$$p_{rt} = \alpha_{ct}(a_{rt})^{\alpha_{1t}} (i_{rt})^{\alpha_{2t}} (s_{rt})^{\alpha_{3t}} (o_{rt})^{\alpha_{4t}} \tag{7.1}$$

where α_{ct}, α_{it} ($i = 1, 2, 3, 4$) are parameters specific to each period: α_{ct} is a constant, characteristic of country c containing region r; α_{it} ($i = 1, 2, 3, 4$) are so-called "elasticities". Table 7.9 reproduces the estimation results.

TABLE 7.9

RESULTS OF ESTIMATING EQUATION (7.1)

Coefficients	1950	1960	1970
α_c			
FRG	40.04	1211.97	5507.08
	(4.43)	(8.56)	(8.58)
UK and Ireland	46.99	1299.84	4023.87
	(2.81)	(1.32)	(8.48)
Italy	45.60	1074.92	4722.06
	(2.23)	(2.42)	(4.67)
France	61.56	1754.61	6502.88
	(8.18)	(7.61)	(4.37)
Benelux	59.15	1495.12	6185.73
	(6.22)	(3.79)	(2.55)
Denmark	58.56	1394.09	5541.39
	(3.80)	(1.78)	(2.30)
α_1	−0.06	0.01	0.03
	(−1.56)	(0.53)	(1.44)
α_2	0.30	0.41	0.44
	(3.97)	(5.81)	(6.23)
α_3	0.57	0.58	0.96
	(4.47)	(6.15)	(8.70)
α_4	−0.15	0.07	0.03
	(−1.37)	(0.79)	(0.34)
$\bar{R}^2$	0.863	0.901	0.897
F	53.35	76.66	73.40

The figures in brackets are Student t-values; the test indicates that the corresponding coefficient differs significantly from zero at the 5 per cent level, if the absolute value of t exceeds 1.96. For technical estimation reasons, the countries had to be regrouped somewhat; for country groups other than the FRG the values in brackets correspond to the Student-t test of an assumed significant difference with respect to the value of the parameter associated with the FRG.

The values of the determination coefficients corrected for loss of degrees of freedom ($\bar{R}^2$) are high and the overall explanation of the domestic regional product per employed person is significant (the computed F-values of the Fisher test statistic exceeding the critical value of 2.79 at the 5 per cent level).

A remaining observation is that Equation (7.1) is in fact an "average" equation (in terms of its parameters) accounting for the set of regional identities

$$p_{rt} \equiv \sum_i p_{irt} w_{irt} \tag{7.2}$$

where the p_{irt} are sectoral productivities, and w_{irt} are sectoral shares in terms of employment; hence the occasional occurrence of negative parameters.

REFERENCES

Ancot, J.-P. 1979 Une approche par analyse discriminante à des problèmes de seuils régionaux et d'analyse de localisation, *Recherches Economiques de Louvain*, **45(3)**: 281–97.

Ancot, J.-P., Paelinck, J. H. P. 1979 A discriminant analysis approach to regional threshold problems with an application to Spanish data, *Papers of the Regional Science Association*, **42**: 139–52.

Ancot, J.-P. 1983 Politique régionale, facteurs de localisation et seuils de croissance, [to appear in] *Revue d'Economie Régionale et Urbaine*.

Ancot, J.-P., Paelinck, J. H. P. 1983(a) The spatial econometrics of the European FLEUR-model, in D. Griffith, A. Lea (editors), *Evolving Geographic Structures*, Martinus Nijhoff, The Hague, pp. 229–46.

Ancot, J.-P., Paelinck, J. H. P. 1983(b) Desarrollo regional: análisis, modelos, programación, [to appear in] *Desarrollo y Sociedad*.

Banque Européenne d'Investissement, Direction des Etudes 1982 (mimeo) *Indices de Disparité du PIB/hab 1979 dans les Régions de la Communauté*, Luxembourg.

Eurostat 1979 *Statistiques Régionales 1970–1977, Principaux Indicateurs Régionaux*, Luxembourg, 1979.

Eurostat 1980, '81, '82, '83 *Comptes Régionaux SEC*, Luxembourg.

Hoffman, L., Klaassen, L. H., Iwema, R., Paelinck, J. H. P. 1977 Wydajność wzrost gospodarczy: wybrane czynniki strukturalne (Productivité et croissance: quelques facteurs structurels), *Wpływ wydajnośc v pracy na wzrost gospodarczy*, Uniwersytet Łódzki, Institut Ekonomiki Produkcii.

Hughes Hallett, A. J., Ancot, J.-P. 1982 Estimating revealed preferences in models of planning behaviour, in J. Paelinck (editor), *Qualitative and Quantitative Mathematical Economics*, Martinus Nijhoff, The Hague, pp. 149–216.

Hutton, J., Hartley, K. 1968 A regional payroll tax, *Oxford Economic Papers*, **20(2)**: 417–26.

Keeble, D., Owens, P. L., Thompson, C. 1981 (mimeo) *Centrality, Peripherality, and EEC Regional Development Study*, University of Cambridge, Department of Geography; document CEE XVI/362/81 of 24 November 1981.

Klaassen, L. H., Paelinck, J. H. P. 1974 *Integration of Socio-Economic and Physical Planning*, University Press, Rotterdam.

Molle, W. T. M. (with B. van Holst and H. Smit) 1980 *Regional Disparity and Economic Development in the European Community*, Saxon House, Teakfield Limited, Farnborough.

Molle, W. T. M., van Haselen, H. W. J. 1980–82 Regional Disparity and Assisted Areas in a European Community of Twelve, *Series: Foundations of Empirical Economic Research*, Netherlands Economic Institute, Rotterdam.

Molle, W. T. M. 1982 *Industrial Location and Regional Development in the European Community*, Ph.D., Erasmus University, Rotterdam.

Netherlands Economic Institute, *Stage V of the FLEUR-Study:* The quantification of the explanatory variables urbanisation, labour markets, regional policy and output markets, Rotterdam, September 1980, January 1981 (a) (mimeo); FLEUR, Stage V, *The Explanatory Variables: Synthesis Report*, Rotterdam, March 1981 (b) (mimeo); *Operationalising the Projection Model*, Rotterdam, July 1982(a) (mimeo); Factors of Location in Europe (FLEUR), *Final Report*, Rotterdam, November 1982(b) (mimeo).

Paelinck, J. H. P. 1978 Une théorie des seuils de croissance régionaux, in *Seuils d'efficacité de la planification et de l'action régionale*, IDEA, Mons, pp. 101–7.

8

Financing Investment

Eric Roll

The emphasis of this book, written to celebrate the jubilee of the European Investment Bank, is on European economic development and on capital investment to that end. It discusses investment as a means of economic recovery (in the short run, given the present depressed state of the European economies) and on sustained economic growth in the longer term. It focuses on investment in relation to current and to be expected technological developments and those, such as energy, related to the basic requirement for economic growth. In the process it also lays stress on the important role which investment can play in removing or mitigating regional disparities with their economic, social and political implications for the member countries and for the Community as a whole. Emphasis is naturally also placed on the role of Community institutions in the implementation of investment.

However, the Community and its members do not live in isolation. They have many, sometimes very close, trading and other relations with other parts of the world, developed and less developed alike. Their own needs for investment for development and technological advance appear, therefore, side by side with those of other countries; and trading relations, in recent decades increasingly freed from artificial barriers, mean that these needs, and, when satisfied, the products to which they will give rise must be considered alongside those of other countries and regions.

This chapter is concerned with the financing of investment. In this context, even more than in that of trade and industrial and technological development in relation to other parts of the world, the world framework is of vital importance. For the need to secure funds to finance investment—however urgent or desirable—is not only common to all the investment objectives mentioned above, but also to investment requirements from many other parts of the world from many different sources and for many different purposes. At the point, therefore, at which money—the ultimate fungible—is involved, the demands of Europe wherever they may originate and for whatever purposes they may be exerted, come into competition with a literally enormous range of other demands. Given the fact that most of the markets in which these demands meet the supplies of investible funds are to a significant degree free—and have become increasingly so in recent decades—the competition is severe, sometimes very severe. It is, therefore, impossible to consider the problem of financing investment in Europe and for Europe's future except through a close study of the various markets in which these requirements can be satisfied, the competition they will be obliged to meet in these markets, and the practices and techniques through which these markets operate.

This chapter is, therefore, mainly devoted to a discussion of the financing of European investment by means of fund-raising activities in the different markets in which these activities are carried on. As a preliminary, there are some general observations to be made on where and how investment demands are generated; on what are the sources of funds to satisfy them; on what markets exist for the purpose of bringing together demand and supply of investment finance; and in what respect these have undergone major changes, both in size and in structure since the end of World War II.

These changes are discussed in greater detail in a subsequent section which also includes reflections on the impact which the large payments imbalances of different countries, particularly as they have appeared in the last few years, have had on the demands for finance not directly, sometimes only very tenuously, related to investment needs in the strict sense of the word. In this connection, some quantitative analyses are also given of the evolution of different markets and of the factors influencing fluctuations in their ability to meet borrowers' requirements or, at least, the terms on which they can meet them.

A following section examines the position of Europe, of individual countries and more particularly of Community institutions against the background of the recent history of financial markets, and the variety of techniques available and utilised for meeting investment demands. Finally, the current position and the outlook are discussed, particularly in the light of the problems for the international financial and banking system created by the large accumulation of debts by certain countries and the difficulties experienced by some of them in servicing these debts.

GENERAL OBSERVATIONS

This is not the place for a lengthy discussion of capital theory, of the factors which determine the volume and character of capital formation at different times and in different economic and social environments. It seems, however, useful to recall a few simple aspects if the more detailed, quantitative and technical considerations are to be properly seen against the background of basic macroeconomic elements.

Without attempting to choose among the deeper wellsprings of the desire for capital formations which theorists and historians have debated for a long time, it is enough to state that the *demand* for funds which would enable investment to take place — that is to say to create the necessary conditions (in the form of fixed plant and equipment and the necessary stock of raw materials) for productive purposes (new production, enlarged production, technologically and economically more advanced forms of production) — originates either from the State or other institutions in the public domain, or from private entrepreneurs. Historically, the balance between the two has tended to fluctuate. From the nineteenth century onwards until the early decades of the present century, the balance in most of the advanced industrial countries and particularly in western Europe has been very substantially in favour of the private entrepreneur, at least as far as 'genuine' productive investment is concerned (that is excluding expenditure on armaments, some, though by no means all public utilities, and a varying, but often substantial, volume of investment for social purposes, such as health, education, etc.).

The depression of the 1930s led to an increase in publicly initiated and financed productive investment, notably in the United States, but also in countries of western Europe; and this trend was enormously strengthened during the war. Commitment to full employment policies, virtually ubiquitous in the western world after World War II, together with the in any event vast requirements for reconstruction tended for a time to reinforce the weight of public demand for funds for investment in the western world; while the pressure for development in the ex-colonial areas of the world with its surge of investment projects added substantially to the demand for funds to a very large degree initiated by the public sector.

As the immediate post-war reconstruction and development needs were satisfied and new, often technologically based, investment opportunities opened up, the market economies reasserted themselves and the proportion of demand for funds from the private sector for investment in private enterprise grew substantially. While the balance between the public and the private sector continued to fluctuate—partly in response to changes in the preponderance of different political and ideological forces and concepts—the net effect was a very rapid growth in the total volume of finance required. The fluctuations between the public and the private sectors are not in themselves of special concern to the theme of this chapter; the size of the total demand is. In considering it, one must also bear in mind that certainly as far as public-sector demand is concerned, that part of it which is strictly for capital investment purposes cannot be totally segregated from other demand which requires financing in one way or another. Both actual practices and the book-keeping conventions which apply to them vary from country to country and from time to time; and the distinction within the public sector— central and local government, governmental agencies and nationalised industries—between financing for capital and revenue purposes is sometimes debatable. Even in the private sector, certainly as between different countries, conventions as to what is to be considered to be in the nature of working capital and what is a fixed investment requirement are variable and not always precise. From the point of view of arriving at a measure of the competition which investment by and for European purposes has to encounter, one has, therefore, often to take into account in the main, and certainly in the first instance, the total volume of demand for available funds, rather than any particular portion of it.

The distinctions are clearer on the side of the supply of investi-

ble funds. The sources of these funds are either internal or external. In the case of the public sector, they are taxation and other
forms of revenue, including in the case of State enterprises such as
nationalised industries excesses of earnings over expenses which
are set aside for investment. In the case of private enterprise, they
are provisions made out of revenue after current expenses (and
taxation) have been accounted for. External finance consists of
borrowing both by public and private entities in different financial markets, the ultimate source which feeds these markets being
savings by individuals or institutions.

HISTORICAL BACKGROUND

In the early phases of modern capital development, some relatively simple categories sufficed to describe and explain the
process of capital formation. As stated, savings out of current
income first directly by individuals, later also indirectly by enterprises which did not distribute the whole of their revenue surpluses, were usually directly translated into funds made available
for productive investment to individual entrepreneurs or groups
of them, associated in more or less loose forms either as participations in the projected investment (carrying a variable income
related to the results of the enterprise) or as loans carrying a rate
of interest, and often secured on the physical properties of the
enterprise. This simple pattern is a reasonable approximation to
the basic process that happened in the older industrial countries,
particularly in Britain with its early development of the joint-
stock company and a capital market in which demand and supply
for investment funds met directly. In Britain, too, as a result of
this early development of a capital market, the structure of the
financial system developed along lines of considerable specialisation, particularly as between the banking system proper (the
'deposit' banks) whose activities were for a long time confined to
the provision — through various forms of credit — of short-term
working capital to industry and commerce, leaving the mobilisation of funds for longer-term capital investment purposes to
the capital market. This market quickly developed increasing size
and complexity, both as a primary provider of funds as well as for
the purpose of secondary trading in the capital instruments
created — stocks and shares.

The development in the rest of western Europe (as indeed in the United States and in other of the developing industrial countries) was not dissimilar, except that their later arrival on the industrial scene had the effect of blurring the distinction between the processes by which short-term (working) capital and long-term (investment) capital were carried on. This was most notably the case in Germany (though it applied also to other countries now members of the European Community), where the some-what more 'hot-house' atmosphere of industrial development, particularly after the Franco-Prussian War and with the added stimulus of protective tariffs and other trade barriers, led the banking system to play a much more direct part in furnishing funds for the long-term capital needs of industry. However, in the continental countries of western Europe also capital markets developed which translated individual savings into investible funds, in which instruments evidencing such investment were created and traded, and in which specialised intermediating institutions operated side by side with the banks.

The above reflections are made not simply to recall some elementary historical facts, but rather to show that on the side of the mechanisms for investment, the countries of western Europe did not all start from the same basis, although over the last hundred years, and more particularly in the decade since the end of World War II, the pattern has tended to become more uniform. Thus on the continent, capital markets, properly so-called, have become more sophisticated and now form one of the most important instrumentalities for producing 'investment for Europe'; and in Britain, the role of the banking system as such, while still that of a provider of credit only — ostensibly for short-term purposes — has widened greatly, partly under the impetus of international competition, and may now in practice extend its provision of funds over a considerable period of years. The British banks still do not take actual shares in their client companies; but the multiplicity of loan instruments, domestic and international, is now such that they are active traders in a variety of markets.

It is important to remember the existence of these 'national' European markets which, notwithstanding their differences in regard to structure and type of institutional specialisation, supply a considerable proportion of the funds needed both for the public and the private sector, particularly in view of the special attention which the more recent development of international capital movements and the international markets through which they take place has attracted. For many potential borrowers the domestic markets still form the basic source of external funds. As has already been stated, in these markets — and as we shall see in international markets also — the demands of the public sector arise not only from productive needs but often for general budgetary purposes. Given the increasing complexity of budgets and the 'virement' which every government naturally possesses (and would wish to preserve), the essential fact for markets — that is for suppliers of funds as well as for other borrowers who are competing for these funds — is the total requirement of government for external finance — i.e. over and above its fiscal revenue. This used to be called the budget deficit, but is in recent years often referred to as the public sector borrowing requirement, thus bringing out even more clearly the significance in market terms of the government's management of its own household. It may be said parenthetically that it is in the national budget that the movement of the great macro-economic categories — consumption, saving and investment — on which the balance of the whole economy depends, can often be most clearly discerned.

RECENT DEVELOPMENTS

The mechanism by which investible funds are channelled to their productive employments has undergone some very important developments in recent decades. The private saver is still very important, but not only does he, more often than not, use newly developed intermediaries to make his savings effective, but also an ever increasing amount of saving is done collectively on behalf of the individual, and is channelled into productive investment with very little — sometimes with no — practical intervention by the individual saver himself. In addition to the traditional repositories of private savings, such as deposit accounts in banks, savings banks, building societies and so on, the individual saver has been increasingly able in recent decades to make investments indirectly in various enterprises through investment trusts and unit trusts. Even more important than these has been the truly enormous growth in pension funds, and in the funds from policy premiums which insurance companies have available to invest, and need to invest, in order to meet their future liabilities.

Thus, though savings in the broadest sense (including private savings) continue to be the ultimate source for investment, the proximate source to which those who need funds have to look — that is to say the proximate lenders and investors — are now largely a multiplicity of institutions whose investments are usually professionally managed on behalf of a large number of ultimate beneficiaries. It is important to speak here of both proximate lenders as well as investors, for given the more varied roles which different types of banks and other financial institutions — not themselves at all, or in the main, to be thought of as, long-term investors — play, they are often the immediate source of funds passing on to ultimate institutional or private investors the claims which they have temporarily acquired.

Another important development of recent years has been the developments of new institutions which act as intermediaries in the provision of long-term investment capital. They raise funds in their own name and on their own credit, and on-lend to those in the public or private sector that are able to apply these funds for productive projects. Most industrialised countries, including the members of the European Community, have institutions of this kind, many of them specialising in particular areas of investment — small businesses, industrial reorganisation and reconstruction, etc. Often these institutions are born of specific industrial difficulties such as economic recessions in which certain sectors of industry have suffered particularly severely; sometimes they are the result of attempts at 'planning', particularly in new areas of industry such as high technology ones. The importance of these institutions (which are often publicly or semi-publicly owned or controlled) and the record of their achievement has varied considerably from time to time and from country to country. Although they are not designed, or calculated, to foster specifically 'European' investment and development in any collective sense, they are mentioned here because they are often an important element in capital and credit markets, both as borrowers and as lenders.

More striking and important from that point of view are the

international institutions which have been created since the war as capital-investing intermediaries. These include the International Bank for Reconstruction and Development (the World Bank), and a number of regional development banks, such as the Asian Development Bank, the African Development Bank, the Inter-American Development Bank, and (especially important for our purpose) the European Investment Bank — which together with the other institutions of the Community that borrow and on-lend (the EEC itself, the European Coal and Steel Community and Euratom) has specific responsibilities for European development.

The appearance of these new institutions is of great importance not only because of their obvious politico-economic significance in the mobilization of funds, and in the direction of these into investments for specific regional developmental purposes. It is also of very great moment, as we shall see presently, because their appearance has meant the introduction of new entities not only as sources of funds but also into the series of borrowers in the market with their own standing in the spectrum of credit-worthiness.

INTERNATIONAL CREDIT AND CAPITAL MARKETS

Finally, among these new developments that have occurred in recent years and have fashioned the character and mechanisms of financing investment, a special place must be given to the internationalization of markets. The movement of capital originating in one country for investment in another is itself by no means new. The history of the nineteenth and early twentieth century is in fact characterised by the growth of capital movements from countries with large capital formation into less developed countries with little or no indigenous capital, but with natural resources offering opportunities for productive investment. The development of some of the most highly industrialised countries in the world, notably the United States and Canada, though not to anything like the same extent Japan, was largely brought about through the import of capital from older countries. This export of capital in the strict sense, that is from countries where capital formation takes place into investment elsewhere, continues. In the form of the raising of loans and credits by borrowers from other countries in these 'national' markets (particularly in the United States, but also in Switzerland, Germany, more recently in Japan, and latterly also in the United Kingdom) it remains a very important source of funds for a large variety of borrowers, including the international and supra-national institutions. It is, however, not by any means the only or always even the major part of international finance for investment.

The most novel and in some ways the most characteristic development in this respect has been the growth of truly international capital and credit markets — that is to say markets which are not tied to any one particular national source of funds. These are markets in which borrowers meet lenders (mainly commercial banks but also other financial institutions) investors both private and above all institutional, and investment banks and other intermediaries, through telecommunication media and virtually without any direct constraints from national regulatory or supervisory authorities. These so-called Euro-currency and Euro-bond markets operate in a variety of national currencies (though the US dollar has throughout been far and away the most important currency in which credits or bonds are denominated), and also, though to a very much smaller degree, in 'artificial' denominations constituted by 'baskets' of currencies such as Special Drawing Rights (SDRs) or European Currency Units (ECUs). The origins of these funds — particularly dollars held outside the national banking system or national capital markets — can be traced to pre-war accumulations of dollars held outside the United States, but the massive post-war outward flows of dollars produced vastly increased amounts, particularly since the dollar being by far the major transaction currency, many accumulations not arising from direct US transactions were denominated in dollars and held outside the United States, or at any rate in accounts freely disposable from outside the United States.

As far as the Euro-bond market is concerned — again the US dollar being by far its most important currency of denomination — this developed at the beginning of the 1960s as the result, very largely, of the measures taken in the United States to correct persistent American balance of payments deficits (such as the interest equalisation tax which put most foreign borrowers in the US capital market at a relative disadvantage). Combined with certain technical obstacles created by American regulations concerning the issue of, and trading in, securities (which have only recently been alleviated), as well as certain tax disadvantages, this created a powerful incentive for the development of an international bond market. In 1963 the first Euro-bond issues took place, to a total volume of US$164 million — the first of these, significantly, being for an Italian para-statal borrower, the Autostrade. The market very quickly developed its own techniques, rules and practices, and apart from having grown, as we shall see, very markedly and almost continuously in the twenty years since it started, now has as clear cut usances as many a national capital market, although it remains less rigid, more rapid in operation and consequently more open to imaginative innovation in regard to the structuring of bond issues than are national markets. Like national markets too, it has grown to a size (and its continued growth contributes further to this) which makes it into a regular and important source of funds: almost automatically as the years pass, an increasing volume of funds becomes available for re-investment as the result of the redemption at, or even before, maturity of previously issued bonds, to which are added new funds resulting from individual and institutional savings.

The mobility of funds and the internationalisation of markets were greatly fostered by the gradual disappearance, accelerated in recent years, of exchange controls and other impediments to the international flows of capital. Until the current world economic recession — which has seen the unfortunate appearance of, at least, threats of a recrudescence of protectionist measures — this process of the liberalisation of financial flows, though not complete, showed steady progress. Without it, the remarkable growth of international credit and capital markets in the last twenty years, and particularly their performance during the last decade after the first oil shock, coming as it did just after the breakdown of the Bretton Woods system, would not have been possible. This is not the place to go into the wider consequences of the collapse of the system of fixed (but changeable) parities painfully constructed and consolidated after 1945, nor into those created by the sudden — though perhaps to have been expected — revolution in the relative value of petroleum. But the consequences for world financial markets of the payments disturbances and the international flows of funds brought about by the oil revolutions of 1973–74 and again of 1979 had a very profound effect on the operation of these markets and, therefore, on the position of borrowers and investors.

Already before these oil revolutions, governments had from time to time had recourse to international credit and capital markets not for specific investment purposes, but either to cover general budgetary needs or, more often, for balance of payments reasons; that is, to cover current account deficits and strengthen their foreign exchange reserves. Sometimes they did this in their own name, sometimes through various State or para-statal entities (in which case the investment requirements of these entities were met in local currency, the foreign exchange proceeds of international borrowing benefitting the central reserves). In the latter cases, the international and supra-national development banks might theoretically have been brought into play, since their on-lending would, of course, have been for investment purposes, but owing to various constraints in the currency borrowing and lending practices of these institutions, their role as a provider (indirectly) of balance of payments facilities would have been only a limited one.

After the oil revolutions, two important developments occurred: on the one hand the current balance of payments situation of the oil-importing countries, including in particular those in the group of less developed countries, suffered a serious deterioration; on the other hand, the oil exporting countries found themselves suddenly in the possession of greatly enhanced surpluses of funds in US dollars (the dollar being the currency in which oil is traded) requiring to be placed. The destinations of these surpluses, both immediate and ultimate, varied a good deal. Some went into a more or less rapid expansion of imports into the oil-producing countries, including imports of capital goods, etc., for development projects in those countries. Some went into direct investments in other countries, or into the acquisition of titles (portfolio investments) or, at least temporarily, into bank deposits for relatively short periods. The latter immediately — and by a multiple — increased the lending capacity of the international banking system. The former, directly or indirectly, eventually increased the funds available for investment through international capital markets. It is useful at this stage to remember that funds seeking employment and the markets in which they do so can be conceived of as being in the nature of communicating vessels — not perhaps perfectly, but certainly to the extent that the varying attractiveness of one employment compared with another and the degree of perfection of different markets (i.e. the facility with which funds may be entered or withdrawn) permits.

Both the credit markets and the capital markets showed the effects of this influx of funds as well as the recourse to them of borrowers: in short, the volume of transactions in both increased very considerably. This widening of the markets also meant that competition both on the supply and the demand side became more acute, and also between the intermediaries — primarily the commercial banks in the credit markets and the investment banks in the capital markets. This increased competition had the effect of increasing the variety of techniques used and the instruments created, thus offering a greater range of possibilities to lenders and investors on the one hand and to borrowers on the other.

It may be useful at this stage to look at the development of these international markets in recent years. Table 8.1 shows the growth of the Euro-bond market in the last twenty years and in the last quarter for which statistics are available at the time of writing. The figures are in millions of US dollars or equivalent, and show the number of issues, and their division, both in absolute figures and in percentages of the total, according to the currency denomination.

The Euro-currency credit markets have also grown enormously, particularly after the imbalances created by the successive oil shocks. By the end of 1971 the total Euro-currency market was estimated to be about US$60 billion. This was then considered a high figure; and it compared with perhaps one-thirtieth of that amount of its nearest pre-war equivalent — what Keynes called the international short-loan fund. By 1973 the market was estimated to be $315 billion; by 1980 over $1500 billion; and by the end of 1982 over $2000 billion. (These figures are on a gross basis, the net figures being about one-half the gross; although for the purpose of having an appreciation of the significance of the volume of liquid funds capable of rapid movement from one centre to another and from one currency to another, the gross figures may be the more telling ones.) As might be expected, the bulk of these Euro-currency liabilities are in US dollars: in 1981–82 a little over 80 per cent. The volume of Euro-currency credits has also grown greatly, and by 1980 the amount granted that year as publicly announced had reached over $77 billion, only to grow to over $133 billion in the following year. Since then, however, the growth has slowed down and in 1982 the total volume of new credits was about $84 billion.

The fluctuation in Euro-currency credits and their distribution among different countries (industrial, non-OPEC developing, OPEC, and communist) as it varies from year to year are of considerable interest for the purpose of analysing the changing attitudes of the banking system to total lending and to their exposure to individual countries or groups of countries, as well as to the fluctuating balance of payments difficulties of different countries and their need for international funds to alleviate these. They are not, however, of primary significance from the point of view of the main theme of this chapter, namely the need for capital development investment and the availability of funds for this purpose.

In this regard, the evolution of the international capital market is of much greater importance. Table 8.1 contains some interesting features in this regard. Ignoring minor fluctuations, it will be seen that the total volume rose steadily in the first few years, but suffered a set-back in the first two years after the oil shock, precisely at a time when, as would be expected, the volume of Euro-currency credits rose sharply. Again ignoring minor fluctuations which are largely the result of fluctuations in the market's absorptive capacity—and based in part on fluctuations in the volume of bonds coming up for redemption and the resulting funds for reinvestment—the next eight years and particularly the last three or four have seen a sharp acceleration of this process. The present year (1983), if the first quarter figures can be taken as an indication, is likely to produce a record figure of over US$50 billion. The breakdown between currencies of denomination is not of special relevance to our main theme, and is largely explainable in terms of relative interest rates and expectations as regards exchange rates, movements in these in turn being traceable to

TABLE 8.1
GROWTH OF THE EURO-BOND MARKET 1963–83
(ALL FIGURES IN US$ MILLIONS OR EQUIVALENT)

Year	Total volume of issues	US$ issues		DM issues		Other issues	
1963	164	102	62%	—		62	38%
1964	794	570	72%	91.2	11%	132.8	17%
1965	1,164	775	67%	105	9%	284	24%
1966	1,138	898	79%	146.3	13%	93.7	8%
1967	1,884	1,622	86%	145	8%	117	6%
1968	3,074	2,280	74%	726.4	24%	67.6	2%
1969	2,730	1,622	59%	1,047	38%	61	3%
1970	2,379	1,733	73%	569.3	24%	76.7	3%
1971	3,349	2,188	65%	827.1	25%	333.9	10%
1972	5,045	3,093	61%	1,167	23%	785	16%
1973	3,128	1,718	55%	902.6	29%	507.4	16%
1974	1,388	797	57%	213.8	15%	377.2	28%
1975	6,090	2,943	48%	1,723.1	28%	1,423.9	24%
1976	11,856	8,024	68%	2,018.7	17%	1,814	15%
1977	15,145	9,951	66%	3,833.4	25%	1,360.6	9%
1978	11,025	5,363	49%	4,956	45%	706	6%
1979	13,782	9,193	67%	2,933	21%	1,656	12%
1980	18,203	12,331	68%	3,413	19%	2,459	13%
1981	24,343	20,203	83%	1,229.3	5%	2,910.7	12%
1982	43,648	35,835	82%	4,312.4	10%	3,500.6	8%
1983 (to 31st March)	13,763	10,329	75%	1,680	12.2%	1,754	12.8%

domestic policies. Table 8.2 breaks down the issues into 'other currencies' for the last four years, and illustrates (together with the preponderance of dollars and Deutsche marks—particularly the former) the fact that from time to time other currencies can play a useful supporting role.

TABLE 8.2

BREAKDOWN OF 'OTHER CURRENCIES' SINCE 1979
(FIGURES IN US$ MILLIONS)

	1979	1980	1981	1982
£	281.6	955.2	508.8	790.1
FF	368.3	819.0	608.6	—
Canadian $	424.1	285.6	516.1	1,331.4
ECU	—	—	189.9	680.9
Yen	116.2	256.9	362.7	382.6
Miscellaneous	465.8	142.3	724.6	315.6
Total	1,656.0	2,459.0	2,910.7	3,500.6

The types of borrowers in the international capital market have varied according to their needs in relation to the opportunities offered them in this as compared with other markets. US corporations, for example, have had frequent and substantial recourse to the market, the fluctuations being almost entirely in accordance with the state of the US bond market by comparison with international markets. At the other end, developing countries (particularly non-OPEC countries) have in general accounted for only a very small proportion of Euro-bond issues; and the volume has recently been declining further with the mounting debt and rescheduling problems encountered by many of them. Thus, while in 1981 non-OPEC developing countries (which included such countries as Brazil, Korea and Mexico) took US$4,338 million through bond issues, the figure was only $3,890 million in 1982, and in the first three months of 1983 the amount was down to $212 million.

TABLE 8.3

ISSUES BY EIB AND OTHER COMMUNITY BORROWERS ON NATIONAL AND INTERNATIONAL MARKETS; ESTIMATED MARKET SHARES 1979–81

Markets	1979		1980		1981	
	Percentage of European Community	Of which EIB %	Percentage of European Community	Of which EIB %	Percentage of European Community	Of which EIB %
(a) International:						
US$	9	6	7	3	4	3
DM	7	3	5	—	11	3
Other	9	8	10	7	6	4
Total (a)	8	5	7	3	5	3
(b) National:						
USA	23	17	17	17	2	2
EEC Countries	58	42	46	28	59	35
Others	5	3	7	5	7	6
Total (b)	18	13	22	15	12	8
Total (a) + (b)	13	9	14	9	8	5

International organisations, the European Investment Bank among them, have been consistent borrowers over the last two decades or so in all capital markets, national as well as international, and have thus been an important factor in the raising of finance for investment in many parts of the world; naturally, in the case of the European Investment Bank, especially in Europe.

For the years 1979 to 1981 the proportions which the European Community has represented as a borrower in different markets and the shares of that proportion taken by the European Investment Bank have been as given in Table 8.3.

For the sake of completeness it should be emphasised again that these institutions are not the only sources of investment funds, even within the channels that are under some form of governmental (in this case, intergovernmental) direction. There are substantial funds made available for productive purposes through bilateral or multilateral aid arrangements, including in a number of cases, for regional development, as is also the case in Europe. On the other side, these agencies do not draw their funds through market borrowings only: they do have their own capital resources and they also borrow, sometimes in very substantial amounts, by placing their obligations directly with the monetary authorities — central banks and other official institutions — of member governments. This is, for example, a major source of funds for the World Bank, accounting for about 30 per cent of its total debt. A significant part of the borrowing that is done by these institutions from major private institutional sources as distinct from official institutions is in the form of private placements — that is, direct-debt obligations placed with or without the intermediation of investment banks. Finally, there are the public bond issues in domestic or international markets.

In managing their borrowing operations, the international institutions (such as the European Investment Bank) must be guided by a variety of considerations. Among these the state of the different markets (i.e. the volume of funds available and the terms on which they can be obtained in each) play an important, but not necessarily an exclusive part — though they are often decisive as regards the timing of any operation. Over a period, borrowing policy in regard particularly to maturity, average rate of interest paid, and currency of denomination, is determined by the lending policy which the institution wishes to follow, having regard to certain parameters or constraints in that regard, created by objective factors such as practical on-lending possibilities or by policy desiderata laid down by member governments. In these regards as well as in their detailed techniques, the various development banks do not necessarily follow the same pattern. One factor which will produce differences is the total volume of borrowing involved: for example, the total outstanding debt of the World Bank in 1982 was over US$37 billion, of the European Investment Bank $18 billion, and of the other regional banks much smaller amounts. These differences, which mirror differences in the volume of their lending, will, for example, account for a greater regularity of borrowing rhythm as far as the bigger borrowers are concerned, including appearances in the public bond markets, and such matters as the choice of intermediaries. The World Bank has a policy of virtually maintaining unchanged its managing syndicates in different public capital markets, while the European Investment Bank has tended to vary these to a considerable extent.

FINANCING EUROPEAN INVESTMENT

Against the background of the preceding sections, the more specific questions relating to the financing of European investment can be considered in greater detail, and in particular, given the general theme of this book, financing of investment in the context of the European Community. Once again, in order to get the right perspective, it is necessary first to look at some overall figures. In the last three years the amounts of total international borrowings in the Euro-currency bank credit market and in the international bond markets (including bond issues in different domestic markets on behalf of foreign borrowers) were broadly as given in Table 8.4.

TABLE 8.4

	1980	1981	1982
International bond issues	42,000	53,000	76,000
Euro-currency bank credits	77,000	133,000	84,000
Total	119,000	186,000	160,000

This Table shows the steady and substantial rise in the volume of Euro-bonds (which has already been shown in Table 8.1 for a longer series of years and which continued in the first quarter of 1983), but a sharp up-and-down in the volume of Euro-currency credits in consequence of the debt-servicing problems which many developing countries experienced in 1982. What is important for our purpose is to note that within the grand total of borrowings Europe was a relatively limited part, and the amount borrowed by European Community institutions a smaller part still.

For example, in 1981 Italy borrowed US$5,800 million in the international banking and $904 million in the international bond market; and France borrowed $3,600 million in the banking and $3,100 million in the bond market. As against these figures for the two largest European Governmental borrowers, the Community institutions as a whole borrowed about $3,300, of which the European Investment Bank accounted for $2,300 million. These figures do not convey a measure of what total funds went into productive investment in Europe, first because they exclude the very large sums raised by the private sector internally and externally, and second because (as already pointed out) in the case of the figures for individual governments they exclude internally generated as well as domestically borrowed funds which were applied for productive purposes. On the other hand, the figures for external borrowings include amounts raised for balance of payments purposes.

Although we are not here concerned with the Community's specific lending activities, it is necessary to have some measure of these in mind when examining the Community's borrowing. Accordingly, Table 8.5 shows the lending activities for 1970–81 (by instrument employed).

Table 8.6 shows the borrowing operations undertaken by the different Community institutions to set against the on-lending set out in the preceding Table. It will be noted that in two years, 1976 and 1977, the Community borrowed substantial sums in its own name — ECU 1,249 million in the former and ECU 571 million in the latter year. While these large borrowings were, of course, very significant in market terms at the time they took place, they are not directly relevant to our subject, since they were under-

TABLE 8.5

LENDING OPERATIONS IN THE COMMUNITY BY INSTRU-
MENTS (EXCLUDING LOANS FOR BALANCE OF PAYMENTS
PURPOSES) (IN ECU MILLION)

Year	ECSC	EIB	Euratom	NCI	Total
1970	31.6	338.6			370.2
1971	112.2	469.0			581.2
1972	188.5	505.9			694.4
1973	286.4	696.8			983.2
1974	377.9	849.7			1,277.6
1975	804.9	917.5			1,722.4
1976	1,063.8	1,086.0			2,149.8
1977	741.5	1,401.3	96.9		2,239.7
1978	797.7	1,966.5	70.3		2,834.5
1979	675.8	2,281.2	152.5	277.0	3,386.5
1980	1,020.3	2,753.2	181.3	197.6	4,152.4
1981	387.6	2,821.5	364.3	539.8	4,113.2

TABLE 8.6

BORROWING OPERATIONS BY THE EUROPEAN COM-
MUNITIES, BY INSTRUMENT, 1970–81 (IN ECU MILLION)

Year	ECSC	EIB[1]	Euratom	EEC[2]	NCI[3]	Total
1970	60	169				229
1971	102	413				515
1972	230	462				692
1973	263	608				871
1974	528	826				1,354
1975	731	814				1,543
1976	956	732		1,249		2,937
1977	729	1,030	99	571		2,429
1978	981	1,863	72			2,916
1979	837	2,437	153		178	3,605
1980	1,004	2,384	181		305	3,874
1981	324	2,243	373		332	3,272

1 Excluding third-party participations in EIB financing, which amounted to
ECU 402.3 million from 1972 to 1980 (44.6 million in 1979 and 83.3 million in
1980).
2 Borrowing to finance balance of payments deficits.
3 The New Community Instrument, or Ortoli Facility, was brought into being
to help stimulate an economic revival by making a contribution to investment.

taken for specific balance of payments assistance to individual Community member countries.

As the European Investment Bank is not only the largest among the Community institutions as a borrower and a lender — and in the latter capacity more particularly responsible to serve as a source of funds for productive investment — it is useful to look more closely at its borrowing operations. Table 8.7 sets out total borrowings by the European Investment Bank from its inception to 1982 inclusive, broken down first into private placements and public borrowings, and then into currency denominations.

Finally, to complete the statistical material, Table 8.8 shows the total amount of debt outstanding for each instrument at the end of each year 1970–80 (the last year for which full figures are available); while Table 8.9 shows the total amount of loans granted by Community institutions to member countries (and to a very small degree to other countries of direct interest to the Community) in the years 1975–80.

COMMUNITY FINANCING: RECORD AND OUTLOOK. THE SPECIAL ROLE OF THE EIB

There are now five Community institutions which are engaged in borrowing and on-lending to finance European investment. Three of these were set up for this purpose by the original treaties founding the Community institutions as such. They are the European Coal and Steel Community, now for its operational purposes integrated with other appropriate Community organs and thus acting also for the second institution, Euratom, and the European Investment Bank. The two new ones are first the Community itself, borrowing and lending in its own name. As we have seen, this has been (and presumably is likely to remain so) for balance of payments support, extending its facilities — as does the International Monetary Fund — subject to the undertaking by the borrowing country of certain programmes in relation to its domestic economic policy. This activity, therefore, need not be further examined here: its impact on the total demand for funds in the markets has already been noted. The second new institution is the New Community Instrument created to stimulate recovery by

TABLE 8.7

TOTAL BORROWINGS (IN ECU MILLIONS) BY THE EUROPEAN INVESTMENT BANK IN ALL MARKETS FROM 1958 TO 1982, WITH A BREAKDOWN INTO THE RESPECTIVE BORROWING CURRENCIES

Year	Private placements (in all currencies)	Public issues	Total borrowed in all currencies[1]	ECU	EURCO	DM	FF	£	LIT	B.Frs.	D.Fls.	L.Frs.	US$	S.Frs.	£LEB	Yen	A.Sch.
1958) 1959) 1960	No medium and long term loan liabilities																
1961	7.6	13.8	21.4	—	—	—	—	—	—	—	19.3+	—	—	—	—	—	—
1962	—	32.3	32.3	—	—	—	—	—	24.0	—	8.3	—	—	—	—	—	—
1963	8.0	27.2	35.2	—	—	15.0	12.2	—	—	8.0	—	1.0	—	—	—	—	—
1964	13.5	53.3	66.8	—	—	32.5	—	—	—	—	8.3	—	25.0	—	—	—	—
1965	—	65.0	65.0	—	—	—	—	—	24.0	10.0	11.0	—	20.0	—	—	—	—
1966	24.0	112.0	136.0	—	—	—	40.5	—	48.0	10.0	—	—	37.5	—	—	—	—
1967	40.0	136.0	179.5	—	—	5.0	40.5	—	24.0	15.0	—	—	95.0	—	—	—	—
1968	112.5	100.0	212.5	—	—	137.5	—	—	24.0	15.0	11.0	—	25.0	—	—	—	—
1969	63.7	89.7	153.4	—	—	128.4	—	—	—	—	—	—	25.0	—	—	—	—
1970	66.6	102.3	168.9	—	—	27.3	20.0	—	—	15.0	16.6	—	90.0	—	—	—	—
1971	208.0	205.0	413.0	—	—	82.0	18.0	—	64.0	30.0	20.7	26.0	120.0	52.3	—	—	—
1972	133.4	328.8	462.2	—	—	54.6	31.5	—	64.0	32.0	27.6	26.0	202.0	24.5	—	—	—
1973	207.0	404.9	611.9	—	30.1	95.6	36.0	—	80.0	52.0	55.2	42.0	149.2	49.0	22.8	—	—
1974	704.2	120.7	824.9	—	60.7	39.8	—	—	—	—	16.0	8.1	665.4	34.9	—	—	—
1975	318.6	495.1	813.7	—	—	180.8	66.8	—	—	33.3	71.8	11.1	298.9	133.8	—	17.2	—
1976	221.0	510.9	731.9	—	—	114.2	—	—	—	—	24.0	11.9	489.3	43.8	—	30.5	18.2
1977	321.9	707.5	1,029.4	—	—	202.4	—	38.2	—	36.7	80.8	12.2	521.6	55.5	—	82.0	—
1978	509.0	1,353.8	1,862.8	—	—	416.8	140.7	38.9	—	82.1	172.6	18.5	861.9	109.6	—	—	21.7
1979	983.2	1,453.4	2,436.6	—	—	534.0	205.1	62.1	—	61.9	276.4	21.3	1,006.7	92.3	—	148.9	27.9
1980	874.6	1,509.0	2,383.6	—	—	814.1	136.6	45.7	42.7	—	226.2	51.7	666.0	234.0	—	166.6	—
1981	974.9	1,267.8	2,242.7	85.0	—	358.3	128.5	106.8	—	51.7	319.1	14.5	615.3	300.0	—	263.5	—
1982	1,319.0	1,826.6	3,145.6	112.0	—	586.0	177.4	262.9	—	79.2	412.9	37.2	745.3	345.7	—	387.0	—
Total	7,110.7	10,918.6	18,029.3	197.0	90.8	3,824.3	1,053.8	554.6	394.7	531.9	1,777.8	281.5	6,659.1	1,475.4	22.8	1,095.7	67.8

1 Not including participations by third parties in EIB loans. In addition, an amount of ECU2.1 million was borrowed and classified as 'other currencies'.
Source EIB Annual Reports 1958–81; 1982 figures from EIB Treasury directly.

TABLE 8.8

BORROWINGS BY THE EUROPEAN COMMUNITIES
(AMOUNTS OUTSTANDING AT END OF EACH YEAR, IN ECU
MILLION)

Year	ECSC	EIB	Euratom[1]	EEC[2]	NCI	Total[1]
1970	741	1,020	—	—	—	1,761
1971	802	1,423	—	—	—	2,225
1972	963	1,784	—	—	—	2,747
1973	1,172	2,287	—	—	—	3,459
1974	1,617	3,124	—	—	—	4,741
1975	2,393	3,926	17	—	—	6,336
1976	3,477	4,732	14	1,161	—	9,384
1977	3,956	5,421	110	1,500	—	10,986
1978	4,416	6,715	182	1,361	—	12,674
1979	4,713	8,541	333	965	178	14,730
1980	5,300[3]	10,598	502	1,016	402	17,898

1 Excluding Euratom figures for the period prior to 1975.
2 Balance of payments financing.
3 Estimate.
(*Sources:* Commission staff and EIB.)

contributing to investment. This has been directed to the reduction of regional imbalances, improving employment prospects, energy conservation and supply, advance factories, housing and assistance to small firms. In essence, these purposes are not very different from those of the European Investment Bank; and the operational implementation of transactions under the NCI has effectively been sub-contracted to the EIB.

The multiplicity of these Community institutions may at first sight raise the question as to whether such variety is really necessary and whether it does not create special problems of potential competition, indeed conflict. Leaving aside balance of payments borrowing and lending as being different in kind, and leaving aside also the necessary diversity which stems from their different origins both as to time and as to their statutory foundations (which in turn has given each a different historical experience), there is little if any evidence — at any rate to the outside observer — of any significant confusion, let alone conflict, arising from the number of channels used for these collective European transactions. It is true that each instrument has its own ultimate source of resources as the basis on which it has recourse to the

TABLE 8.9

TOTAL AMOUNT OF LOANS GRANTED BY THE COMMUNITY IN MEMBER COUNTRIES AND OF DIRECT INTEREST TO THEM, 1975–80[1] (IN ECU MILLION)

	1975 EIB + ECSC		1976 EIB + ECSC		1977 EIB + ECSC + EUR[2]		1978 EIB + ECSC + EUR		1979 EIB + ECSC EUR + NCI		1980 EIB + ECSC EUR + NCI		Total 1975–80	
	Value	Percentage	Value	Percentage	Value	Percentage	Value	Percentage	Value	Percentage	Value	Percentage	Value	Percentage
Belgium	52.9	3.1	55.2	2.6	15.9	0.7	64.1	2.3	139.6	4.1	264.6	6.4	592.3	3.6
Denmark	40.7	2.4	9.1	0.4	33.2	1.5	119.5	4.2	15.9	0.5	103.5	2.5	321.9	1.95
FRG	150.9	8.7	297.7	13.8	221.0	9.9	218.9	7.7	196.9	5.8	143.3	3.4	1228.7	7.5
France	275.1	16.0	193.3	9.0	490.8	21.9	486.4	17.2	391.5	11.6	653.5	15.7	2490.6	15.1
Ireland	37.9	2.2	58.1	2.7	79.9	3.6	117.4	4.1	353.5	10.4	377.1	9.1	1023.9	6.2
Italy	535.4	31.1	530.4	24.7	599.2	26.7	1007.3	35.6	1126.0	33.3	1430.0	34.4	5228.3	31.7
Luxembourg	1.1	0.1	0.1	—	0.6	—	73.9	2.6	19.8	0.6	68.6	1.6	164.1	1.0
Netherlands	30.4	1.7	69.0	3.2	0.5	—	42.8	1.5	0.6	—	4.9	0.1	148.2	0.9
United Kingdom	597.9	34.7	936.9	43.6	749.8	33.5	704.0	24.8	1103.3	32.6	1056.0	25.4	5147.9	31.2
Non-EEC	—	—	—	—	48.8	2.2	—	—	39.4	1.1	57.5	1.4	145.7	0.9
Total	1722.4	100	2149.8	100	2239.7	100	2834.5	100	3386.5	100	4159.0	100	16491.6	100

1 The EIB statistics for the Community include operations of direct interest to the Community carried out under the second sub-paragraph of Article 18(1) of the Bank's Statute, which stipulates that the Board of Governors may authorize loans for investment projects outside the Community.

2 EUR = Euratom.

(Source: Borrowing and lending instruments in the context of the Community's financial instruments (updated), European Economy, July 1980, No. 6.)

market. The EEC itself has the Community budget, the ECSC, its levying powers, the Bank its capital. Yet, their standing in the market does not seem now to be directly related to these factors, whatever may have been the case when they first started borrowing. Given their different purposes and needs and hence the pace and rhythm of their entries into the market, it has been argued by the Community—and experience supports the argument—that the ability to come to the market with different 'names' increases the total volume of funds which can be secured. Furthermore, any doubts which may exist concerning coordination between the different institutions, particularly at the operational level, have been effectively dispelled as the result of enquiries both from member governments and the European Parliament. An interesting example can be found in the speeches made in a recent debate in the British House of Lords on a report of its Select Committee on the European Communities Lending and Borrowing (House of Lords *Hansard*, Thursday, 14th April 1983). It was generally acknowledged that the Community's practices were beyond criticism.

The record of achievement of the Community, and since it is the largest instrument in our present context, particularly of the EIB, in other respects can be judged first by its lending and second by its borrowing history. On the former, that is to say on its ultimate success in fostering European productive capital investment, the other chapters in this book can throw most light. But there is ample evidence from all the member countries (an example, as far as the United Kingdom is concerned, can again be found in the above-mentioned debate) that the activity of the Community institutions in these respects is very highly appreciated and forms one of the most tangible and solid achievements of European integration. In purely financial terms the statistical material provided has already shown that certainly as far as the amounts of funds made available are concerned there has been steady and substantial progress. Moreover, the loan experience of the EIB has been most enviable. It has not suffered any default and has had to have recourse to loan guarantors on only very few occasions indeed—an eloquent testimony to the skill and prudence which have gone together with the imaginative and energetic pursuit of its wider objectives.

As far as the Community's borrowing history is concerned, the record is equally impressive. From a relatively modest start in 1954, and fairly slow growth in the first two decades, the volume of borrowing has increased in the last decade, by a factor of nearly seven, a very rapid rise even allowing for inflation. With this rise in total volume, has gone a great increase in what might be called sophistication. The EIB and the other Community instruments have taken full advantage of the growth in the size of the market and the variety of techniques available, though always, and necessarily, with an eye not only to the need to preserve their status, but also to their ultimate objective, namely their on-lending obligations.

As far as status is concerned, the EIB and the other Community borrowers enjoy the best ratings, and are therefore able to borrow at the finest available rates. It is generally acknowledged that the Community has raised funds in a highly efficient and knowledgeable manner. Its expert knowledge is well recognised in the markets not only by the investors, but also by the intermediaries, the investment and merchant banks who manage and underwrite the EIB's, ECSC's etc, public bond issues or act for them in private placements. While many large and regular borrowers in capital markets — large corporations, governments and government agencies — have highly expert staffs, it is perhaps fair to say that the World Bank, the EIB, ECSC and the Community generally occupy an outstanding place in this regard. In the recent debate already referred to, a special point was made of the excellent relations existing between the various banking intermediaries and the Community institutions which were described as being "among the most professional borrowers in the world". To have these qualities recognised is valuable in a most tangible way. While the technical rating in the markets of the Community borrowers may ultimately rest on their resources and their credit-worthiness as evidenced by their record, the skill of their experts in the actual operations ensures that while the precise measure of success of individual issues may vary one from another (as is inevitable), the average rate of success, which depends on skill in timing and 'tailoring' of particular issues to circumstances prevailing at the relevant time, has been extremely high. This, of course, is of crucial significance in the carrying out of the Community's task (to which borrowing serves as a means to an end) — namely to provide substantial funds for productive investment which the investing instrument, whatever it might be, could not otherwise secure at all, or not on as advantageous terms. Even for the most credit-worthy among the Community's clients, it could well be argued that through the channel of the EIB, or whichever Community institution may be involved, their effective credit is significantly expanded.

The very progress and success of the Community's on-lending and borrowing has sometimes led to the question whether the total size of their transaction was not too large, that it might 'get out of hand', in the sense of over-straining the markets in which it borrows; and, on the other side, might lead to relaxing the criteria for on-lending with consequential ill-effects on the structure of investment in the ultimate place of destination. As we have already seen, large though the Community's borrowing is in absolute terms it represents only a relatively small proportion of the total size of financial markets; and many Community members — and other European (non-member) borrowers — sometimes borrow equally large and even larger amounts. If there are dangers of the kind mentioned on both the borrowing and lending side, they do not seem to arise in respect of that group of transactions for which the Community is responsible. The criteria which have been applied have been both strict and discriminating, such as any private financial institution would be happy to be able to point to.

Enough has already been said, and emerges clearly from the historical record portrayed in the statistical Tables that the benefits of Community borrowing and lending are considerable. The Community can rightly claim that its presence has improved the availability of investment finance for specifically European purposes. In some — perhaps many — parts of the Community the mobilisation of investment funds is less than perfect, be it through an overall shortage of investment finance, or be it through balance of payments constraints on maintaining high levels of investment, which can be mitigated by the inflow of funds for investment from Community sources. In other countries, internal market mechanisms and experience and skill in tapping external markets are inadequate. Apart from increasing the total of funds, the

Community's ability to borrow in different currencies has widened the choice of currency to the ultimate borrower, but also by accepting the exchange risk, has enabled him to borrow at lower interest cost. A further advantage has been that broadly speaking, Community borrowing has relieved the charge on the Community's budget.

The record also shows that the Community instruments have not been slow in taking advantage of new technical developments in markets and of the opening of new markets, such as the 'Samurai' market (domestic yen market for foreign borrowers), the Euro-yen market, the fairly recently opened 'Bulldog' market (UK domestic sterling market for foreign borrowers), as well as the Euro-sterling market, and the long-established Euro–dollar, DM, and 'Yankee' (domestic US market for foreign borrowers) markets.

It is not easy to forecast what developments the next few years will bring. The general availability and mobility of investible funds will depend on many important but hard-to-forecast world economic and financial developments. For example, the decline in the price of petroleum has already led to major financial changes. While it has reduced (or will in due course reduce) the price of imported oil to many developing and industrial countries — easing the balance of payments problems of the former, and assisting economic recovery in the latter — it has sharply reduced the flow of funds out of the oil-producing countries into credit and capital markets; and the full consequences of this cannot yet be foreseen. A vigorous and sustained economic recovery in the United States will increase US domestic demand for funds, which, together with large governmental borrowing requirements (if they persist), may reduce the funds available to foreign borrowers — or, at least, increase the rates of interest on which they can be obtained. Sharp increases of company profitability in European countries — a consequence of economic recovery with improved productivity — would increase internal funds available for investment, but would also increase the total investment requirement. On the other hand, an aborted recovery, continued debt-service difficulties and their associated balance of payments and banking problems may intensify the already threatening pro-tectionist and restrictionist tendencies and reverse the development of recent years towards greater freedom of capital movements, with deleterious consequences for the functioning of the markets.

The framework within which the Community institutions will operate both in their borrowing and on-lending activities could thus be subject to an unpredictable variety of influences which could make the task of these institutions either easier or much more difficult. So could political developments which affect favourably or unfavourably the cohesion of the Community and its further progress. Apart from these very broad questions of the climate in which the EIB and its sister institutions will operate, there are certain to be many developments of a more technical character which will affect their operations. These too are not easy to forecast. One example is that of currency of denomination: one can be confident that the major national currencies in which borrowing has hitherto taken place (US dollar, Deutsche mark, yen) will continue to play a major part, with the others such as sterling and guilder fluctuating more. What is less clear is how far the ECU can develop as a currency in which borrowing can take place. It is, of course, highly unlikely to be able to rival for a long time to come the dollar, which is so overwhelmingly the world's major transaction currency. Moreover, there is a clear limit to the use of the ECU, since the requirements of those who borrow from the Community are mainly in terms of national currency. Nevertheless, an expansion and consolidation of the European Monetary System might enlarge the opportunities for using the ECU.

Maturity is another factor on which one cannot be dogmatic, although it is certain that the vast bulk of the Community's lending and, therefore, its borrowing, will continue to be for relatively long terms in view of the purposes for which the funds are ultimately needed. Nevertheless, some greater variation in maturities might well develop, partly in response to changing circumstances on the on-lending side, partly through changing developments in the markets in which the Community borrows. Moreover, the increasing size of the Community's total borrowings and outstandings makes some variation in maturities possible. The World Bank has in fact recently made some move in that direction by embarking on a discount note programme. Such a development cannot be ruled out for the Community. On one aspect the Community has maintained a steady view and policy, despite suggestions by some member countries for a change, and that is that it borrows on fixed rates of interest only — a policy hitherto adhered to also by the World Bank. The rationale here is clear (and is similar to that applying in respect of maturities): those who borrow from the Community do so for longer-term investment purposes, and require, therefore, certainty as regards cost.

It would be hazardous from the outside to urge a change of policy in this regard upon the EIB and the other institutions, the policy being so much dependent on prudent judgement of a very large variety of considerations for which those directly responsible alone can have a knowledge of all the relevant facts. It is not, however, too difficult to envisage circumstances which might make a modest move in the direction of variable rate borrowing acceptable, as it has proved for some individual borrowers in international markets.

What is clear is that with the adaptability to changing circumstances which the Community institutions have shown so far, they can be relied upon to respond to market changes and opportunities.

As has repeatedly been stressed in the earlier parts of this chapter, Europe, and within Europe the Community institutions, must compete for quality borrowers to whom to make investible funds available. Similarly it has to compete for finance from investors. What investors are interested in are essentially two things, the balance of which (not always the same) determines their investment decisions: security and return. In the end, therefore, the extent to which European investment is able to attract funds will depend on what it offers to investors in these two respects. Clearly the performance of the Community institutions cannot, in the last resort, be better than the security and the profitability of European investment as such; this, in turn, depends — political considerations apart — on the fortunes of the European economy. Within that broad limitation, the role which the Community institutions can and will play will be determined by the cohesion and progress of European integration. In the light of the remarkable success which the European Investment Bank in its twenty-five years' history, and its sister institutions have had, one must hope that neither constraint will prove inhibiting to continued and accelerated progress.